Playing God:
Medieval Mysteries on the Modern Stage

Religious drama was one of the most vital art forms of the medieval era. Until very recently, however, the revival of interest in medieval culture has not included drama, because of a lingering fear of blasphemy associated with the representation of God on the stage. In Britain this fear was the legacy of the theatrical censorship which had been exercised by the Lord Chamberlain's office for hundreds of years. Since 1968 and the abolition of that power medieval religious, or mystery, plays are once again appearing on stages of many countries.

John R. Elliott jr studies the modern context of this important medieval genre. He begins by describing general attitudes towards religious drama from the time of the Reformation, the popularity of the Oberammergau Passion Play in Victorian times, and specific attempts by producers to overcome official hostility to religious plays. He traces the history of the major modern productions of the mystery cycles, such as the York Festival and the Bristol University performance of the Cornish *Ordinalia*, up to 1980, and provides information about the careers of the two leading pioneers of modern mystery-play production, Nugent Monck and E. Martin Browne. The concluding chapter discusses the chief practical and aesthetic problems involved in staging mystery plays for modern audiences, and assesses the overall importance of their revival in the larger context of British theatre today.

JOHN R. ELLIOTT jr is Professor of English at Syracuse University. He is the author of *The Prince of Poets: Essays on Edmund Spenser*, co-editor, with Graham Runnalls, of *The Baptism and Temptation of Christ*, and editor of the Oxford University records for Records of Early English Drama.

STUDIES IN EARLY ENGLISH DRAMA 2

General Editor: J.A.B. Somerset

JOHN R. ELLIOTT jr

Playing God:
Medieval Mysteries
on the Modern Stage

UNIVERSITY OF TORONTO PRESS
Toronto Buffalo London

© University of Toronto Press 1989
Toronto Buffalo London
Printed in Canada

ISBN   0-8020-5606-7

Printed on acid-free paper

Canadian Cataloguing in Publication Data

Elliott, John R.
  Playing God : medieval mysteries on the modern stage

  (Studies in early English drama ; 2)
  Includes bibliographical references and index.
  ISBN   0-8020-5606-7

  1. Theater – England – History – 20th century.
  2. Mysteries and miracle-plays. I. Title.
  II. Series.

  PN 2595.E 54 1989   792.1'6'0942   C 87-095197-1

Permission to reproduce photographs has been obtained from the following: (plates 2 and 3) Monck Papers, courtesy of Mr and Mrs John Hall; (plate 4) Stewart Lack; *Yorkshire Evening Press*, York; (plate 5) Stewart Lack; (plate 6) Stewart Lack; *Yorkshire Post, Yorkshire Evening Post*, Leeds, and *Doncaster Chronicle*; (plate 8) *Yorkshire Evening Press* and *Gazette and Herald*, York; (plate 9) Bristol University Drama Department; (plate 11) Stewart Lack; *Yorkshire Evening Press* and *Gazette and Herald*, York; (plate 12) Department of Tourism, York

Contents

For my sons
Richard and Mark
who continue to share mysteries with me

Preface

This book attempts to supply a previously unwritten chapter in English theatrical history – the story of the revival of the medieval mystery plays in the twentieth century. Ours is an age committed to the conservation of the past, yet few forms of art, dramatic or otherwise, have followed so tricky a path from oblivion to recognition as these fifteenth- and sixteenth-century Biblical dramas. Today performances of the mystery plays are enjoyed by audiences throughout England and other countries, but less than four decades ago they were almost totally unknown on the English stage and virtually unread anywhere except by a handful of scholars.

The reasons for the long neglect of the medieval mysteries, and the theatrical experiments through which they have at last come to be recognized as the dramatic masterpieces they are, constitute the subject of this book. Because of their religious content, the mysteries have posed problems for modern producers of a sort not encountered in other theatrical revivals. 'Playing God' is a dangerous occupation under any circumstances, even when considered as a purely theatrical undertaking. The solutions to these problems devised by modern producers have had far more than a temporary or local importance. The frequency with which such names as William Poel, Nugent Monck, Dorothy Sayers, T.S. Eliot, and E. Martin Browne appear in the following pages indicates that the revival of the mysteries has not been an isolated phenomenon, but rather a part of the broader development of twentieth-century English religious drama as a whole.

The progress of the mysteries on the modern stage has to a large extent paralleled the progress of our scholarly knowledge of medieval dramatic practices, both drawing on its theories and inspiring its discoveries. The last two chapters of this book describe some of the more ambitious attempts to reproduce as accurately as possible the setting, style, and atmosphere of a medieval performance. The motive of most twentieth-century productions of medieval plays, however, has been religious and aesthetic rather than archaeological, and to understand the forms that these productions have taken one needs to know as much about the cultural milieu in which they occurred and the purposes for which they were performed as about the history of medieval staging practices. The attitude of the majority of modern producers toward the mystery plays was expressed by a reviewer as early as 1904 in the following terms:

It ought not to be forgotten that an undiscriminating revival of methods which appealed to the feelings of the fourteenth, fifteenth, and sixteenth centuries, such as the representation in dramatic art of the Person of God the Father, is not without its dangers, and it is to be hoped that, with a view to real devotion, the dramatic representation of the mysteries of our Faith may be adapted to the requirements and necessities of the present.[1]

In one way or another, virtually all twentieth-century peformances of the mystery plays have been adaptations to 'the requirements and necessities of the present.' The bulk of the present study is accordingly devoted to an account of the forms that these adaptations have taken, concluding with an assessment of the relative merits of 'authentic' versus 'adapted' scripts, an issue not nearly as clear-cut as it might seem. The major share of attention has been given to those performances that took place prior to 1970, a year which marked a turning point between what may be called the local and devotional presentation of the mysteries and their adoption by the academic and professional stages. The principal performances since that time are noted in the final chapter. The year 1980 has, for practical purposes, been chosen as a cut-off point for a story whose continuation must, of necessity, be written by someone else.

My study has been restricted, with a few notable exceptions, to performances of the mystery plays in England. Those already familiar with the subject will know, of course, that within the last twenty years practical interest in the staging of medieval plays has spread widely throughout the English-speaking world and that it could well be argued at the present moment that North America has taken the lead in such ventures. The rediscovery of the mysteries, however, began in their native country and followed a course peculiar to the spiritual and cultural life of modern England. American, Canadian, and other Commonwealth productions came late into the picture and present few consistent patterns or traditions, with the important exception of the series of academic performances, most of them in the original language, recently initiated at the University of Toronto, which are discussed in chapter 6. Linguistic differences and the close association of the plays with their individual places of origin have, however, kept them a distinctively English phenomenon, not easily exportable in all their Englishness to the outside world.

For those coming to the subject for the first time, a brief definition of what a mystery play actually is may be in order. Of all those that have been attempted, perhaps the most useful remains the following one, written by Dorothy Sayers in 1951:

The *mystery* is the fundamental form [of medieval drama]. It deals, as its name shows, with the central Mystery of Redemption; and its whole end and purpose is to show forth the *Myth*, beginning to end. Properly speaking, a complete Mystery Cycle (though all the extant cycles differ in detail) should begin with the Creation, Fall of the Angels, and Creation and Fall of Man; should show the chief Old Testament types of redemption, such as the Flood, the Sacrifice of Isaac and so forth, and the Old Testament prophecies; should then proceed to the events of the Gospels, and should conclude with the Harrowing of Hell, the Resurrection, Ascension, and Last Judgment. Its characters are for the most part scriptural, though they may include invented or traditional minor characters, such as Pilate's son, Longinus, citizens, servants, and various Angels and Devils. The dialogue (usually in verse) is partly scriptural and partly invented, but always in contemporary idiom; and the costumes are likewise partly scriptural and partly contemporary. The productions were for the most part as costly, lavish, and elaborate as the management could afford, making full use of the most up-to-date machinery and stage effects; comedy was freely permitted; and there was no aesthetic mystique about simplicity and stylization: the aim was the greatest possible realism and a determination to show the events as living, historical fact.[2]

In 1951 Dorothy Sayers was one of the very few persons, even among scholars, who possessed an accurate historical understanding of the medieval mystery plays. Many of the qualities she perceived in them, such as their humour, their realism, and their theatrical splendour, had long been ignored or misunderstood, and would only be proved real to audiences through the experiments in production that began in that year and that have continued to reveal new, or forgotten, features of these plays to the present day.

The many friends and benefactors who have helped to make this book possible are acknowledged in a special section at the close. I wish to mention here, however, an earlier study of this subject without whose existence the present book would have had to be extended beyond any practical boundaries. In 1946 Harold Gardiner, SJ, published an account of the suppression of the medieval mystery plays in the sixteenth century by Queen Elizabeth I's government, entitled *Mysteries' End*. There he described how 'every one of the four great cycles which have come down to us were put down through the intervention of authority within the period 1569–80, for religious motives.'[3] The present book is a sequel to the story that Father Gardiner told, though one which he could hardly have foreseen in 1946. I myself had little idea that there could be a sequel to such a tragical history when I first read his study many years ago. It was, however, *Mysteries' End* that showed me the connection between the reasons for the decline of the mystery plays as living dramas and the conditions under which they once again struggled back to life under the reign of the second Queen Elizabeth. I have alluded to this debt in my choice of several chapter titles, and trust that Father Gardiner might take pleasure in the fact that the sixpence paid to Robert Brown in 1483 for 'playing God' is still yielding its dividends half a millennium later.[4]

'To Robert Brown playing God, six pence':
item in a theatrical expense account, 1483

1 Oberammergau, the Passion Play Theatre, mid-nineteenth century

2 Newspaper article announcing the prohibition of Nugent Monck's production of the *Ludus Coventriae*, London, April 1909

3   Final tableau in Nugent Monck's production of the Norwich Passion Play,
Maddermarket Theatre, Norwich, 1952

4 The Last Judgment, York Festival, 1954

5 Judi Dench as Mary, York Festival, 1957

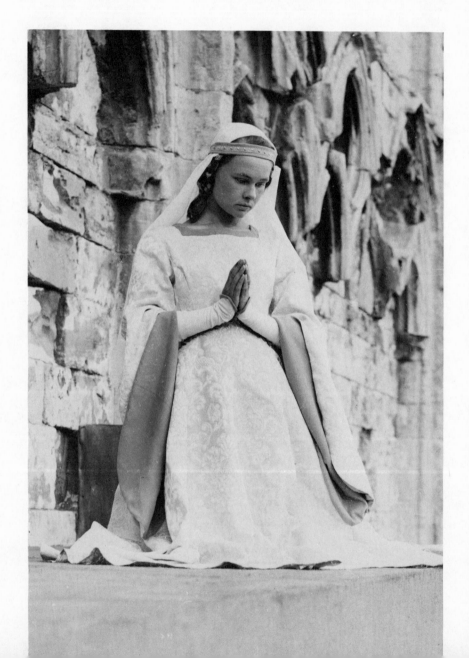

6 Christ's Ministry, York Festival, 1960

7 The Creation of Adam and Eve, York Festival, 1969

8 The Expulsion of Adam and Eve, York Festival, 1969

9 Model of Piran Round, Cornwall, as reconstructed for the performance
of the Cornish Cycle, 1969

10 The Trial of Jesus, Cornish Cycle, 1969

11 Christ's Ministry, York Festival, 1973

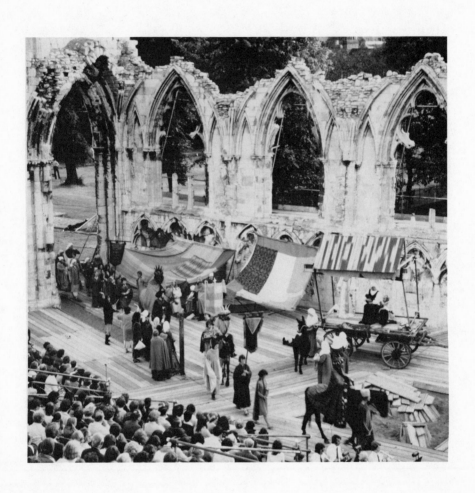

12   Entrance of the Three Kings, York Festival, 1976

PLAYING GOD:
MEDIEVAL MYSTERIES ON THE MODERN STAGE

1

Mysteries Suppressed

The Catholics in honor of Corpus Christi feast ... caused a show or stage-play to
be acted, wherein was represented the Court of the King of Heaven, and God the
Father sitting in Majesty, together with God the Son (O blasphemy, prophanesse
beyond all expression) offering up the Blessed Virgin his mother, taken out of her
sepulchre, unto his eternal Father. What wickedness, what blasphemy like to this,
as thus to deify a player, and to bring the very throne, the Majesty of God himself,
yea, the persons of the eternal father, son, and god of glory on the stage!

William Prynne, *Histriomastix* (1633)

The English mystery plays during the Middle Ages were among the most
ambitious dramas the world has ever known. Seldom has so much energy
been poured into a regularly recurring dramatic event. Annually in cities
throughout England plays depicting the history of the world, as told in the
scriptures and medieval legend, were enacted in performances that sometimes
lasted as long as eleven days. (In medieval France, *misteres* occasionally took
as many as twenty-five or even forty days to perform.) The earliest references
to such dramas are found in the mid-fourteenth century, and they continued
to be regularly performed for the next two hundred years, until the last
decades of the reign of Queen Elizabeth. There could hardly have been an
inhabitant of England during those two centuries who did not see the mystery
plays performed at least once in his lifetime. The clerk Absolon, in a tale
Chaucer wrote in the 1390s, was already an experienced hand at playing
Herod. And Shakespeare's Hamlet evidently heard one of his more memorable performances.

From surviving records we know of at least fifteen English cities that
regularly sponsored such performances, and there is every reason to suppose

that there must have been more.[1] Only five complete texts, however, together with a few fragments, have come down to us. Three of the complete cycles can be traced to a particular place of origin, those from York, Chester, and Cornwall. One, often called the 'Towneley Cycle' after a former owner of the manuscript, is now generally assigned to the city of Wakefield in Yorkshire. The remaining manuscript, usually called either the 'N-Town' Cycle or *Ludus Coventriae* ('Coventry Play') after ambiguous phrases found in the text, has been variously assigned to Lincoln, Norwich, and Bury St Edmunds. That it does not come from Coventry, despite the appearance of that name in the manuscript, is one of the few things we know for certain about it, as a fragmentary text of the actual Coventry Cycle survives in a different manuscript. All of these cycles except the Cornish were written in Middle English, originally in the first half of the fifteenth century, though they continued to be copied and altered down to the end of the sixteenth century.

As Harold Gardiner has demonstrated, such a popular and long-lived form of theatre did not pass out of existence simply because it came to seem crude and old-fashioned to a later age. Rather, it was deliberately legislated out of existence by Protestant government officials and their allies in the pulpit, who resented the very effectiveness with which the plays brought home the tenets of Catholic doctrine to their audiences. When the sectarian disputes of the Reformation cooled, however, the plays, instead of benefiting from the renewed interest in medieval art, met an even more comprehensive opposition in the continuing hostility toward religious drama that was one of the chief cultural legacies of English puritanism. If we are to understand why the mysteries lay dormant for so long and why their rebirth on the modern stage took the particular form that it did, we must first look briefly at the way in which they died.

'MATTERS OF DIVINITY AND STATE, UNFIT TO BE UTTERED' (1539–1603)

At the close of the fifteenth century, when the mystery plays were at the height of their popularity, no mechanism existed in England for regulating the drama. There were, of course, as yet no theatres in the modern sense. All dramatic activities were occasional events, falling automatically under the control of those who commissioned them – royalty, nobility, town, and city councils, or the church. By the end of the following century, however, under pressure of the conflicts unleashed by the Reformation, a system had grown up to regulate the drama that was to continue to do so in much the same way for the next 350 years. To this system the mystery plays fell victim.

The earliest instance we know of governmental interference with the mystery plays is an undated letter, probably from the 1530s, from Henry VIII to the Justice of the Peace in York, instructing him to watch carefully for 'any papists who shall, in performing interludes which are founded on any portions of the Old or New Testament, say or make use of any language which may tend to excite those who are beholding the same to any breach of the peace.'[2] Henry's letter was sent in response to a 'late evil and seditious rising' in York after the performance of a 'religious interlude of St. Thomas the Apostle.' What was inflammatory about St Thomas the Apostle we do not know. Henry makes no mention of any objection to the play itself, but only of the use to which it appears to have been put by those bent on resisting the King's reforms. In 1543 Henry affirmed the right of all his subjects to stage whatever entertainments they pleased so long as they did not 'meddle with interpretations of Scripture, contrary to the doctrine set forth by the King's Majesty.'[3]

Just what constituted 'meddling' with interpretations of scripture Henry did not spell out, but it is clear that this was not synonymous with simply performing plays drawn from the Bible, as later came to be the case. Under Henry the mystery plays continued to be performed much as before, with the exception of those episodes which touched on the sacraments, definitions of which Henry was concerned to 'set forth' as a part of his reforms.[4] Protestants, despite the language of the Act, also succeeded in giving their own versions of Biblical history on the stage – as, for example, in John Bale's trilogy of *God's Promises*, *John the Baptist*, and *The Temptation of our Lord* (c 1538), a kind of protestantized mystery cycle. So far as we know, no one objected to this practice. Both sides in the war of religion tacitly assumed the stage to be a fitting and potent weapon in the service of their cause.

Under Queen Mary this situation began to change, despite the fact that Mary was evidently fond of plays and eager to bring them back into the service of the True Religion. At her coronation Nicholas Udall's anti-Protestant morality called *Respublica* had been performed for her court, and on the occasion of her marriage to Philip of Spain there had been various interludes and pageants, all with a religious theme. But Mary soon found that all this dramatic activity was only encouraging her Protestant enemies to more vituperative efforts. In August 1553, for the sake of public peace, she issued a proclamation which forbade all 'Interludes, books, ballads, rhymes, and other lewd treaties in the England [sic] tongue, concerning doctrine in matters now in question and controversy, touching the high points and mysteries of Christian religion.'[5] The role of the stage as a teacher of doctrine was over – not because it had done its work crudely or badly, as Puritan critics of medieval plays were later to insist, but because it had done it so well. Ironically, England's foremost Catholic drama had received its death-blow from England's last Catholic monarch.

Mary's proclamation was only the first in a series of governmental edicts over the next fifty years banning plays on controversial subjects. Queen Elizabeth issued an even harsher decree upon her accession to the throne in 1559, forbidding any plays 'wherein either matters of religion or the governance of the estate of the commonwealth shall be handled or treated.'[6] In 1581 the Privy Council set up a special censorship commission to read every play-script in advance and to 'strike out or reform' anything that they found 'unfit or undecent to be handled in plays, both for Divinity and State.'[7] Periodically during the 1580s and 1590s whole companies of actors, and even the London theatres themselves, were shut down because they had ventured too far into sensitive areas either of politics or religion.

Gardiner has recounted the resulting death-throes of the mystery plays under this barrage of governmental decrees. In York the annual productions of the Corpus Christi play continued precariously through the troubled reigns of Edward and Mary, only to come to an abrupt halt with the issuing of Elizabeth's proclamation in 1559. The festival was cancelled in that year and in the year following. In 1561 the guilds decided to try again and succeeded in performing the cycle in exchange for agreeing to omit the play about the life of the Virgin. But from 1564–6 the festival was suspended once again, and in 1568 the Commission for Ecclesiastical Causes in the North condemned the plays as 'disagreeing from the sincerity of the gospel.' The Catholic rebellion of 1569, which drew its strength from York and other northern cities, ensured that the plays would be stamped out for good. The last performance of the York Cycle in that year was got together 'with more than usual alacrity,' and in the following year the newly appointed Archbishop of York, Edmund Grindal, effectively killed the plays by the simple expedient of calling in the play-book and failing to return it. A deputation of city aldermen tried pathetically in 1575 to get back 'all such play books as pertain to this city now in his grace's custody,' but their request went unanswered. In the following year the Diocesan Court of High Commission, an arm of the Privy Council, gave strict orders to the neighbouring town of Wakefield that no play be performed in which 'the Majesty of God the Father, God the Son, or God the Holy Ghost ... be counterfeited or represented.' The civic pageants of other towns and cities throughout the country experienced the same fate, and a precedent was set that would be followed in England for the next three and a half centuries.[8]

In addition to furnishing the Puritans of the following century with a precedent for muzzling religious drama, the Tudor monarchs also provided the machinery. At first this was clumsy and inefficient. In the early years of the century, under Henry, Edward, and Mary, the sovereign's wishes in theatrical matters seem to have been administered chiefly by the Privy Council, who in most cases passed on the burden to those who were closest to the suspected offences: the noblemen who sponsored companies of players, the Lord Mayor of London, the Lord Lieutenants of the provinces, or the bishops. They in turn were likely to turn over specific tasks of surveillance or punishment to justices of the peace or other local officials. Elizabeth's proclamation of 1559 was addressed generally to magistrates all over the country. Such a system soon proved inadequate. Centralized control of the theatre was clearly desirable, and the next forty years saw a struggle between the various factions in English society who were most interested in exercising it. By the latter part of Elizabeth's reign these factions had narrowed to three: the Crown, the Church, and the Lord Mayor of London. At times each proclaimed its authority over plays independently of the other. In the end, however, it was the Crown that carried the day, and to its servant, the Master of the Revels, and later to his superior, the Lord Chamberlain, fell the duty of keeping watch on plays, players, and playing-places throughout the kingdom.

A royal patent in 1581 authorized the Master of the Revels 'to warn, command, and appoint ... *all and every* player or players, with their playmakers' to appear before him with their plays and to 'order and reform, authorise and put down' these plays 'as shall be thought meet or unmeet unto himself'[9] Elizabeth's Master of the Revels, Edmund Tilney, served in the office for thirty-two years, and by the time he died in 1610 there was little question where authority over the stage in England lay. Years later, when Charles II's Master of the Revels sought to reassert his authority over theatres after the Restoration, he could argue that the job had been the prerogative of his office 'from time immemorial.'

Not all the efforts of the Elizabethan censors were successful. Plays continued to be performed in churches until at least 1592, despite the ban on such performances in Canon 88 of the Church of England. Plays drawn from the scriptures, such as Peele's *David and Bethsabe*, still appeared at odd intervals on the public stage, even if they were careful not to 'meddle' with interpretations of them. Some mystery cycles, or parts of them, continued to be performed in the provinces, despite all the royal decrees, right down to the last decade of the century. There was even, if we can believe William Prynne, a private performance of a Passion Play given in London on Good Friday, 1605, under the very noses of the censors. But such instances were the exception rather than the rule, and their days were clearly numbered.

The gradual demise of Catholic – and Protestant – plays under the Tudors had a significance far greater than the temporary discomfort that it may have brought to guild-members in York or the disappointment that it may have caused to audiences in Chester, Wakefield, or Coventry. It signalled a permanent change in the character of English drama. The edicts of the Tudor monarchs against religious drama established for centuries to come the precedent of governmental control of the theatre for reasons of state. As early as Shakespeare's time, actors and playwrights had to accustom themselves to thinking of the theatre as a circumscribed area in which all might not be said. If censorship did not stifle the genius of the Elizabethan theatre, it certainly altered its character from what it might otherwise have been. Instead of man's relationship to God, a subject explored in every other sixteenth-century medium so intensely, theatrical censorship insisted that a play should treat only man's relationship to man. If Shakespeare and his contemporaries were not thereby prevented from creating plays of lasting value, the growth of the censorship system would in later years produce a stage on which anything might be said except that which was important to be heard.

'THE VERY HOUSE AND SYNAGOGUE OF THE DEVIL' (1603–1737)

The motives of the Tudor monarchs for keeping religion off the stage were generally political. Given a guarantee of good order, they were perfectly prepared to compromise on good doctrine. Had there been a return to political stability in the country, religious drama might well have resumed its place on the English stage and kept it indefinitely. Instead, however, a new force grew up in English life that carried hostility to religious drama to lengths undreamed of by the Tudors. When the Puritans launched their attack on the theatre in the 1590s, they were attacking not just the abuse of the stage but the very idea of drama itself. So far as religious drama went, their victory was almost complete. If their political triumph was short-lived, their reformulation of the traditional relationship between religion and the stage took hold of the minds of Englishmen and maintained its grip there almost down to the present day. The story of theatrical censorship in the seventeenth century is the story of the conversion of the royal censors to the views of the Puritans.

The turning of the tide occurred almost simultaneously with the accession to the throne of James I in 1603. During the last years of Elizabeth's reign the London theatrical companies lived a precarious existence, under constant threat of extermination by their enemies. To save them James decided to take the three principal companies under the direct patronage of the royal family. In return he was obliged to put his name to an Act of Parliament designed to ensure that even the mention of religion would henceforth be banned from the London stage. The act was called 'An Act for the Preventing and Avoiding of the great abuse of the holy name of God in stage plays, interludes, May games, shows, and such like' (3 James I, c 21). Its sole provision was for penalties against anyone who 'jestingly or profanely speaks or uses the holy name of God, or of Christ Jesus, or of the Holy Ghost, or of the Trinity, which are not to be spoken but with fear and reverence.'

If the language of this act implied that it was only abuses of sacred words that were under concern, the administration of the act soon proved otherwise. The rooting out of verbal impieties extended far beyond the hunt for blasphemous oaths and covered any mention by name of God, Christ, or the Trinity, however pious in intent. One of the few surviving play-manuscripts of the period, that of the anonymous *Second Maiden's Tragedy* (1611), is covered with corrections in the hand of the Master of the Revels, Sir George Buck, who crossed out any reference to the Bible or to religion that he could find, regardless of their context. Sir Henry Herbert, who succeeded Buck in the office and held it off and on for fifty years, compiled a list of taboo phrases which included such blasphemies as 'faith,' 'troth,' 'by all that's good,' "fore George,' 'the devil take 'em,' and 'send him to Abram's bosom.' On occasion he even suggested improvements to erring authors, recommending such substitutions as 'believe me' for 'by Jesu,' 'by my sword' for 'by the gods,' or 'by these hilts' for 'by heaven.'[10]

Plainly, there was not much hope for staging a drama whose principal characters could not even be mentioned by name. What little hope there might have been was soon swallowed up in the Puritan advance. By the 1630s the attack on the language of plays had shifted to an attack on their contents, and the blasphemy of preaching Christianity from the stage formed the backbone of the Puritans' tirades against the theatre. The more persuasive of these opponents of the stage developed an aesthetic philosophy not unlike Plato's in the *Republic*, and there can be little doubt that their redefinition of piety struck a warm response in the minds of Englishmen as a whole. 'What a stupendous impiety, a desperate blasphemy and prophaneness it is for men, for Christians, to turn the most serious oracles of God's sacred word into a play, a jest, a fable, a sport, a May-game!' argued William Prynne in his *Histriomastix*.[11] The synonyms which he gives for the word 'play' tell us how he conceived of a drama, and explain the sneer which the word so often brought to the lips of his successors. A 'play' for the Puritans was not limited to acting in the strict theatrical sense: a 'game' was a play, as was a joke or a story or a football match. A play on the stage was no different from these and no better. All were alike in that they were not serious, not real, not true. The word of God, as pure truth, could have nothing to do with mere shows.

The showiness of medieval Catholic drama was a favourite theme with Prynne's supporters. As early as 1599 John Rainolds had attacked 'the profane and wicked toyes of Passion-plays ... procured by Popish priests,' who, he said, 'as they have transformed the celebrating of the Sacrament of the Lord's Supper into a Mass-game, and all other parts of the Ecclesiastical service into theatrical sights, so, instead of preaching the word, they caused it to be played, a thing put in practice by their followers, the Jesuits, among the poor Indians.'[12] Rainolds' emphasis, like Plato's, is on 'theatrical sights' rather than spiritual nourishment, on the feeding of the outward senses rather than the inner soul. The same emphasis is found again in Prynne's exclamations against scriptural plays: 'to make the sin-slaying, the lust-mortifying, soul-converting word of God ... a mere pander to mens' beastly lusts, their ribaldrous mirth, their graceless wits, and carnal jollity, yea a very instrument to the devil himself, who rules in stage plays!'[13] For the Puritans, to rely on the senses to move men's souls was to use the very tools of the devil. They insisted instead, as Jonas Barish has noted, on shifting 'the drama of salvation from an outer to an inner and invisible stage.'[14]

If the Puritans were eager to stress the unreality of the stage, they nevertheless displayed a curious literal-mindedness about what happened when a man undertook to play a part upon it, an attitude that was to figure heavily in later objections to the revival of the mystery plays. The substance of his part may have been unreal, but a man risked his soul by playing it. 'What wickedness, what blasphemy like to this, as thus to deify a player,' Prynne exclaimed about the actors who had impersonated God the Father and Christ in the medieval drama. The Biblical injunction to 'speak plainly' and the commandment against idolatry were used to bolster the arugment against impersonation. Stories were told of notorious instances in which stage devils had been carted off to hell by their real counterparts. For different reasons than Stanislavsky, the Puritans were convinced that an actor must become the thing he imitates. Despite their insistence that plays were only games, they believed that the effect of plays upon audiences was to trick them into believing that they were seeing the real thing – plainly an impossible goal where the Deity was concerned.

Perhaps the most effective of the Puritans' arguments against religious drama, because the closest to the truth, was their denunciation of the

introduction of the sacred mysteries of religion into the confines of a 'theatre.'
It is hard for us today to appreciate how a mere physical structure could be
thought of as 'the very house and synagogue of the devil.' The reason had
to do only partly with the nature of the plays that were presented there:
from the Puritans' point of view, Restoration plays were to be far more
scandalous than anything seen on the stage in Shakespeare's time. But the
London theatre of the sixteenth and seventeenth centuries housed more than
plays and players. They housed the audience as well, and the frequent
complaints from municipal authorities that theatres were havens for pimps,
prostitutes, pickpockets, and other assorted denizens of the London under-
world were not without truth. If this was not the fault of the players and
managers, it was nevertheless an inevitable concomitant of drama in England
once the system of permanent, commercial theatrical buildings had been
established in 1576. When Prynne inveighed against the wickedness of 'pol-
luting those sacred histories in the theatre,' of bringing 'the very throne,
the Majesty of God himself, yea the persons of the eternal Father, Son, and
God of glory on the stage,' he was thinking less of the subject than of the
propriety of the surroundings. Even if the Puritans had had no *a priori*
grounds for condemning play-acting, it is unlikely that, once English secular
drama had begun, God would ever again have been allowed to resume his
place on the public stage beside Bottom, Touchstone, and Mosca.

   All of these arguments – the charge of untruthfulness, the fear of blasphemy, the denunciation of the 'theatre' – were quite foreign to the spirit
of the medieval drama that the Puritans condemned. The mystery plays had
never pretended to be anything other than 'plays' or 'games.' 'In play we
purpose for to show,' they plainly advertised.[15] To their audience they had
offered, not real life, but a frankly theatrical version of it. Their subject was
not the visible but the invisible – a mystery, literally speaking, which could
only be known through outward symbols. Their Herod was not a real Herod
any more than their God was a real God. They were, instead, purely theatrical
characters. Real Herods, after all, do not strut about and reveal their weak-
nesses for all to see, for if they are real Herods they are much too clever
for that. And whatever God really looks like, no one in the medieval audience
ever believed for a moment that he wore a gold mask. Nor is there any
evidence that the actors who played these parts worried about their personal
worthiness of them, or that producers cared about any qualifications other
than histrionic ones. As V.A. Kolve has written, 'The aim of the Corpus
Christi drama was to celebrate and elucidate, never, not even temporarily,
to deceive. It played action in "game" – not "earnest" – within a world
set apart, established by convention and obeying rules of its own. A lie

designed to tell the truth about reality, the drama was understood as significant play.'[16]

In the changed intellectual climate of the seventeenth century, however, the Puritans' arguments against the theatre carried the day, even after their wider objectives had been lost. The reopening of the public theatres after the Restoration of Charles II did little to affect the status of religious drama. One of Charles' first acts was to 'strictly command and enjoin' William Davenant and Thomas Killigrew, whom he had picked to manage the two royally licensed theatres in London, 'to correct and purge ... any passages offensive to piety or good manners,' whether they occurred in new plays or 'old and received plays.'[17] At the same time the Master of the Revels reasserted his authority over plays, claiming that the purpose of his powers was to detect 'all prophaneness, oaths, ribaldry, and matters reflecting upon piety and the present government ... before there be any action in a public theatre.'[18]

Political events gave added impetus to Restoration officials' determination to keep religion off the stage. The Popish Plot of the 1680s brought about a situation not unlike that under the early Tudors. Any references to religion on the stage were bound to have political overtones, and as a result plays were screened as vigilantly for any improper references to religion as they were later to be for improper references to sex. During the years 1680–6 more plays were prohibited by the Censor than in any other period, with the exception of the years from 1890 to 1910. None of these were 'religious' plays in any devotional or doctrinal sense. Indeed they could not have been, when even passing references to religious subjects were taboo. Throughout the whole of this period we have not a single mention of any religious drama, properly speaking, being attempted anywhere in England.

In such circumstances the medieval mystery plays could only go 'underground.' During the seventeenth and eighteenth centuries they managed to keep up a shadow existence in such popular theatrical forms as puppet shows and village mummings, far from the vigilant eyes that were kept on the commercial theatre. Shakespeare's Autolycus gives us one of the earliest references to these survivals. Among his many accomplishments at country fairs and festivals Autolycus boasts that he has 'compassed a motion [i.e., devised a puppet show] of the Prodigal Son.'[19] Much later, during the reign of Queen Anne, there are records of puppet shows depicting the Creation, the Flood, and the story of Dives and Lazarus. One playbill promised to show 'Noah and his family coming out of the ark, with all the beasts two by two, and all the fowls of the air seen in a prospect sitting upon the trees; likewise over the ark is seen the sun rising in a glorious manner; moreover, a multitude of angels will be seen in a double rank.' Another, conflating the mysteries with Milton, promised to resurrect 'the whole story of the Old Creation of the World, or Paradise Lost, yet newly revived, with the addition of Noah's Flood.' In 1709 the *Tatler* reported the performance of an even more ingenious hybrid, a puppet show in Bath in which Punch and his wife were introduced dancing in the ark.[20]

Later forms of popular entertainment occasionally contained similar echoes of the past. In 1823 William Hone described a kind of magic-lantern pantomime called a 'Gallantee show,' which presented such stories as the Prodigal Son, the Flood, and 'Pull Devil, Pull Baker.' The last was based on a familiar theme in the medieval Judgment plays – 'the just judgment upon a baker who sold short of weight and was carried to hell in his own basket.'[21] The episode of the Ale-Wife in the Chester Last Judgment is a close analogy. A Protestantized version of the Last Judgment also occurred in a play called *The Coronation of Elizabeth*, performed at Bartholomew Fair in 1680, which showed the Pope, assisted by the devil 'in the shape of a Jesuit,' plotting Queen Elizabeth's death. After being shown a vision of 'Hell full of Devils, Popes, and Cardinals,' the Pope was then ceremonially burned by the Queen's loyal subjects.[22] An actual ceremony called 'Burning the Pope' was carried out annually during the late seventeenth and early eighteenth centuries on the anniversary of Queen Elizabeth's accession day (17 November), eventually merging with the more secular celebrations of Guy Fawkes Day (5 November).[23]

Such were the mutations of the medieval mystery plays in a society which had banned them from its official theatre. The plays themselves were virtually forgotten, their texts surviving only in the hands of a few antiquarian collectors. When the first volumes of Dodsley's *Old Plays* began to appear in 1744, no medieval plays were among them. In the last decades of the eighteenth century, when Thomas Warton and Edmond Malone attempted to write histories of English drama, the only medieval plays available to them in print were the first five plays of the *Ludus Coventriae*, the Newcastle *Noah*, and the Digby *Herod*.[24] Lack of acquaintance with the plays did not prevent critics from expressing judgments as to their quality, however. Thomas Rymer, the historiographer-royal, confidently declared that 'the Company for acting *Christ's Passion*, or the *Old Testament*, were Carpenters, Coblers, and illiterate fellows, who found that the Drolls and Fooleries interlarded by them brought in the rabble and lengthened their time so they got Money by the bargain,' and that 'in a church acting their play called *The Incarnation* [they] had usually the *Ave Mary* mumbled over to a stradling wench (for the blessed Virgin) straw-hatted, blew-apron'd, big-bellied, with her Immaculate Conception up to her chin.'²⁵ Dodsley, despite equal unfamil-iarity with the texts, wrote that 'the Mysteries of Religion were made very free with all over Europe, being represented in so stupid and ridiculous a manner that the stories of the New Testament in particular were thought to encourage Libertinism and Infidelity.'²⁶ Thus did the myth arise that the mysteries had been composed by licentious monks and acted by incompetent neighbours of Bottom the Weaver.

The last and most successful attack on the theatre came with the publication of Jeremy Collier's *Short View of the Profaneness and Immorality of the English Stage* in 1688. Collier, unlike Prynne, gave short shrift to religious drama for the simple reason that by this time there was none. 'To go to Heaven in jest is the way to go to Hell in earnest,' he reminded his readers, but saved most of his invective for the ridiculing of religion that he detected in the plays of his contemporaries.²⁷ Collier's views found favour in the highest circles of English life. Within a few weeks of the publication of his book, King William himself issued a proclamation with an identical title through the Lord Chamberlain's office, directing players not to act anything in their plays 'contrary to religion and good manners.'²⁸ In the following decade new convictions were brought in against actors under the old Profan-ity Act of James I.²⁹ By the time that Parliament was ready, in 1737, to endorse by statute the traditional system of theatrical censorship in England, it had become virtually axiomatic that one of the censor's prime duties would be to keep references to religion off the English stage.

'NOW I AM EXAMINER OF PLAYS' (1737–1843)

From about 1680 onwards the Lord Chamberlain gradually took over the censorship duties of his subordinate, the Master of the Revels, whose office eventually passed out of existence in the early eighteenth century.³⁰ In 1737 the powers of the Lord Chamberlain were confirmed by an Act of Parliament which provided that all plays be sent to him for licensing at least fourteen days in advance of performance, and which gave him absolute authority to allow or disallow them as he pleased.³¹ Upon acquiring this power, the Lord Chamberlain's first act was to delegate it, creating the post of Examiner of Plays to handle the work of reading and licensing scripts. During the eighteenth and nineteenth centuries the Examiner himself frequently appointed deputies to help him, and on more than one occasion the deputy duly succeeded to the office at the death of the incumbent. In this way the system became largely self-perpetuating, and over the years the Exam-iners evolved a set of 'unwritten rules' to guide them in censoring plays which they came to regard as being as binding as the laws of the realm.

The activities of the censors in the late eighteenth and early nineteenth centuries may be studied in detail in the Larpent Collection, now in the Huntington Library in California. This contains (at least theoretically, for a few are missing) copies of every play submitted for licensing in England between 1737 and 1824.[32] The bulk of the scripts, for obvious reasons, have little to do with religious drama *per se*, and are thus beyond the scope of this study. A fair number of them, however, have to do with religion in one form or another, and the scripts reveal that, like their predecessors, the eighteenth-century censors were particularly sensitive to anything in plays that might hint of profanity, disrespect for the Bible, or ridicule of religious sects.[33]

Under the tenure of office of John Larpent (1778–1824) references of any sort to religion virtually disappeared from the theatre. Larpent, himself a Methodist preacher, zealously cut out of all the scripts that were submitted to him even the most harmless of Biblical echoes, extending to the very words 'Heaven' and 'Hell.' In this attitude he had the full support of both the King and the government. The royal patent issued by George III to the Drury Lane theatre in 1812 contained a clause imposing restrictions on the performance of religious plays that went far beyond any previous official guidelines:

We have thought fit to declare that henceforth no representations be admitted on the stage by virtue or under colour of these Our letters patent, whereby the Christian religion in general, or the Church of England, may in any manner suffer reproach, strictly inhibiting every degree of abuse or misrepresentation of sacred characters, tending to expose religion itself, and to bring it into contempt, and that no such character be otherwise introduced or placed in any other light than such as may enhance the just esteem of those who truly answer the end of their sacred function.[34]

Among the pre-Victorian censors by far the most important figure, from the point of view of religious drama, was Larpent's successor, George Colman the Younger. Son of a popular playwright, Colman followed in his father's footsteps until his advancement to the office of Examiner of Plays. His own plays had more than once been condemned by Larpent for their indecency, but upon taking over the office in 1824 Colman underwent a conversion. He prohibited plays and deleted offending words and passages with a zeal that made his predecessors look like libertines. 'Mr. Colman has been rather particular,' complained the playwright W.T. Moncrieff to the Parliamentary Commission on Dramatic Literature in 1832. 'He would not let one mention the word "thighs;" he said those were indecent. And he would not let me insert "goblin damned," for he said it was blasphemy, and a number of things of that kind.' When Colman was asked by the Commission how he reconciled his present linguistic fastidiousness with the vulgarity of some of the language in his own works, he replied disarmingly: 'If I had been the examiner, I should have scratched them out, and would do so now. I was in a different position at that time. Then I was a careless immoral author; now I am the Examiner of Plays.'[35]

On the subject of Biblical plays, Colman was equally forthright. 'I conceive,' he said, 'that all Scripture is much too sacred for the stage, except in very solemn scenes indeed, and that to bring things so sacred upon the stage becomes profane.'[36] Colman thus became the first Examiner of Plays to announce publicly what in fact had been the policy of his office since it was founded, namely that plays on scriptural subjects were considered *ipso facto* to be unsuitable for the stage. The qualification 'except in very solemn scenes indeed' seems not to have meant anything in particular and was contradicted in the next clause. In practice, the nineteenth-century Examiners made no inquiries at all into manner of performance but simply refused outright to read any play submitted to them on a scriptural subject. 'Solemn scenes' constituted their vision of what a religious play ought ideally to be like, but it was commonly agreed that nothing of the sort was to be found in the drama of the Middle Ages. Historical accounts of the drama continued to show the bias of Rymer and Dodsley, such as the following, written in 1830:

When the church had become corrupted under the dominion of the Popes, spiritual dramas became frequent in most countries of Europe; and from the manner in which they were conducted, tended greatly to diminish respect for the holy mysteries of religion, and to turn into ridicule everything sacred. Nothing but the grossest superstition could have tolerated them as religious spectacles. Monks and friars were the actors, and they performed in churches, monasteries, or even in the open air, like common jugglers.[37]

That such plays could ever be purged of their grossness or replaced by better ones of their kind seemed scarcely conceivable. 'It is impossible for the stage to become good, in a Christian sense,' the same writer concluded, 'because its character must be faithfully congenial with that of its supporters, and they consist chiefly of the most trifling, irreligious, and immoral part of the community.' These sentiments were shared by Colman's deputy, John Payne Collier, who agreed that 'it is a very ancient complaint against theatres that they collect a bad neighbourhood around them.'[38] It was to protect God

from such company that the censors of the remainder of the nineteenth
century saw as their duty.

'FEELING HOT': THE VICTORIAN CENSORS (1843–1909)

> You may lampoon and you may libel,
> Double entente you may employ,
> But you mustn't use the Bible
> For your purposes, my boy.[39]

The personal records of the Victorian Examiners of Plays have been preserved
in the Public Record Office in London. Through the files of letters, play-lists,
and memos one can trace their efforts to keep religion off the English stage,
while at the same time perceiving the growing opposition to their views that
eventually made possible the revival of the mystery plays.

The only significant piece of theatrical legislation to be enacted during
the Victorian era was the Theatres Act of 1843, a modification of the 1737
Act which was to govern the licensing of plays and theatres for the next 125
years. The main purpose of the new act was to extend the Victorian principle
of free trade to theatres. It abolished the monopoly of the patent theatres
on legitimate drama in London and empowered the Lord Chamberlain to
license as many theatres as the city wished to support. But if free trade was
to be extended, free speech was not. The clause in the 1737 Act requiring
prior submission of playscripts to the Lord Chamberlain for licensing was
repeated almost verbatim, though a phrase was inserted which attempted to
define the grounds on which a play might be denied a license. The Lord
Chamberlain was empowered 'for the time being, whenever he shall be of
opinion that it is fitting for the preservation of good manners, decorum, or
of the public peace so to do, to forbid the acting or presenting of any stage
play anywhere in Great Britain either absolutely or for such time as he shall
think fit.'[40]

The vagueness of these guidelines made them useless from the start, and
there is no evidence that the Examiners paid any attention to them. Instead,
they made their decisions much as they had before. A report issued in 1866
listed 2,816 plays submitted for licence during the preceding dozen years,
of which nineteen had been banned. Of these, 'two were from Scripture
subjects, seven were of the swell mob and burglary school, and the bulk of
the remainder were French plays of an immoral tendency or English versions
of them.'[41] Occasionally the Examiner's task was lightened by the appearance
of a play which was objectionable on both religious and sexual grounds,

such as Oscar Wilde's *Salome*, which E.F.S. Pigott described, accurately enough, as 'half Biblical, half pornographic.'[42]

Support for the censors' position was widespread. The files of the Lord Chamberlain's office bulge with letters, often anonymous and most of them from either clergymen or worried mothers, urging him to take harsher measures toward indecency and irreverence in the theatres. One anonymous clergyman, for example, protested against licensing plays which showed 'insufficient respect to the matrimonial tie,' informing the Lord Chamberlain that at one such play several friends of his had 'felt hot from beginning to end.'[43]

Such letters lend credence to the Examiners' claims that when they erred it was always on the side of leniency. Narrow-minded as some of their views seem to us today, the attitude of the general public toward the theatre appears to have been far more stringent. Recognizing this, we can better understand the quandary which the Examiners found themselves in when it came to religion on the stage.

Unlike sex, which found few adherents brave enough to defend its discussion in public, religion was a topic that found expression in every Victorian medium other than the stage. The ban against scriptural drama, while it continued to be rigorously enforced, was open to question in a way that the ban on sex was not. With the advent of the new 'serious' drama of the 1890s, led by George Bernard Shaw (who was, by his own lights, a 'religious' dramatist), it was inevitable that some writers, as well as a substantial section of the public, would wish to add religion to the list of subjects available for treatment on the stage.

Against this movement the Examiners stood firm, but it is a measure of the trouble that Biblical subjects caused them that they consistently referred the more important cases to higher-ups: to the Lord Chamberlain, to the Bishops, even to the Queen and the Prince of Wales. There is evidence that as early as the 1850s the Examiners themselves felt that an easing of the restrictions against Biblical plays might be advisable. An instance of this is the struggle that William Bodham Donne underwent in attempting to determine whether a play based on an apocryphal book of the Old Testament was, legally, a scriptural play. Unwilling to take so tricky a matter upon himself, he addressed a memo to the Lord Chamberlain requesting guidance and expressing his own opinion that 'nearly as much liberty should be allowed to the theatre as to Literature in the choice of subjects.' The Lord Chamberlain, however, was more cautious and declined to issue a licence on the grounds that it might set a precedent, though he saw nothing objectionable in the play itself. As a way out of the difficulty he suggested that the author be encouraged to change the names of his characters to non-Biblical ones, or better still to find another story in secular history, 'the main facts of which would tally with those of the story in question.' As a precedent he cited the transformation of Rossini's *Mose in Egypto* into *Pietro l'Eremita* and Verdi's *Nabucco* into *Nino and Zorro*. Donne accepted the decision stoically, though not without a grain of humour. 'There is now,' he wrote, 'what the lawyers call a 'ruled case,' and in future I shall have no doubt whenever a drama founded on the Apocrypha is submitted to me for examination.'[44]

All this was over the Apocrypha. There was no suggestion that Biblical drama itself should be allowed, nor could there be. The man who had once objected to a play on the grounds that it was 'a little too dramatic for Passion Week' could hardly be expected to show much mercy to the drama of the Passion itself.

Donne's successor, E.F.S. Pigott, was equally vigilant where scriptural subjects were concerned, even if they had only a peripheral connection with the play in question. In 1873, for example, he became alarmed over a play by Wilkie Collins called *The New Magdalen*, a story of a girl driven by poverty into an 'evil life,' who, after undergoing a conversion, becomes a sister of charity in the Franco-Prussian War and eventually marries a clergyman. Pigott found the theme 'painful' and insisted that at least the title be changed. When a poster advertising the re-christened play hinted at its Biblical content by referring to 'Luke xv.7,' Pigott was incensed. 'This unprecedented and unnecessary allusion to a verse of Scripture,' he told the producer, 'far from attracting visitors to the theatre may keep many away.'[45]

Toward the end of the 1870s, however, the battle between religion and the censorship began to come to a head. In 1879 an organization was formed called the Church and Stage Guild. Its founder, Stewart Headlam, was an Anglican priest who had been relieved of his curacy by the Bishop of London for preaching a sermon which, according to the Bishop, 'encouraged young men and young women to be frequent spectators at Ballet Dancing.'[46] Headlam was a Christian Socialist, who, like William Morris, sought to bring spiritual nourishment to the industrial masses through the arts. The purpose of the Church and Stage Guild, he announced, was 'to promote religious and social sympathy between the members of the Church and the Stage, to hold meetings for these purposes from time to time, and to meet for worship at least once a year.' A journalist of the time promptly rewrote Headlam's aims as 'the introduction of curates to actresses and the promise of stage players to go to church once a year.'[47] Undaunted, Headlam proceeded to attack 'the unchristian prejudices' of Englishmen against the theatre, and particularly the legal system which upheld these prejudices, accusing the Lord Chamberlain's office of having reduced English drama to an arena of trivia, of 'licensing adultery while forbidding religion on the stage.'[48]

Throughout the 1880s and 1890s the Church and Stage Guild kept up its attack, publishing a report each year which chronicled its efforts. In 1901 the Society disbanded, satisfied that it had succeeded in breaking down the prejudice of the English Church against the theatre. As evidence of their success they cited the fact that in 1897 Henry Irving had been granted permission to give a dramatic reading of Tennyson's *Becket* in Canterbury Cathedral, as well as the fact that quasi-religious spectacles like *The Sign of the Cross* had gained a foothold on the public stage. As far as Biblical drama went, however, their success was negligible. Early in 1895 a proposal to perform the Oberammergau Passion Play in London was vetoed by the Lord Chamberlain, after careful consultation with his superiors, including Queen Victoria herself.[49] The decision had the effect of reconfirming the general ban on Biblical plays.

Later in the same year George Alexander Redford took over the office of Examiner of Plays. A man even more fearful of setting dangerous precedents than his predecessors, Redford proceeded to turn down every play that came before him with even the faintest hint of Biblical origin. He seems to have taken it for granted that the issue had been settled by the highest authorities and that his job was simply to enforce the rule, without regard to the merits of individual proposals.

The number of such proposals, however, increased strikingly during Redford's tenure as Examiner. He had scarcely taken office when a Tyneside vicar who had composed his own Passion Play wrote for permission to perform it in an exhibition hall in Newcastle. Redford duly replied 'privately, as a matter of courtesy,' calling the vicar's attention 'to the Regulations,' and adding that 'Passion Plays have never received the License of the Lord Chamberlain for representation in Great Britain and I see no reason to make any exception in this case.'[50] It was perhaps the influence of the Queen that had elevated an unwritten rule to a 'Regulation.'

Scarcely two months later a similar application, this time by a visiting Australian clergyman, the Reverend G. Walters, arrived at Redford's office for an Old Testament play on *Joseph and his Brethren*. Redford rejected it summarily with the curt notation: 'The episode with Potiphar's wife is the central situation. Quite impossible.'[51] In this decision Redford received ample support from the public. When the possibility of a performance of *Joseph and his Brethren* was reported in the press, a barrage of letters reached the Lord Chamberlain's office, of which the following is a sample:

It is with surprise and much concern I notice a statement in the newspapers that a Rev. Mr. Walters has come to England from Australia to introduce his plays on the English stage. It appears that he has dramatized sacred subjects out of the Bible such as Joseph in Egypt which all Christians regard as the Word of God. This causes me and other Christians much pain of our moral sense and we consider it will be a shocking thing if he is allowed to carry out his intentions – trafficking in sacred things, parading solemn and holy things to be laughed at and ridiculed by worldly minded men and women and I trust, My Lord, that you will prevent such a sacrilegious perversion of Holy Writ being made a stage spectacle to amuse people many of whom have no regard for the Bible as the Word of God to sinful men who have no respect for things holy and I consider it is a most dangerous folly to jest with things holy. Such exhibitions are calculated to bring the Holy Book into contempt. It is degrading the Holy Scriptures to drag them before a profane multitude to make sport of before the ungodly and amounts to a practical denial of the sanctity of the Bible and committed by a professing clergyman (!) it appears to me to amount to the unpardonable sin against the Holy Spirit.[52]

The rhetoric of this letter, no less than its opinions, shows how little had changed in the attitude of at least some Englishmen toward religion on the stage since the days of William Prynne. In Redford they found an official sympathetic to their views. During the next fifteen months he turned down two plays, *Barabbas* ('a Scriptural Play involving the trial and crucifixion of Christ') and *The Conversion of England* ('a series of tableaux with dialogue of very religious tendency unsuitable for representation in a licensed theatre').[53] Two other plays he rejected solely because of their titles, though in fact they had nothing whatever to do with the Bible. The offending titles were *No Cross, No Crown*, and *A Crown of Thorns*. (A precedent for this policy had been set by Pigott in 1883 when he banned a play called *God and the Man* on the grounds that 'some people might think the title referred to the Incarnation.')[54]

By the time that Redford had completed his second year in office, there could be little doubt as to what the fate of even the most respectable Biblical dramas would be if submitted to the Examiner of Plays. He even had a form letter specially designed for the contingency:

Dear Sir, – I have no power as Examiner of Plays to make any exception to the rule that Scriptural plays, or plays founded on or adapted from the Scriptures, are *ineligible for licence* in Great Britain. It would appear ... that your play would come under this rule, and I may say for myself that I am glad to be relieved of the difficult and delicate duty of deciding on the fitness of treatment in each particular case.[55]

Between 1897 and 1907 Redford's ban fell upon such works as Rubinstein's opera *Christ*, which was prohibited at Covent Garden even though the part of Jesus was written for an offstage tenor; Saint-Saens' *Samson and Delilah*; a 'Hebrew Operetta' on the Sacrifice of Isaac, sung in Yiddish; Housman's *Bethlehem*, a retelling of the Nativity story; and Hauptmann's *Hannele*, a modern allegory performed in German which was licensed only on condition that its Christ-figure should not have a beard. Even a play about Mohammed was prohibited after a worried telegram from the Home Office asked 'what the feelings of people would be in any Christian country if it was proposed to produce a play in which Jesus Christ was one of the characters.' [56]

In 1907, however, seventy-one of the leading literary figures of the day, including Conrad, Galsworthy, Hardy, James, Masefield, Shaw, and Yeats, announced in a letter to *The Times* that they had lodged a 'formal protest' with the government, demanding that the licensing of plays be abolished. [57] Four months later, a delegation of the signers met with the Home Secretary, Winston Churchill, and secured the promise of an investigation. On 29 July 1909, the Joint Select Committee of the House of Lords and the House of Commons on Stage Plays opened public hearings in London.

The evidence presented to the Committee was devastating to the censorship, none more so than that of the Examiner himself:

Q   On what principles do you proceed in licensing the plays that come before you?
A   Simply bringing to bear an official point of view and keeping up a standard. It is really impossible to define what the principle may be. There are no principles that can be defined. I follow a precedent.
Q   It is no part of your duty to give any reason whatsoever for vetoing a play?
A   No, it is no part of my duty to give any reason for vetoing a play ... I have no critical view on plays at all. I simply have to maintain a standard. [58]

Redford's testimony on the subject of scriptural plays was equally revealing:

Q   Is it a rule of your office that scriptural plays or plays adapted from Scripture are ineligible for license in Great Britain?
A   Yes. I do not even read them. If they are obviously scriptural, I point out the fact and the play goes back to the person who submitted it.
Q   That is the rule?
A   Yes.
Q   Can you tell me by whom that rule was made?
A   No, I cannot.

Q   Or when it was made?

A   No; it was in existence before my time.

Q   Has it ever been clearly laid down for the information of authors?

A   It is very generally understood in the theatrical profession.

Q   But you cannot point to anything which definitely lays it down?

A   No, I cannot.

Q   What objection do you think there would be to producing the Passion Play in London?

A   Religious feeling would be outraged at seeing the Crucifixion, for instance, enacted on a public stage in a theatre.

Q   Do you recollect a play being submitted to you by Mr. Lawrence Housman called 'Bethlehem'?

A   Yes.

Q   And you consider that the Christmas story was not proper for representation on the stage?

A   It was not a question of propriety at all; it traversed the custom.

Q   You are bound by the rules of your office, of course?

A   And custom and precedent; the unwritten law you may call it ... I have simply endeavoured to carry on the office on the principles which I had learnt from Mr. Pigott and which I have since learned from my connection with it during the last 14 years.

Q   That is to say, the matter has not been considered from the consideration of what are the definite instructions under which the authority should be exercised?

A   No, I know nothing of any definite instructions.

Q   I may take it then that you have no means of judging, and you have not attempted to judge, whether the rules under which you act are merely precedents which might possibly be unauthorised and at any rate are not authorised by the Act of Parliament?

A   No.[59]

But if the Examiner stood on shaky legal ground, his procedures and opinions received some prominent endorsements. Against the protests of playwrights appeared the united support of the theatre managers for the licensing system, because of the protection it afforded them from common-law prosecution. On the subject of religion, the Bishop of Southwark defended the Examiner's reluctance to license plays representing the deity on the stage. While allowing that there might be no objection to such characters as the Queen of Sheba, he insisted that there was grave danger of irreverence in 'bringing anything like very sacred matter into the general context of a theatre.' To represent Christ and the Apostles, as was done in the Oberammergau Passion Play, he declared, and to make 'fancy speeches in their character' would be 'an absolute shock of a most scandalous kind to reverence.' Warning the Committee that 'the opinion of Churchmen at large would be likely to be even more sensitive and stricter than my own,' he finished by urging them to 'limit very closely the area of things of that kind' permitted in the theatre.[60] A Roman Catholic spokesman endorsed the Bishop's views.

The report issued by the Committee following the hearings recommended only partial changes in the censorship system. It endorsed the continuation of the office of Examiner of Plays, though under closer supervision by the Lord Chamberlain. It urged the relaxation of the ban against scriptural plays, but advised that this should not extend to 'dramas in which Persons held to be divine are represented.' It further recommended forbidding a licence to any play found 'to do violence to the sentiment of religious reverence.'[61] No legislation on the subject was ever introduced, but in the years that followed the Lord Chamberlain's office voluntarily adopted most of the Committee's suggestions. In 1912 the rule against scriptural plays was relaxed to the extent of permitting Old Testament characters and non-sacred New Testament figures to appear on the stage. But the ban on impersonating the Deity remained legally in force, with a few specially granted exceptions which we shall examine in later chapters, until the final abolition of the censorship system by Parliament in 1968. It was thus that as late as 1932 E. Martin Browne, the foremost modern producer of medieval religious plays, could still write that 'the Lord Chamberlain has ruled that "neither God nor Jesus may appear on the stage or take a speaking part." It is, moreover, at present axiomatic in England that the person of Christ shall not be shown even in church.'[62]

Such were the conditions under which the revival of medieval Biblical drama during the twentieth century was obliged to begin. Producers who wished to take up these plays found themselves under a double handicap. First, they had to skirt, as best they could, the Lord Chamberlain's restrictions. Second, and equally important, since there was no continuous native tradition of Biblical drama to draw on, they had to look elsewhere for any existing theatrical models on which to base the style of their productions. When the first tentative revivals of these plays finally came about, they were to bear the unmistakable imprint not of medieval English theatrical traditions but of modern Bavarian ones.

2

Oberammergau and the Victorians

'Here we see a performance unstained by any artificial and professional tinge, the performers unslurred by the filth that has hung about the modern stage.'

Henry S. Holland, 1870

'The *Passionspiel* at Oberammergau is as different from the miracle play of England as the noblest tragedy from the commonest farce.'

Henry Blackburn, 1870

'The consumption of beer is appalling.'

The Archdeacon of Westminster, 1890

The one Biblical drama which Englishmen did approve of was the Oberammergau Passion Play. Some insisted that it was the exception that proved the rule: only in the remote mountain valleys of Bavaria, insulated from the decadence of modern life and untainted by theatricality or commercialism, could such a performance be allowed. For others, however, it was the exception that proved the possibility of further exceptions: if Bavarian peasants could stage the sacred drama without offence, why could English actors not do the same? Both sides agreed that in Oberammergau a unique formula had been found that overcame all the objections that had traditionally been raised against the enactment of Christian history on the stage. The search for the ingredients of that formula became the preoccupation of nearly every producer of religious plays in England in the early years of the present century.

The English fascination with the *Passionspiel* dates from the introduction of the railroad to Europe and coincides with the institution of the Grand Tour. Before 1850 the Passion Play had been a purely local affair, performed in the village churchyard on a temporary stage. There is no record of a single Englishman ever having visited it. After that, however, they came, first in a small stream, then in a flood. A description of the 1860 performance mentions 'the Englishmen, very few in number, with serious but complacent faces, contrasting grimly in their business-like grey cloth suits with those picturesque costumes of the natives.'[1] Eleven years later, at the next performance (the 1870 performance having been cancelled due to the Franco-Prussian war), Matthew Arnold noted that 'everybody has this last Autumn been either seeing the Ammergau Passion Play or hearing about it.' Most remarkable among the English visitors, Arnold found, were the numbers of clergymen. 'Anglican ministers were sympathisers to be expected. But Protestant ministers of the most unimpeachable sort, Protestant dissenting ministers, were there too, and showing favour and sympathy.'[2] By 1900 the Passion Play had been almost taken over by foreigners, the *Church Times* marvelling on how 'English people have associated – one might almost say identified – themselves with the performance of the Passion Play at Oberammergau.'[3] Given the seal of approval by visiting clergymen and romanticized in the memoirs of prolific novelists like Mrs Howitt-Watt, the Passion Play had become a three-star entry on the itinerary of every English tourist.

What accounts for the extraordinary popularity of Oberammergau with the Victorians? Their attitude toward it appears to have been much the same as their attitude toward Germany as a whole. They went to Oberammergau for the same reasons that they went to Heidelberg and Berlin, Munich and Vienna, and a little later to Bayreuth. Germany was the centre of nineteenth-century romantic culture. It was the home of musicians and poets, philosophers and scholars, all of whom had one thing in common: they showed no sign of ever having heard of the Industrial Revolution. Along the Rhine and in the Alps the English traveller could think high thoughts without stumbling over the unemployed, could contemplate the past without having his landscape marred by smokestacks and chimneys. His way to Oberammergau had been prepared by the Germans themselves, especially the scholars from Heidelberg and Berlin who had declared the Passion Play to be a true example of the Folk-Art to which all the best modern German art was once again aspiring. Wagner could only imitate it, but here was the real thing, preserved in all its purity and artlessness to astound the sophisticated and convert the cynical. The Passion Play was, everyone believed, a genuine relic of the Middle Ages, even if it had been purified of some of its original grossness by sensible editors. In Oberammergau relevant tradition and enlightened progress appeared side by side, combined to elevate the spirit of man.

The Englishman who visited Oberammergau did not go there just to see a play. He came also to breathe the atmosphere in which that play took place and to see the people who performed it. Accounts of the experience always began with the picturesque journey through the mountain passes from Munich, the roads marked by carved wooden crosses and quaint Bavarian church-towers, to the Eden-like village in the Ammer valley. Along the way qualms occasionally set in. 'Two friends of mine,' recalled a canon of Westminster in 1890, 'were so deeply moved by the doubt of whether it was *right* to witness a play which presented the Lord Jesus Christ that even when they arrived within three miles of Oberammergau they were on the point of turning back.'4 The first sight of the town and its inhabitants was generally enough, however, to allay their fears. 'The sweet, pure, happy, and deeply religious population of this Tyrolese village,' the canon reassured his readers, were totally incapable of approaching their task with 'anything but the most solemn reverence.'5

The idea that the Passion Play was not acted but lived was perhaps the most important ingredient in the Oberammergau mystique. Everyone knew that only those who modelled their private lives on that of the Saviour could be chosen for the principal parts. The roles were allocated by secret ballot and any known misconduct was enough to disqualify a candidate, except for the role of Judas or the Jewish priests. Only unmarried women under the age of thirty-five were eligible for the part of the Virgin Mary. No make-up of any kind was permitted in the performance, and no artificial lighting was used, so that the 'real-life' faces of the actors had to meet the requirements of the parts. The accounts of English visitors invariably dwelt on this mingling of the real and the imaginary. The first sight of bearded peasants in the streets of the village stirred feelings of awe in the visitors as great as any they were to feel in the theatre. When the actor who was to play Christ was pointed out to them, whether behind a shop counter or seated at a table in a tavern, they lapsed into hushed silence as though in the presence of the Galilean himself. When Mrs Howitt-Watt was introduced to Tobias Flunger, the Christus of 1850, she felt that she was seeing a ghost:

As he removed his fez we saw his dark glossy hair parted above the centre of his brow, and falling in rich waves upon his shoulders, and that his melancholy dark eyes, his pale brow, his emaciated features, his short, black beard, all bore the most strange and startling resemblance to the heads of the Saviour as represented by the early Italian painters.

There was something to my mind almost fearful in this resemblance, and Tobias Flunger seemed to act and speak like one filled with a mysterious awe. If this be an act of worship in him, this personation of our Lord, what will be its effect upon him in after life? There was something so strange, so unspeakably melancholy in his emaciated countenance, that I found my imagination soon busily speculating upon the true reading of its expression.[6]

The conduct of the performance itself was calculated to sustain this atmosphere of reverence and awe. Both actors and audience behaved more like a church congregation than like a theatrical crowd. The play began at eight o'clock in the morning, preceded by the village bells calling visitor and resident alike to Mass. Before the curtain went up the cast assembled behind it to pray. No one was seated after the performance began and no interruptions were permitted, other than the one-hour lunch interval, after which the play was resumed for another four hours. The one sour note was struck by a few local members of the audience who were in the habit of slipping out the side doors as occasion permitted to refill their beer-steins, a custom noted with alarmed disapproval by a visiting Anglican deacon. Otherwise all was as decorous as in church, permitting the spectator uninterrupted meditation on the spectacle before him. Visitors were warned in the guidebooks not to whisper, or pass chocolates, or smoke. Ladies were advised to keep smelling-salts on hand in case of faintness at the Crucifixion. A program note warning that applause was out of keeping with the nature of the play proved superfluous.

The character of the inhabitants of Oberammergau and the manner in which they conducted their Passion Play did more than anything else to secure its approval by people who might otherwise have been ashamed to admit setting foot in a theatre. 'The Passion Play is the medium for the expression of reverential and God-fearing peasants,' wrote the theatre critic Archibald Henderson, 'simple in thought, simple in expression, simple in creed – who do not act, but actually live and move and have their being in an antique world of omnipresent actuality.'[7] The fact that this 'antique world' was actually a modern innovation was generally unknown to visitors from abroad. In actuality, however, the Passion Play as performed in the nineteenth century bore practically no resemblance at all to its 'antique,' or medieval, original. On the contrary, virtually everything that Englishmen admired most in it was the product of changes that had been introduced into its original script during the previous one hundred years. The misconception of many spectators that they were watching a genuine survival from the Middle Ages only served to make them more intolerant of the crude examples of the genre that survived from their own country, with which they could not help comparing the purity and grandeur of the German version. Oberammergau was simply one more example of Victorian Gothic, but one that succeeded in fooling more people than usual.

Strictly speaking, Oberammergau never had a medieval Passion play. The first performance took place in 1634, during the high tide of the Counter-Reformation, as a thanksgiving for the deliverance of the town from the plague. The text used on that occasion was borrowed from the nearby city of Augsburg, which did have a tradition of performing Passion plays going back to the fifteenth century. Such medieval features as the Oberammergau play had were thus borrowed ones, and even these quickly disappeared to be replaced by texts of a more elevated and respectable kind. A comparison of the one surviving text from the seventeenth century with the one in use during the nineteenth century shows how much the Oberammergauers had done to 'improve' their play by the time of the Victorians' arrival.

The 1662 text of the Oberammergau Passion Play shows all the hallmarks of the medieval original from which it was copied.[8] Written in rhymed couplets, it includes such allegorical figures as Death, Sin, Avarice, and Envy, plus a host of 'Diabolical Fiends.' It appears to have been written for mansion-and-place staging, with a 'proclamator' or prompter to organize the action and explain it to the audience. The play opened with Satan, seated on his throne, surrounded by Sin and Death, declaring war on Christ. The pace of the drama that followed was swift, the action violent and spectacular. A stage direction at the Crucifixion warned: 'Now remove the rope from his feet, and bind him with strips of linen round the body, hands, and arms, round the breast and loins, so that, should he become unconscious, he will not fall from the Cross.' The climax of the play, however, was not the Crucifixion but the Harrowing of Hell, the focus of the audience being not on Christ's suffering but on his destruction of his enemies. An angel discourteously plucked the halo from Judas' head as he left the table of the Last Supper, while Satan danced jubilantly at the betrayal. At Judas' suicide a swarm of devils cut down his body and proceeded to devour his entrails (made, we are told, of sausages and sweetened pancake-butter) before carting him off to hell. Equally juicy fates awaited the other villains of the piece – Annas, Caiaphas, Herod, Pilate – presented not as victims of circumstance or as misunderstood colonial governors, but simply as henchmen of the devil.

Whatever may be said for its theology, the Oberammergau Ur-Text was simple, passionate, and theatrically exciting. Under the pressures of the

Counter-Reformation and later of Romanticism, however, the efforts of revisers over the next two hundred years were to rid the play of its crudities and *diableries*. The first to take it in hand were the Jesuits. In 1750 Father Ferdinand Rosner wrote a completely new play, casting out the devils and converting the production to a baroque spectacle.[9] The doggerel rhymes of the original were replaced by dignified Alexandrines. Satan and his companions were banished, their places taken by stately allegorical characters and by what Father Rosner called 'plastic figures,' that is, Old Testament models elucidating the New Testament story, the forerunners of the nineteenth-century *tableaux vivants*. A chorus of singing genii anticipated the sombre Greek choruses of later productions, transforming the play partially into an oratorio.

Even in this form the Passion Play came under attack by the authorities during the Enlightenment, and further revisions were necessary to save it from extinction. In 1770 the Archbishop of Salzburg issued a proclamation prohibiting Biblical plays, for reasons curiously like those of the English Puritans. The Archbishop denounced their 'mixture of the sacred and the profane,' the distraction they offered 'from more edifying modes of instruction, such as sermons,' the promiscuity encouraged 'in assemblies of large numbers of persons,' and, perhaps most important at this time, 'the exposure of sacred subjects to the criticism and ridicule of free-thinkers.'[10]

Only the personal intervention of the Emperor Maximilian saved the Oberammergau play from suppression. To prevent any recurrence of the Archbishop's objections, the Oberammergauers decided to rewrite their play once again, this time in such a way as to render it free from the slightest suspicion of impiety or theatricality. This task they entrusted first to Father Magnus Knipfelberger in 1780 and then to Father Othmar Weis of the neighbouring monastery of Ettal in 1815, who may be called the father of the play as it is known today. Weis' major innovation was to stick strictly to the words of the Bible, a practise that was to be greeted with surprised delight by visiting English clergymen in the decades to come. The spoken text of the play was recast into scriptural prose, verse hymns being reserved for the stately Greek chorus, set to music in the style of Haydn and Mozart. Soon afterwards, in 1830, the setting of the play was moved from the church-yard to a permanent theatre of classical design erected in the village meadow, holding five thousand spectators and provided with a stage, 138 feet wide, that permitted the use of movable perspective scenery while managing to look not like a theatre but a Greek temple. (See plate 1.) A contemporary description of 1830 reveals how much this illusionary setting blended into the natural landscape of the Alps:

The stage proper represents the city of Jerusalem and consists of three streets: the one in the middle is covered and provided with wings and curtains; the two at each side are not covered and are separated from the central one by the houses of Pilate and Herod; the latter are provided with balconies on which Pilate and Herod occasionally appear and pronounce judgement. The stage is so deep and is in so peculiar a light that people appearing in the background seem to be coming from afar. Imagine at the same time the wild valley of the Ammer, surrounded on both sides and on the east by high chalk peaks whose lower slopes are covered with green forests, open on the west with many grand mountain giants in the distance; a country such as the old Romans were wont to choose for their theatres, in which the two mountain ranges form the wings.[11]

The comparison with Roman theatres is, of course, a misconception. Roman drama was an urban art, and Roman theatres were equipped with a *scaena* high enough to blot out any distracting views of nature. What the writer was thinking of – and what the Oberammergauers designed – was a Greek theatre, and a ruined one at that, bereft of its civilized surroundings, set in a lonely wilderness and conjuring up visions of decayed antiquity. For the nineteenth-century spectator Oberammergau thus provided a heady mixture of traditional Christian piety, classical gravity, and romantic nature-worship. The finishing touches were put on this blend in 1850 by Father Alois Daisenberger, a classical scholar who pruned Father Weis' prose and cast the choral hymns into the form of Greek strophes and antistrophes. The result was described in the most popular English account of the period as follows:

And whilst they sang, our hearts were strangely touched, and our eyes wandered away from those singular peasant-angels and their peasant audience, up to the deep, cloudless sky; we heard the rustle of the trees, and caught glimpses of the mountains, and all seemed a strange, poetical dream.[12]

The script finally produced by all these efforts resembled a medieval Passion play only in length. The Oberammergau play as performed in the nineteenth century – and substantially as still performed today – had eighteen acts and took nearly eight hours to perform. Each act followed a three-part formula. First, the chorus appeared, 'plumed and fancifully decked in a sort of operatic attire,' as the German medieval scholar Karl Hase described them in 1850.[13] They were led by a Choragus, costumed in a slightly different manner from the rest, and proceeded to sing verses introducing and explaining the scene to follow. Everything the chorus did was symmetrical and uniform. The individual members were arranged according to height, the taller in the centre, the shorter graduated toward the wings. The colour schemes of their costumes were similarly arranged to form a harmonious progression. The gestures they were permitted to use to illustrate their verses fell into three prescribed categories: attention, exhortation, and warning. The uniformity of the chorus's movements and the perfect timing with which they were executed never failed to impress English visitors: 'The curb that was set on the imagination here was worthy of Hellenic moderation,' one of them enthused, 'of Sophoclean tone.' [14] A sample of the verses written for the chorus by Father Daisenberger, in a contemporary English translation, conveys something of the elevated style of the production (the lines are from the end of the Conspiracy scene):

Ah! are they gone, the ruthless sons of spite?
Their sordid forms and aims are brought to light!
From sin's vile garb the shreds of grace are torn,
By keen remorse the face is sear'd and worn! [15]

Following the chorus came the tableau. The tableau took place on the central curtained stage and depicted an Old Testament scene deemed to be analogous to the forthcoming incident in the Passion story. In more than half the acts there were not one but two tableaux preceding the main scene in the drama. The scene of Christ's departure from his mother in Bethany, for example, was preceded by tableaux depicting, first, 'Young Tobias Taking Leave of His Parents' and, second, 'The Lamenting Bride of The Canticles.' The principles governing the selection of these Old Testament episodes in the Oberammergau play were quite different from those which had operated in the medieval mysteries. Medieval dramatists had limited their choice to those incidents in the Old Testament which they imagined had a direct historical connection with events of the New Testament. In Oberammergau, on the other hand, any resemblance would do, however remote. The resemblance, moreover, was generally an emotional rather than a theological one, all traces of historical typology having disappeared. 'The Lamenting Bride of the Canticles' could only have meant, to a medieval dramatist, a type of the Church separated from its husband, Christ – an apt figure for the Babylonian Captivity, perhaps, but hardly for the Saviour's leave-taking from his mother on the way to his victory on the cross. In Oberammergau, however, the general emotional content of the incident was enough: 'a pathetic heart-melting scene,' commented the official English guide-book in 1880.

Occasionally the tableau was used to give a significance to the following episode that it might otherwise not have had. The scene of Christ's last journey to Jerusalem, for example, was preceded by a tableau depicting the repudiation of Queen Vashti by King Ahasuerus and the Elevation of Queen Esther in her place. The chorus explained the Esther story as an allegory of Christ's rejection of the 'proud and disdainful Jews, as punishment for their sins,' and his decision 'to elect for himself a better and more worthy people.' It then concluded: 'Thus will the synagogue be abolished, and the kingdom of God instrusted to another people – a people that will bring forth fruits of righteousness.' In such ways did the notorious anti-Semitism of the play creep in.[16]

The execution of the tableaux was for most visitors to Oberammergau the high point of the performance. Devoid of all but the most essential movement, the scenes enabled the spectators to meditate on their subjects in complete tranquillity. 'The performers stand so still that you can hardly believe that they breathe,' exclaimed one admirer in 1870.[17] The groupings were modelled on familiar poses from the Old Masters, and no expense of scenery or costume was spared to duplicate the originals with the minutest fidelity. For the German poet Eduard Devrient, the Oberammergau tableaux were 'as if pictures of medieval painters had become endowed with life.' For Mrs Howit-Watt they were an intoxicating blend of the Pre-Raphaelite and the Hellenic:

We felt at times as though the figures of Cimabue's, Giotto's, and Perugino's pictures had become animated, and were moving before us; there was the same simple arrangement and brilliant colour of drapery; the same earnest, quiet dignity about the heads, whilst the entire absence of all theatrical effects wonderfully increased the illusion. There were scenes and groups so extraordinarily like the early Italian pictures, that you could have declared they were the works of Giotto and Perugino, and not living men and women, had not the figures moved and spoken, and the breeze stirred their richly-coloured drapery, and the sun cast long, moving shadows behind them on the stage. These effects of sunshine and shadow, and of drapery fluttered by the wind, were very striking and beautiful; one could imagine how the Greeks must have availed themselves of such striking effects in their theatres open to the sky.

The most spectacular of the tableaux were the Grapes of Canaan and the Delivery of Manna to the Israelites, preceding the Last Supper, each requiring casts of several hundred performers marshalled with precision about the stage. Other favourites were the tableau of Adam and Eve which began the play, Eve appearing in flesh-coloured tights, Adam bare-shouldered but clad in leggings, and the vision of the brazen serpent that introduced the Way of the Cross.

The costuming of Adam and Eve was as close as the nineteenth-century Oberammergau play ever came to shocking the sensibilities of its audience. The main episodes of the drama which followed the tableaux were acted with a dignity deemed suitable to their sacredness. These episodes consisted of scenes beginning with the Entry into Jerusalem and following the Passion story through the Conspiracy, the Last Supper, Judas' Betrayal, the Trial, Crucifixion, Resurrection, and Ascension (but omitting the Harrowing of Hell). The tableau method was carried over to a number of these so as to render them free from any unseemly motion or violence. The Scourging, for instance, took place behind a curtain, which was then raised to reveal the static pose known in art galleries as 'Ecce Homo.' 'The painful sight is lost in a torrent of tears,' wrote one spectator.[18] The same technique was used for the Crucifixion: the nailing took place offstage, the unpleasant sounds covered by a choral dirge. The curtain was then pulled to show the cross already in place, the slumping figure motionless and quiet. The effect thus created was described by a visiting English clergyman in 1870:

The Crucifixion, without perhaps specially resembling any one representation, is so much more like a picture than a reality that its painful effect is thereby much diminished. The Descent from the Cross is an exact copy of Rubens' famous painting. ... Only when the motionless silence of the Central Figure is broken by the few words from the Cross, is the illusion dispelled which might make us think that we were looking on a sculptured ivory image.[19]

Even with such care taken, the Crucifixion was too much for some spectators to endure. Canon Farrar confessed that 'up to the Crucifixion I could watch and listen with profit, but from the moment that the Cross was raised my imagination was perturbed and over-whelmed with the doubt whether this scene was not far too majestically sacred for such presentation.'[20] Mrs Howitt-Watt recalled turning her head away, 'sick with horror,' when she heard 'from behind the curtain the strokes of the hammer as the huge nails were driven into the cross, and, as your imagination believed, through His poor, pale hands and feet.' It was, she felt, 'our Lord's Passion stripped of all its spiritual suffering, – it was the anguish of the flesh – it was the material side of Catholicism.' Yet both writers felt almost guilty at their own reactions, hastening to emphasize the good taste with which the horrifying scene had been presented. There was not 'a single feature,' Farrar said, 'at which the most refined spectator need take the least offence.'[20] And Mrs Howitt-Watt felt that the simple reverence of the peasants put her own emotional reaction to shame: 'Such an earnest solemnity and simplicity breathed throughout the whole of the performance, that to me, at least, anything like anger, or a perception of the ludicrous, would have seemed more irreverent on my part than was this simple, childlike rendering of the sublime Christian tragedy.'

The other main scenes in the drama were acted with comparable solemnity. There was nothing in the whole play, Farrar noted with satisfaction, 'at which the most frivolous spectator could venture even to smile.'[21] Visitors were struck by the deliberately anti-theatrical quality of the acting. 'The acting of the principal characters was something quite unique and remarkable. They never turned towards, or appealed to, the audience; they seldom walked with a stage stride; they never kept the 'stage waiting' as the saying is, and even the little children never took a wrong position or attitude.'[22] The actor who portrayed Christ bore himself throughout with singular restraint. 'Great as is the brutality with which Christ is treated,' wrote a German critic admiringly, 'His calm carriage, firm nobility, and the elevated dignity in His conduct never waver.'[23] Even when he fell off his stool during the scourging scene he managed to do it, according to Eduard Devrient, in a manner 'so as not to detract from his dignity.'[24] The rest of the cast strove without exception to emulate the 'classic dignity, authority, and impressiveness' of the Christus' style.[25] Mary Magdalen, for example, acted her part – even in her moving scene of repentance – with 'solemn resolution' rather than with the 'impetuous passion' which one might have expected.[26] Pilate was a very model of a modern major-generalship, as befitted a production which costumed the Roman soldiers distinctly from the Jewish Temple Guards and made sure that the scourging, buffeting, and nailing were done by the latter. 'Every movement of Pilate, and even of his attendants,' noted the Dean of Westminster, 'is intended to produce the impression of the superiority of the Roman justice and the Roman manners, to the savage, quibbling, vulgar clamours of the Jewish priests and people.'[27] In contrast to the pompous tyrant of the medieval plays, the Oberammergau Pilate was an admirable, even likeable figure. 'The conception of this character,' wrote a Scotsman who saw the performance of 1860, 'was the least painful that could be produced. He was not represented as a brutal and tyrannical Roman governor, as the illiterate are apt to conceive him ... He was, as an intellectual gentleman of the Court of Augustus and his immediate successors, deeply impressed with the dignity of law and the majesty of Rome ... The conception of the character was thus a good one, and to some extent original ... The natural dignity and grandeur of the Roman procurator sat well upon the man who played his character.'[28] For the Englishmen in the audience, at any rate, Pilate appears to have been the easiest character to identify with, and he behaved with impeccable Foreign Office manners.

Even Judas, whose part offered the greatest range of histrionic possibilities and who seldom failed to make a deep impression on spectators, managed to keep his role within the bounds of good taste. 'The wildest gestures of Judas,' remarked one visitor, 'would have seemed tame to a London audience.'[29] Judas' suicide scene offered perhaps the clearest illustration of the general softening of the play's theatrical effect over the centuries. In the original seventeenth-century version, the scene had been one of the dramatic highlights of the play, brought off with all the stage-tricks at the producer's command. The hanging took place in full sight of the audience and, as we have noted, a swarm of devils carted his body off to hell after devouring his entrails. (Satan had already examined the body and declared it to have no soul.) By the eighteenth century the devils had given way to a herd of swine, who enjoyed the same meal. In the 1850 performance – the first to use a curtained stage – the scene was brought to an abrupt, cinematic end just as Judas was about to jump from the tree limb. An offstage shriek as the curtain went down was all that the audience was permitted to see of Judas' fate, the physical details of the suicide having been replaced by a long Faustian soliloquy delivered as Judas contemplates the girdle with which he is about to hang himself:

> Where can I go to hide my fearful shame?
> How rid my conscience of its dreadful guilt?
> No forest fastness is there dark enough!
> No mountain cavern deep enough! O earth,
> Open wide thy jaws, and swallow me! I can
> No longer here remain.

Finally, in the 1860 performance even the shriek was cut, the curtain falling before Judas began to climb the tree. Oddly enough, a number of English visitors reported that the local audience broke into gleeful laughter when the curtain fell, as they had always done before, even though nothing was now left of the scene which had once produced such joyful satisfaction at the downfall of a villain. The audience is also reported to have laughed habitually at the entrance of Barabbas, at the cock-crows during Peter's denial, and at the rolling of the Bad Thief's head on the cross to signify his death. There were, evidently, at least some members of the audience with long memories.

The Oberammergau play as performed in the nineteenth century was thus guaranteed to appeal to Victorian tastes and to overcome any objections that might be raised against Biblical drama. Yet it preserved its repute with Englishmen only by remaining in its traditional home. Unlike most tourists, they had no wish to bring back souvenirs. The thought of exporting the play from its 'antique' world to the capitals of Europe filled Englishmen with horror. 'There cannot be a doubt,' wrote the Dean of Westminster in 1870, 'that the same representation in London, in Paris, in Munich, would, if not blasphemous in itself, lead to such blasphemous consequences as to render its suppression a matter of absolute necessity.'[30] To have suggested performing the play in an ordinary theatre was equally unthinkable. 'The conscience of Christendom might well cry out in alarm,' exclaimed another clergyman, 'against the hideous profanation of transplating such a spectacle from its true surroundings in the hearts of a simple, believing peasantry to pollute it into wicked and blasphemous vulgarity by setting it upon the boards of some coarse rendezvous of idlers, or worse, in Paris or in London.'[31] When an adaptation of the Oberammergau play was staged at the *Théatre des Variétés* in Antwerp in the 1860s, an English reviewer exclaimed his disgust:

A dingy little theatre, where one would expect to see broad farces and bloody melodramas, was to be the scene of a mimic representation of the most solemn and affecting of stories – a story so sacred that to Protestant feelings there is something shocking in the idea of its being brought into the remotest relation with anything like amusement, especially theatrical amusement.[32]

As we might expect, the Lord Chamberlain's office fully shared these sentiments and played an active role throughout the last half of the century in thwarting any attempts by unscrupulous producers to profit by the popularity of the Passion Play in England. When the first suggestion of this sort arose in 1878, Mr Pigott wasted no time in turning it down, boasting afterward that he had succeeded in 'averting a scandal.'[33] For the next two decades Pigott devoted a large part of his time as Examiner of Plays to outwitting entrepreneurs determined to present the Bavarian Biblical spectacle, or facsimiles thereof, to London audiences. In 1879, for example, a proposal was made to bring the 'San Francisco Passion Play' to London. This was an imitation of Oberammergau, written by an American Jew named Salmi Morse, who had produced the play, though not without police harrassment, in the San Francisco opera house, with James O'Neill (Eugene O'Neill's father) cast as the Christus. A furor erupted as soon as the proposal was made known. The *Theatre* magazine exclaimed that 'the production of a religious play in this country could do no good and might do much harm ... The cause of religious progress would in all probability be materially retarded by the introduction of Passion Plays. ... The devout would regard a Miracle Play as a profanation.'[34] Dion Boucicault stepped forward with advice on how the show might be made acceptable: 'To gain a success it would be necessary to have an immense edifice that would allow of the grandest spectacular effects, as represented in the open air at the Ober-Ammergau, and, as in Oratorio, every word should be sung, combined with the grandest creations in sacred music. By this method the very natural prejudices that many felt on the subject would be allayed, and the cause of religion might, as in olden times, be greatly benefited by the production of the sacred drama.'[35] This project, too, came to nothing, though Boucicault's splendid imaginings gave a foretaste of those religious extravaganzas, such as Max Reinhart's *The Miracle*, with which the mystery plays would, a few years later, be confused.

By the 1880s the public interest in Passion plays, coupled with the Lord Chamberlain's refusal to license them, had made the very name 'Oberammergau' a hot property, shamelessly exploited by ambitious producers. In 1884 the suburbs of London were placarded with bright orange posters featuring a large black cross, advertising the performance of a 'Passion Play' at Wandsworth Town Hall. In the centre appeared, in large lettering, the word 'Oberammergau,' followed by a description of the German play and excerpts from reviews. Alarmed letters from residents of Wandsworth flooded the Lord Chamberlain's office and the police were sent to investigate. The producer, as it turned out, was indulging in advertising chicanery. The show was not to be a Passion play at all, but a 'series of Dissolving Views with vocal and instrumental accompaniment.' A lecturer from time to time was to read an accompanying narrative. Even the suggestion that the Saviour might be represented on the stage, however, was 'obnoxious' enough. The police advised the Lord Chamberlain that while the show was not legally a 'stage-play,' he might treat it as one if he saw fit. The producer made a hurried visit to the Examiner of Plays, now eager to make it plain that his 'entertainment' was nothing more than some 'very correctly and artistically painted views' of the passion scenes. Nevertheless, the performance was forbidden and the proprietors of the theatre absolved from their contract. 'The Oberammergau Passion Play,' Mr Piggott declared crisply, 'was not licensed in this country.'[36]

The issue of performing the Oberammergau Passion Play in London arose again, more respectably, in 1895, and this time it was referred directly to the Lord Chamberlain, who in turn appears to have consulted the Queen herself. The outcome showed how little had changed in the Lord Chamberlain's views over the years. The details of the deliberations are preserved in a memo from an official of the Lord Chamberlain's office to the Queen's private secretary, dated 23 January 1895:

Mr. Page came here today *privately* to ask if the Lord Chamberlain would entertain the question of licensing the Oberammergau Passion Play – with the original cast of characters, specially brought over from there – dresses and scenery. I told him that the Lord Chamberlain had carefully considered the question and taken reliable advice from others, and had decided that the Passion Play was under any circumstances unsuitable for performance in a *London theatre*, and that he therefore declined to give his License for it here.

The Lord Chamberlain does not consider that the Passion Play could be properly given in a London theatre, and will not therefore grant a license for it as a 'Stage Play.'

His jurisdiction extends no further than this – i.e., if it is proposed that it should be performed in the Albert Hall, Exeter Hall or some other such place not licensed as a theatre, the Lord Chamberlain has no jurisdiction.

As a matter of private opinion he thinks that transplanting the simple Peasants from their native homes where they have been used to perform the Drama as a religious Service to London would entirely alter the whole character of the performance, which must therefore degenerate into a theatrical spectacle.

It was not for him to offer an official opinion as to its being performed elsewhere, i.e., in a Hall or Building not licensed by him, but his own private opinion was that it would entirely alter the character of the performance from a solemn religious function to an ordinary melodramatic performance, and the company of simple religious Peasants to Strolling players.[37]

How much the Lord Chamberlain's arguments owed to the 'reliable advice' he sought from 'others' we can only guess. But there is no doubt that his decision found favour in the highest quarters. A few days after receiving his memorandum, Queen Victoria instructed her secretary to tell the Lord Chamberlain that she 'entirely concurs in the view that he takes and is very glad that he has acted as he has done in the matter.'[38] The Bishop of Southwark was even more forthright, declaring that it would have been a 'religious calamity' if there had not been 'some power which could have stopped, without hesitation and without discussion, the performance of the Oberammergau Passion Play in London.'[39] George Bernard Shaw, who almost certainly was not consulted, confidently predicted in the teeth of the evidence that 'we shall have a Passion Play in Shaftesbury Avenue, and the sooner the better; depend on it, we shall see Mr. Wilson Barrett crucified yet.'[40] But the time was not yet ripe, and Shaw's prediction proved as vain as did Squire Bancroft's dream in 1900 of producing the Oberammergau play in the West End with Henry Irving as Judas, Beerbohm Tree as Pilate, and Forbes-Robertson as Christ. Neither Wilson Barrett nor anyone else was about to be crucified in the British Isles.

The failure to secure a performance of the Oberammergau Passion Play in England made, in all probability, little difference to the fortunes of the medieval mystery plays in the nineteenth century. The two types of play were so different that the mystery plays would hardly have been better off for the precedent, even if there had been a chance of their being produced. The underlying aesthetic of the Oberammergau play was, as we have seen Germanic-classical rather than medieval. It aimed at an effect of stasis, at the quality of tension frozen in repose that Lessing thought was the secret of all the greatest Greek art. A German cultural historian described the final impact of the Passion Play on its audience as follows:

Filled with contentment to the inmost depth of the soul, the noblest yearnings stilled, and with calmed feelings, the spectator departs, having found everything which he had longed and sought for.[41]

Of the sense of life as a violent drama which the medieval cycle plays conveyed there was little at Oberammergau. Nor were the spectators encouraged to see their own place in the drama against the backdrop of a divinely ordained history that was impelling them forward toward either heaven or hell. The events enacted at Oberammergau were timeless, otherworldly, and above all comforting. Practically the only historical lesson they taught was that Germanic races, as heirs to the Empire, had been bequeathed the salvation which the Jews had forfeited.[42] In the decorous, dignified, and picturesque scenes of the Oberammergau *Passionspiel* there was nothing that might upset the spectator's feelings of his own worthiness or his conviction that the highest requirement of sacred art was good taste.

One effect of the Passion Play on Englishmen was to make them even more ashamed of the religious drama of their own country. Against the solemnity and calm grandeur of the Oberammergau play they set the 'vulgar, profane, indecent and horrifying incidents' of the English miracles, with their mixture of the sacred and the profane, their hotch-potch of high tragedy and low comedy, and their primitive superstitions. Victorians who shuddered even at the thought of transporting the Oberammergau play to England could have little interest in seeing a revival of the primitive religious drama of their own country. Nevertheless, a precedent of sorts had been set, and when the revival of the medieval plays eventually came, the shadow of Oberammergau inevitably hung over it. Nearly every producer of medieval Biblical drama in the early years of the twentieth century was eager to claim the purest Bavarian pedigree for his work. To the extent that they earned it, they invariably falsified the true nature of their subject. But the Oberammergau style at least permitted them to introduce a type of drama to audiences who would have found it unpalatable in any other form. The work of these producers and the gradual liberation of English medieval drama from the protective cloak of German romantic piety forms the remainder of our story.

3

Mysteries Revived

You cannot show Divinity on the stage; you cannot get an actor to impersonate Divinity. You may show humanity in juxtaposition to Divinity, acted upon by Divinity and responding in one way or another to the contact – but Divinity itself: no! The thing is impossible. The sentiment against the appearance of Jesus on the stage arises from a sound apprehension of dramatic values and possibilities on the part of the great masses of humanity.

Don Marquis, *The Dark Hours* (1926)

WILLIAM POEL AND NUGENT MONCK

Despite the controversy that surrounded religious drama at the turn of the century, the first modern performance of a medieval religious play in England passed almost unnoticed by the censors. In 1901 in the courtyard of the Charterhouse in London William Poel staged the early Tudor morality play *Everyman* for the Elizabethan Stage Society. The production was to make theatrical history. For many years before, Poel had been the leading advocate of open-stage drama in England, performing Shakespeare in Elizabethan fashion, without footlights, curtains, or intervals. His production of the First Quarto *Hamlet* in 1887 was already a legend., Yet none of his productions caught the public enthusiasm like *Everyman*. Partly because of the stunning pre-Raphaelite beauty of Poel's staging, partly because of its novelty (increased by the fact that a woman played the leading role and that God the father was impersonated on the stage), *Everyman* went on to an astonishing run in commercial theatres all over Britain and America during the next twenty years.

It is hard for us today to imagine the apprehension which *Everyman* aroused in its first Edwardian audiences. Accustomed to a steady diet of melodramas and French farces, theatre-goers of 1901 were suddenly confronted by a drama of unalleviated seriousness, preaching a doctrine of renunciation and spiritual perfection. The directness of its moral invective caused more than one reviewer to squirm uncomfortably. 'It is something of a shock,' wrote *The Times*, 'to find that the character that follows the introductory Messenger is no other than the Creator Himself, and that He starts the drama by lamenting from His heavenly throne the waywardness and wickedness of the leading human character.'[1] To assuage the misgivings of his audience, Poel made a few judicious cuts in the script. God the Father was called not God but 'Adonai,' and the description of the Crucifixion in his opening speech was omitted. The sermon by Five Wits about the sacramental nature of the priesthood was cut, as was Knowledge's later reference to priests' 'lechery.'[2] Most of all, the style of the production disarmed all but the sternest of critics with its solemnity and reverence, from the design of the costumes (lent for the occasion by Holman Hunt, who had copied them from Flemish tapestries) to the very speaking of the verse (God spoke his lines in something approaching Gregorian chant, marked 'recitativo' in Poel's prompt-script). 'Applause,' noted the program, 'is naturally checked during the presentation of such a theme.' The warning was unnecessary. Audiences were described as 'breathlessly quiet, polite, and respectful', and reviewers were left little alternative but to praise Poel's discretion in handling 'matter which under ordinary circumstances might seem horribly blasphemous.'[3]

Poel avoided the wrath of the Lord Chamberlain's office by a combination of good timing and good luck. The Charterhouse was not a commercial theatre (it had been a medieval monastery and was now a pensioner's home) and the Elizabethan Stage Society was a private group, so that the Lord Chamberlain could have no official interest in what they did there. Moreover, plays written before the Licensing Act of 1737 were technically assumed to be already licensed and did not have to be submitted to the Examiner. When Poel, out of caution, approached Mr Redford about the matter beforehand, he was told that *Everyman* 'came under the head of a Shakespearean play' and need not be sent in. The best luck of all was that Redford, as he revealed later to the Select Parliamentary Committee, had never before heard of *Everyman* and had no idea that God was a character in it. He knew only that it was an 'old play' that had been discovered in a 'muniment chest in Ely Cathedral' and that it had something to do with death. When notices turned out to be favourable and no one complained, the production went on to ever greater success without interference from the authorities. The only change made in it when the play moved to commercial theatres was that the part of 'Adonai' became 'The Voice of Adonai' and was kept off stage – a precaution followed in most future performances. Scarcely noticed in all the hubbub was the second half of the program that day at the Charterhouse, a performance of the Sacrifice of Isaac from the Chester Cycle. *Everyman* carried the day, and went on to take its place in almost all subsequent anthologies of drama as the typical medieval morality play. Of the Abraham and Isaac performance – the first of a mystery play since the sixteenth century – little notice was taken by the reviewers, most of whom compared it unfavourably with the masterpiece which had preceded it.

Those who hoped for a change in the official attitude toward religious drama as a result of the success of *Everyman* were doomed to disappointment. Asked by the Select Committee in 1909 why he had allowed God to appear at the Charterhouse, Redford absolutely denied, in the face of the evidence, that He had appeared there at all.[4] Would-be producers of other medieval plays soon found that, despite Poel's achievement, their prospects were little better than before. The person who discovered this most painfully was a young man who was destined to have almost as great an impact on the medieval revival in England as Poel, Walter Nugent Monck.

Nugent Monck could not have been more aptly named. The bachelor son of a clergyman, he became at an early stage a disciple of Poel and devoted the rest of his life to propagating what he called 'the power of the stage for good.' In 1901 he began his acting career by playing Fellowship in a touring production of *Everyman* that Poel took to cathedral cities in England and Scotland. (Monck later recalled that 'in Scotland it was not a success, being considered too papist for the Church of Scotland, and too heretical for the Catholic Church.')[5] In 1905 Monck decided to give up acting and to follow in Poel's footsteps as a producer. He hired an abandoned concert room in London, in which Mozart had once given a recital, renamed it the Fortune Theatre, and founded his own group of players, called the English Drama Society. For the next four years the English Drama Society gave private performances of Ibsen's *Ghosts* (one of the plays on the Lord Chamberlain's black list), three Shakespearean dramas, plays by Browning, Rossetti, and Symons, a Jacobean masque, four plays by Monck himself, the Chester Nativity Play (a play which, according to the *Church Times*, 'coarsened the idea of the Incarnation and ought to be stopped'),[6] and *The Interlude of Youth*, an early Tudor morality play. All this was only a warm-up, however, for Monck's most ambitious project, a public performance of the Passion sequence from the *Ludus Coventriae* cycle of mystery plays at Easter, 1909.

On 7 April 1909, the cast of the 'Coventry' Passion Play, as Monck called it, assembled in their tiny theatre for a dress rehearsal. The play, as edited and modernized by Monck, was to open with the Council of the Jews, followed by the episodes of the Casting of the Devils, the Last Supper, the Agony in the Garden, the Trial before Pilate, the Stations of the Cross (in what Monck called 'the medieval style' – up and down the room through the audience), and finally the Crucifixion. As they were about to begin, there was a knock on the door and two policemen entered the theatre. They escorted Monck to the Vine Street station in Piccadilly, where they informed him that by selling tickets to the public for the performance of an unlicensed play in an unlicensed building he was committing an offence against the Theatres Act of 1843. For good measure, according to Monck, they also read him sections of the Blasphemy Laws.[7] Finally, they ordered him, on the authority of the Lord Chamberlain, to abandon the performance. A personal call by Monck late that afternoon to the Lord Chamberlain's office was to no avail. The theatre was closed and ticket-holders given their money back.[8]

What had happened? Monck himself never knew for sure, and the files of the Lord Chamberlain's office are ambiguous on the matter. The likelihood is that Monck was the victim of a common informer. A poster ornamented with a purple cross advertising the production had been distributed in the neighbourhood beforehand, advising prospective customers that tickets might be had in advance from Messrs Chappell & Co. or from the theatre, but that 'No Money Can be Taken at the Door.' Why anyone should object to his play merely on the basis of pre-show publicity, Monck could not understand. 'All suggestion of a theatrical atmosphere would have been kept out,' he protested at the time. 'There would have been no footlights and no top-lights ... We have done all we can to present the play in a reverent spirit.'[9] The poster itself had declared that 'the Grouping, Costumes, and Properties have been specially designed from pictures of the period, and every care will be taken to give the representations with due reverence.'[10] That mystery plays should come under the same ban as plays prohibited on moral grounds was even more incomprehensible to Monck. 'All of these plays,' he observed ironically, 'were written in an age when people believed in the power of the stage for good.' Monck must have been, at this time, either ignorant or contemptuous of the rules and regulations of the Lord Chamberlain. The odds are, according to those who knew him, on the latter. He was to live to outwit the censors, but not until many years afterward. For the moment the 'Coventry' Passion Play was dead, and with it the English Drama Society, which quietly went out of business the following week.

What would Monck's production of the 'Coventry' Passion Play have been like? Only fragments of the script have survived and a few scattered notes and newspaper clippings (see plate 2). From them, and from what we know of Monck's other productions at the time, we can make a fair estimate of what the experience of an audience would have been like at the Fortune Theatre on the evening of 8 April 1909, had the Lord Chamberlain not intervened. To begin with, Monck had chosen the play because he believed that the mysteries could serve as an antidote to the reigning commercialism and frivolity of the contemporary London theatre. Where Shaw sought to argue his audiences out of their complacency, Monck hoped to transport them to a higher and nobler world. In a lecture which he prepared the following year on 'The Rise of the Mystery Play,' he wrote: 'You may ask whether there can be any profit in taking these old plays from the musty bookshelves. I think so. Apart from the antiquarian interest, there seems to me a possibility that from the study of these old plays we may be able to create a new drama, to do, in fact, what the pre-Raphaelites tried to do.'[11]

Monck had already shown what might be done toward this goal in his earlier productions of episodes from the mystery cycles. A *Times* review of his version of the Chester Nativity plays in December 1906, unsigned but bearing the unmistakable style of G.K. Chesterton, described it as a 'quaint and pleasing spectacle, as pale and sad as any Burne-Jones ghost.' The stage was set up to resemble a church, complete with accessories such as incense and an organ. The audience was assured in advance that the play would be presented 'reverently in accordance with the sacred subjects.' The humour of the shepherds' scenes was 'toned down' to avoid offending delicate sensibilities; a priest made the sign of the cross over the audience as the play ended.

Chesterton's judgment of the performance was predictably caustic:

What we see is not the Chester plays as our ancestors saw them, but as we see them looking back on the Middle, or youthful, Ages from the middle, or old, age of our civilization ... We cannot be, or even pretend to be, medieval nowadays; we succeed only in being pre-Raphaelite – in the worst sense of that abused term. Copy your stage from old French prints (and do away with the altar and the dangerous candles on the right); dress all the characters in 'medieval' costumes; give, as often as you can remember to do so, the authors' medieval words and inflections; get a (stage) priest to make the sign of the Cross over the audience as the play ends, and the result must still be a curious, but spurious, imitation.[12]

Other reviewers, however, were more impressed. One wrote that 'it was very fine pictorially, and fine in a choice and dignified way ... The actors moved and posed with a contained simplicity, holding gesture well down and keeping to a serious, austere delivery of the lines ... Probably the plays were never either acted or heard so reverently before.' Another praised the performance in similar terms and expressed his relief at the 'entire absence of any such unseemliness as eventually led the priests, the original producers of such works, to abandon further association with them.'[13]

There can be little doubt that Monck's production of the Passion Play would have followed along similar lines. 'No painted scenery would have been used,' he told a reporter the day after the production had been called off. 'The awe-inspiring events would have been shown in front of a plain background of black velvet against which the white figures would show grimly. The peculiar method of lighting adopted gave to the scene the appearance of a great altarpiece in some dimly lit cathedral.'[14] Stage directions contained in the few surviving actors' parts indicate that the design of the stage was to be 'Elizabethan,' derived from the theatrical archaeology of William Poel and anticipating the stage that Monck was later to build at the Maddermarket Theatre in Norwich. The directions contain references to 'upper stage,' 'lower stage,' 'rostrum,' and 'curtains.' The nailing to the cross, it is clear, was to take place 'behind the Curtain,' and the Crucifixion to be staged as a 'Tableau' – i.e. the actor playing Christ was to get into place on the raised cross from the balcony while the curtains were drawn, the scene then being 'revealed' to the audience – exactly as it was presented at Oberammergau. Humour of any sort was to be suppressed; Monck had, in fact, picked this particular Passion sequence because he believed it to be 'entirely free from all that coarseness and buffooning which mar so many medieval plays.'

Such was the blasphemy that London audiences were spared in the spring of 1909. After the Lord Chamberlain's intervention, Monck first announced that the Society would go ahead with performances during the following week to invited audiences only, admission free. 'The whole series of episodes,' he once again assured his public, 'will be treated with the greatest sincerity.' But on 19 June 1909, the Home Office wrote to the Lord Chamberlain with satisfaction that the entire scheme had been abandoned.[15] The English Drama Society was disbanded, and with it, temporarily, the revival of the medieval mystery plays.

THE UNSEEN GOD

If the time for reviving the mystery plays had not yet come, a renewed taste for religion on the stage definitely had arrived, and nothing the Lord

Chamberlain could do could prevent producers from catering to it. During the next forty years a great many religious plays found their way onto the English stage, and the subjects that they treated, as well as the manner in whch they presented them, were to profoundly influence the methods by which the mystery plays would be staged when the time for their revival finally came in the 1950s. For that reason it will be useful to look briefly at some typical examples of religious drama written during these years, and in particular to record some of the ways that playwrights found to skirt the restrictions placed by the Lord Chamberlain on their trade.

Broadly speaking, relgious plays in England during the early years of this century fell into two distinct categories. One was the religious spectacular, catering to the popular taste, then as now, for a mixture of religion, spectacle and sex. *Quo Vadis* and *Ben Hur* are examples of the genre still familiar to us through films. Under the guise of romantic melodrama, these plays tried to bring back at least some hint of the supernatural into a theatre dominated by realism, although in most of them the miracles of religion took second place to the miracles of modern set-design and lighting. The other type consisted of psychological studies of the effects of religion on characters drawn close to the life of modern times. Some of these plays presented the gospel in modern dress, others reworked the scriptural narratives into humanistic dramas from which all trace of the supernatural had been removed. In the first, Christ was treated as a god; in the second as a man. It was generally agreed by critics and playwrights alike that in modern drama, despite the doctrine of the Incarnation, he could not be both.[16] Most importantly, in neither of these types of plays was he ever to be seen.

The most celebrated example of the religious spectacular was Max Reinhardt's production of *The Miracle* in London in 1912. Subtitled 'a wordless mystery spectacle,' Reinhardt's play was based on a scenario by the German writer Karl Vollmoeller, taken from an Old High German legend, and it featured original music composed by Engelbert Humperdinck. The work was performed in the Olympia exhibition hall in Earl's Court, otherwise famed for housing annually the world's largest dog show. Size was the essence of the production. 'Olympia's very atmosphere is bigness,' gushed the program, 'not merely the bigness of spaciousness but the amplification of consummation.' Whatever that meant, the consummations of *The Miracle* were devoutly attended by thousands of spectators hungry for its mixture of piety and prurience. More than ten thousand people attended the performance of 29 February 1912, to see a story about a runaway nun whose place was taken at Mass by a statue of the Virgin. While her sisters gazed in panic at the empty pedestal, the nun underwent a series of adventures that included erotic dancing, rape, marriage, seduction, and an illegitimate child. Finally she returned penitent to the convent, enabling Our Lady to resume her more restful role as a statue.

For the occasion, the interior of the arena was transformed into the nave of a Gothic cathedral, complete with coloured windows, hanging lamps, a peal of bells, and a gigantic crucifix perched on top of a rood-screen. A cast of two thousand actors and dancers was backed by a two-hundred-man symphony orchestra and an invisible choir of five hundred voices, as well as a specially built organ 'with pure cathedral tone.' A critic hailed the show as a revival of 'the passion plays of the Middle Ages, inspiring reverence and pure emotional contemplation of what is most sacred to all who profess to follow a Christian creed.' Originally Reinhardt planned a scene in which the nun was to be condemned to death as a witch and ordered to be crucified. At the last moment the scene was cut, 'in order to avoid offending the susceptibilities of any of the audience.' No other care for good taste appears to have been taken, and the judgment of one reviewer – its religion is sham religion, its poetry sham poetry, and its drama sham drama' – seems hard to improve on.[17]

The future of such religious spectaculars lay largely in films. For the theatre, those plays which attempted more modestly and subtly to adapt Christianity to modern life were plainly preferable, and formed by far the largest category of religious drama in the early twentieth century. Between 1910 and 1950 some hundreds of 'modern passion plays' were written in England, some for performance in churches, some for commercial theatres. In all of these the figure of Christ had to be, either out of prudence or out of principle, veiled from the eyes of the audience. Playwrights were all the more willing to comply with this restriction if they agreed with George Bernard Shaw in regarding Christ as a totally passive figure who went 'dumb to the slaughter' and who therefore was best kept in the background in favour of his more human and passionate disciples.[18] Whatever their motives, writers proved highly ingenious at circumventing the Lord Chamberlain's restrictions without loss to their theme, and thereby provided a model for the kind of treatment that would eventually succeed in enabling the mystery plays to be performed before nervous audiences. Few of the plays that they wrote merit analysis in themselves, but a survey of the methods they found to present the Christian story on the modern stage will help us to understand the atmosphere in which the first revivals of the mysteries were to take place. The following are typical examples of their kind.[19]

Servant in the House, by Charles Rann Kennedy. 1908
This popular and widely praised play inaugurated the fad for disguising the
Saviour as a Stranger, Upstairs Lodger, or Travelling Salesman, who had
come back to teach the modern world its sins. A contemporary reviewer
wrote: 'With a daring quite his own, Mr. Kennedy stops short only at
naming the character in his play ... Hardly a passage but teems with overt
references ... When asked "Who are you?" [the Stranger] answers, "I am – "
and is interrupted by the great bell of the church sounding the Sanctus.'[20]

Other examples of this genre are *The Passing of the Third Floor Back* by
Jerome K. Jerome, produced by Sir Johnston Forbes-Robertson in 1908,
and Hauptmann's *Hannele*. An interesting variant is Shirley St Clair's *The
Third Day* (1945), in which alternative endings are provided, depending on
whether the performance is in a church or a theatre. In the first, an anonymous 'Man' appears at an inn to his disconsolate followers, wrapped in a cloak
and keeping his back to the audience at all times. In the second, only a shaft
of sunlight shines through an open door, throwing the shadow of a man on
the floor. The followers look through the door and kneel as the curtain falls.

The Upper Room, by R.H. Benson. 1915
This play inaugurated what subsequently became the most useful of all
staging devices for the Christ-less Passion Play: the so-called Upper Room
or the Room of the Last Supper. From this room the disciples watch the
Trial, the Scourging, and the Way of the Cross, reporting the events to each
other and to the audience.

Variations on this theme included 'a room adjoining the Upper Room'
(*Greater Love Hath No Man*, by May Creagh-Henry, 1920); 'the roof
adjoining an upper room' (*The Housetop: A Play on the Passion of Our
Lord Jesus Christ*, by Cecil Tugman, 1964); 'beside the walls of Jerusalem,
near to the house of Caiaphas the High Priest' (*Passover in Jerusalem: A
Passion Play*, by Donald Dugard, 1939); and 'in front of the gate of the
Roman citadel in Jerusalem' (*Good Friday*, by John Masefield, 1917).

With such examples in mind, E. Martin Browne, who would one day
direct the first modern performance of the York Cycle, wrote in his guide
to producers of religious plays in 1932 that 'those plays which put the Via
Dolorosa outside the window, or the Courtroom through the inner doorway,
are usually the most successful.'[21]

A Man's House, by John Drinkwater. 1934
This play paired the Upper Room with an exhaustive use of the device of
the Leading Question. In it a father cranes his neck out the window and

describes what he sees to his young son behind him. A sample of the dialogue:

Q 'What does Jesus look like Father? Can you see him?'

A 'Yes. He must be a tall man.'

Q 'Is he lovely?'

A 'Yes, child, he is lovely.'

Examples of this technique in other plays are abundant, often involving apostolic straight-men: 'John, did the Master speak as He hung on the cross?' and 'Who can have taken Him from out the tomb?' (*Greater Love Hath No Man*, by May Creagh-Henry, 1920); 'What happened, John, when I had left the Court?' (*The Victory of the Cross: A Passion Play*, by the same author, 1948); and, perhaps most memorably, 'Now tell us, dear, why did Judas kiss Jesus?' (*The Room of the Last Supper*, by Alan Wilkin, 1969).

The Cup of Salvation, by Raymond Birt. c 1950

This play was saved from blasphemy by its ingenious use of lighting. The scene: 'Friday afternoon: about 3.0 p.m. On Calvary. It is dark ... but against the sky the darker shape of the Cross is to be seen. From the angle of its arm and its length it would seem that we see it from behind and half-right, and that we are somewhat below the brow of the hill. The foot of the cross is out of sight, and so – screened from us in the angle of vision – is the body of Jesus which hangs there still.'

Among other examples of what may be called the Shadow-of-the-Cross technique, the most notable occurs in *The Dark Hours*, by Don Marquis (1926). In it a darkened stage allows only the faces of the disciples to be 'dimly discerned' as they look up 'toward a knoll at upper left ... The effect is that we are at the edge of the hill of Calvary and that Jesus is hanging on the Cross just off stage, and that all are looking at him there.' At the fatal hour, the stage goes completely dark, the 'Voice of Jesus' is heard briefly offstage, the lights come up suddenly, and the shadow of the cross is thrown across the backdrop as the curtain comes down.

Bright spotlights could also be used to suggest the unseen presence of the Deity on the stage. This became a common practice in plays of the 1920s and 1930s, and was officially endorsed by the Lord Chamberlain as a permissible substitute for an actor playing Christ. The technique was first devised by Gordon Craig for his production of Housman's *Bethlehem* in 1902. Craig rewrote Housman's play after it had been banned by the Lord Chamberlain to provide a scenic climax at the Adoration of the Shepherds. When the Shepherds approached the crib, light suddenly streamed up from its depths into the faces of those gathered around it. The presence of the Christ-child was thus indicated by the radiant faces of the onlookers, illuminated by the hidden spot.[22]

Christ Crucified: A Passion Play in Six Scenes, by Margaret Cropper. 1932

This play invoked angelic help. Despite the title, the Saviour does not appear. His place is taken by a character called 'The Angel of the Mind of Christ.' In some scenes 'The Voice of Christ' is also heard offstage. Yet a third angel narrates the Passion. Cropper explained, 'Those scenes in Gethsemane and on Golgotha which we may not represent, are presented to us through the voice of an Angel, the Angel of the Passion, who in the words of the Gospel recounts them to the expectant Angels, and to us.' The stage directions call for the Angel of the Passion to mime appropriate gestures while speaking Christ's words, including the stretching out of his arms.

Like the device of the spotlight, the use of an angelic *alter ego* derived ultimately from Laurence Housman and Gordon Craig. In *Bethlehem* an 'Earth-Angel' had stood by the Virgin Mary throughout the play to speak her lines, the Lord Chamberlain having ruled that she could appear in the play only if she remained silent.

The Way of the Cross, by Henri Gheon. 1932

This was the most frequently produced of all church plays during the period. It is about St Helena's search for the True Cross. In order to purify herself for the task, she re-enacts in Jerusalem the stations of the cross. In the play the re-enactment is conveyed through mime. Each station is introduced by four lines of verse, spoken by a reciter. Four other actors, two men and two women, enact various roles as 'watchers or characters in the Passion.' Through their gestures they 'attempt to make one *see* what was beyond representation – Christ Himself.'[23]

The technique of miming the gospel narrative goes back in modern English drama at least to 1887, when a pastor in the London docks area, Charles Lowder, sought to increase his congregation by rewriting some of the medieval Nativity plays for Greek chorus and mimed tableaux. He, in turn, was copying the tableaux vivants of the Oberammergau Passion Play.[24] The technique had the advantage of eliminating speaking parts for the actors portraying divine personages and of sticking literally to the words of the Bible in the narration. The poses in the tableaux were copied from famous religious paintings, such as the Rubens *Deposition from the Cross* which was also used in Martin Browne's production of Gheon's *Way of the Cross*. The fact that the outstretched arms of the Virgin held only empty air instead of the body of the Saviour does not appear to have struck anyone at the time as incongruous. Other popular subjects for imitation were Guido's *Annunciation*, Domenichino's *Adoration of the Shepherds*, Leonardo's *Last Supper*, Millais's *The Carpenter Shop*, and Holman Hunt's *The Finding of Christ in the Temple*.

'In rehearsing a scene planned round such a picture,' Browne wrote, 'it is usually best to arrange the finished picture first, and then go back and plan how the characters get to those positions.'[25] An earlier author of a handbook for producers of Biblical tableaux, published in 1913, contrasted the 'esthetic appeal' of the serenely beautiful tableau with the 'grotesque and licentious' acting out of Biblical scenes in the medieval mystery plays, and asserted that 'nothing could be more antagonistic to the spirit of worship than speech and movement.' The Bishop of Worcester, in a preface to the volume, endorsed this view, declaring his approval of church drama only if it could be kept free from 'any theatrical desire for applause' and from the 'snares into which the medieval miracle plays fell.'[26]

Good Friday, by John Masefield. 1917

Despite the connotations of its title, this play was not about Jesus at all, but about Pilate. It was the first of a series of Pilate plays which saw in the dilemma of the Roman governor an analogue of the British colonial experience. Nearly all these plays presented Pilate in a sympathetic light; some of them were explicitly anti-Semitic. (By contrast, the favourite character in French and German Biblical plays of this period was Mary Magdalen.) Masefield's Pilate is dignified, wise, and resigned. He considers the Jews to be 'mad rabble' and rather likes 'this Jesus man,' but is forced to give in to Herod and Caiaphas for the sake of preserving peace in his province.

Such was the sympathy for Pilate in plays of this type that it is not unusual to find authors hinting at the end, usually through a chorus, that Pilate is to be saved at the Last Judgment – a feature that was to find its way into some of the later stagings of the medieval Judgment plays. Some Pilate plays were, in fact, little more than thinly disguised allegories of Lord Curzon in India. Nugent Monck's play called *Pilate* gave perhaps the most sympathetic treatment of Pilate as a misunderstood colonial governor:

You know, Marcus, we are right to be proud of our Empire. Other people might indeed rule as well as we do, but in fact no other nation has. We make our mistakes, but other people would make more, if they would ever take the trouble to shoulder the responsibility of governing the barbarians.[27]

Occasionally, to be sure, a Pilate appeared who was less certain of his ground. 'What is truth? We Romans don't know – don't even dare to know.

We have thrown away our gods: the faith of our ancestors is too simple for this complex modern world.' (*Caesar's Friend*, by Campbell Dixon and Dermot Morrah, 1933). But the tragic victim of imperial politics continued to dominate plays on this subject even into the 1960s: 'They'll recognize in me a man who is doing a job, doing it fairly and doing it to the best of his ability ... Whether I like it or not, I have to govern them' (*The Day's Beginning*, by Willis Hall, 1963).

Sympathy for Pilate came naturally to authors whose main motive in writing religious plays was to use Christianity as a weapon against Bolshevism. The Pilate plays are only one branch of a class of twentieth-century religious drama that has been largely politically inspired. May Creagh-Henry, for example, the author of several of the plays mentioned above, specialized in a type of Biblical drama that was designed to strengthen the conservative convictions of her audience. In 1922 she founded a group called the Mystical Players and proceeded to write a number of dramas for them. These 'Mystical Plays' turned out to be thinly disguised tracts against red agitators, based on such plot-motifs as the Anarchist who is converted to Law and Order through a vision of God (M. Creagh-Henry, *Four Mystical Plays*, 1924).

THE CHURCH AND THE MYSTERIES

Paralleling the return of the gospel narratives to the public stage was the reintroduction of drama into the church, a development which proved even more important to the revival of the mystery plays. Partly as the result of the renewed interest of modern playwrights such as Masefield, Eliot, and Yeats in religious subjects, partly as the result of its own need to find new methods of evangelism in a materialist age, the attitude of the English Church toward drama began to change. Ever since the sixteenth century it had forbidden the performance of plays within the precincts of a church, but as early as the closing years of Queen Victoria's reign this rule was occasionally relaxed. Biblical tableaux, such as those described above, gained general acceptance during the 1880s and 1890s. The first modern performance of a play with speaking parts in a church took place in 1889. The play was *The Conversion of England*, an historical drama in 'ten tableaux' about St Augustine by the Reverend Henry Cresswell, which had been turned down by the Lord Chamberlain for theatrical production (see above, chapter 1), but which was eventually performed in the Great Hall of Church House in Westminster. As a play *The Conversion of England* was not very distinguished, but the mere fact of its performance was momentous enough. 'It has come at last,' wrote George Bernard Shaw in his review of the occasion; 'the parson has carried the war into the enemy's country.'[28]

Shaw's words were prophetic, even if the war was to look more like a skirmish for some time to come. Following the success of *The Conversion of England*, a number of similar plays on post-apostolic ecclesiastical history were produced, mostly by amateur authors for amateur acting groups. Many of these were animated tableaux rather than genuine dramas, and few of them touched at all on the Bible. When the Lord Chamberlain's ban on Biblical subjects was finally relaxed in 1912, Old Testament scenes were the first to be taken up. The honour of being the first Biblical play licensed by the Lord Chamberlain went to *Joseph and His Brethren*, by Louis N. Parker in 1912. The Joseph story was by far the most popular Old Testament subject at this time, perhaps justifying Mr Redford's fears about Potiphar's wife. In 1905 the Colosseum Music Hall staged a skit on that subject, described as 'a series of scenes in dumbshow, linked by a narrator in strict evening dress who sang his part from a side-box.' The *Church Times* complained that 'the incident in Potiphar's house – could we expect it otherwise? – is dwelt upon at some length.'[29]

Not until 1921 was the character of Christ first introduced into a church play. The play was B.C. Boulter's *Mystery of the Passion*, modelled on the Oberammergau Passion Play and inspired by the author's visit there in 1920. Unlike the Oberammergau play, Boulter's script called for Christ to appear only during the early scenes of the ministry; the Crucifixion took place off stage. In a note to the published text of the play Boulter wrote: 'Special care will, of course, be taken in the selection of the Christus. In the scene of the Last Supper, in order to avoid any possibility of misunderstanding, it is better that the paten and chalice should be empty at the Institution of the Eucharist.' Boulter's caution was rewarded. The play was performed annually on Good Friday at the Church of St Silas the Martyr in London for several years, winning the endorsement of the clergy as well as of the *Times* critic, who singled out for praise 'the impressive feeling of restraint' of the actor who played Christ.[30] Tentative as it may have been, the precedent had been set, and the principle of church drama accepted. The seal of approval came formally in 1929, with the formation of the Religious Drama Society under the presidency of George Bell, Bishop of Chichester, dedicated to 'fostering the art of drama as a means of religious expression.'

The Religious Drama Society was founded specifically to promote Christian drama, and from the beginning showed itself to be remarkably broad-minded. It acknowledged earlier pioneers in the struggle to 'to bring seriousness back to the theater' whose own religion could hardly be called Christian, such as Ibsen, Pinero, Shaw, and Granville-Barker. One of its founders, Sir Francis Youngblood, was inspired equally by performances he had seen of the Oberammergau Passion Play and of the Hindu classical religious epics in India, as well as by the use that Asian communists were making of drama to spread their doctrine, a use he felt Christians would do well to emulate.[31] Above all, the Religious Drama Society was eager to get away from the amateurishness that marked most church drama of the time and from the 'sentimentality' of most religious scripts. In the first few years of its existence it helped to bring some of England's leading dramatic talents into the service of Christian drama. In 1928 Bell, then Dean of Canterbury, had inaugurated the Canterbury Festival by commissioning John Masefield and Gustav Holst to produce *The Coming of Christ* in Canterbury Cathedral. Over the next two decades the Society was at least partly responsible for turning such writers as T.S. Eliot, Dorothy Sayers, Christopher Fry, and Charles Williams to the writing of plays, culminating with the commissioning of Eliot's *Murder in the Cathedral* for Canterbury Cathedral in 1935.

The plays of Dorothy Sayers were especially successful in dispelling old misconceptions about Biblical drama. In *The Man Born to Be King*, a series of radio dramas about the Passion broadcast by the BBC during 1941–2, Sayers introduced Christ as a modern prophet speaking colloquial modern English. Despite instense opposition by the Lord's Day Observance Society and the Protestant Truth Society, the BBC directors refused to cancel the programs and the show proved to be enormously popular.[32] (The Lord Chamberlain gave it his blessing on the condition that no audience be allowed in the studio.) In *The Just Vengeance*, commissioned for Lichfield Cathedral in 1946, Sayers took up the question of representing the deity on the stage and gave it a distinctively medieval answer, drawn from her life's work as a scholar of Dante:

> We, who are actors, bid you not forget
> That all these images at which you look
> Are but as pictures painted in a book –
> No more like that they bid you think upon
> Than this small yellow disc is like the sun;
> Though, in a picture, this might stand for that,
> And the great sun take no offence thereat.
> (Opening chorus)

Following such medieval precedents as the twelfth-century *Jeu d'Adam*, Sayers referred to her divine character not by his 'real' name but by the name of his stage incarnation, 'Persona Dei.' (In the *Jeu d'Adam* he is 'Figura Dei.') Persona Dei's opening speech sought to make a clear distinction in the audience's mind between the imitation and the thing imitated, describing himself as 'the image of the Unimaginable / In the place where the Image and the unimaged are one.' Having re-established this basic but long-forgotten theatrical principle, Sayers went on confidently to include both Christ and the Crucifixion in her play, having first obtained special permission from the Bishop of Lichfield to do so. In *Christ's Emperor*, produced in 1951 at the Church of St Thomas in London, she also took a swipe at the time-hallowed prohibition against audience applause: 'The presentation of a play in this Church is an offering to Almighty God, in which you partake by your presence. Your laughter and applause are an act of courtesy to your fellow-men the actors, and as such cannot surely be displeasing to our most courteous lord.'

The plays of Dorothy Sayers are a good example of how well the Religious Drama Society had succeeded in changing the general attitude toward Biblical plays in England. It was now possible to imitate divine beings, within the very precincts of a church, without fearing either heavenly or official retribution. At the same time, however, some of Sayers' ideas proved to be a good deal more advanced (or reactionary, since in essence they were medieval) than her contemporaries were willing to accept. Many of the old attitudes still survived, partly as the continuing legacy of puritanism, partly out of prudent fear lest reform be carried too far. If the Religious Drama Society and its supporters were anxious to professionalize church plays, they were equally anxious to affirm the special nature of these plays as religious dramas, distinct from the ordinary kind of theatrical entertainment. 'Religious drama is not a nice Christmas occupation for the young people of the parish: it is not something which all the mothers will love to come and see,' wrote one Anglican bishop. 'It is something which men do, and can only do, because God has done it first. It is the recreation, by re-thinking and reliving them, of actual events.'[33] Only the most reverent treatment was therefore deemed appropriate for such a subject. The three words that occur most frequently in discussions at this time of the proper style to be aimed at in religious drama are 'solemnity,' 'simplicity,' and 'sincerity.' When Robert Speaight praised Martin Browne's productions of T.S. Eliot's plays as 'triumphs of virtue over virtuosity,' he only varied the alliteration in order to express the ideal of nearly every practitioner of the art.[34] It was an ideal that was to have an important influence on the style of the first productions of the mystery cycles.

E. MARTIN BROWNE

When these productions finally came it was inevitable that the Religious
Drama Society should be asked to supervise them and that E. Martin Browne
should be appointed to direct the most important of them. During the 1920s
and 1930s Browne had emerged as the most distinguished director of religious
plays in England, and his experience during this time determined the shape
that these productions would take. He had begun his work in the theatre
while still an undergraduate at Oxford in the early 1920s, and passed up an
early calling to ordination to continue in it. Upon leaving Oxford he began
a career that was soon to embrace amateur, educational, and professional
theatre, sometimes all at once. In 1923 he became producer of the Angmering
Shakespeare Festival in Sussex, then spent a year as warden of Educational
Settlement in Doncaster, where he had his first experience producing
medieval drama – the 'Shearmen and Tailors' Play' from the 'true' Coventry
cycle. He followed this with three years in the United States at the Carnegie
Institute in Pittsburgh, where he produced Claudel's *L'annonce faite à Marie*
and the Nativity Play from the York Cycle.

In 1930 Browne came back to England, where he took up a new appointment as Director of Religious Drama for the Diocese of Chichester. In the
same year he travelled to Oberammergau to see the Passion Play, an event
that was to have a marked influence on his later treatment of the medieval
cycles. Bishop Bell, in appointing Browne to the Chichester post, noted the
spectacular success of the Oberammergau play and the 'new attitude of the
Church' toward drama: 'I hold,' he wrote, 'that the presentation of religious
drama in a right spirit and an excellent form is itself an offering of worship.
I wish to lead some to make that offering as artists or as players, and as
audience, who have not found an avenue of worship before.' Of Martin
Browne's duties as director he wrote:

He will desire, and, I trust secure a high standard, in which sincerity and simplicity
have an important part. The Plays which he will himself produce, as opportunity
offers, will be good plays, honestly acted, well and worthily presented. Some may
be given in Church (and for this my special permission will be required), others in
halls or out of doors, especially at the Church's seasons, or linked with some particular
festival or saint, both in town and country. I hope that not a few plays may be taken
out by the players from the town to neighbouring villages and stir a local effort
there. The task of the Director is great and very varied, though it will require time
to accomplish; and it is in the fullest sense religious.[35]

In this way Martin Browne found himself in a unique position as the professional director of an amateur theatre, responsible not to the authorities who had traditionally controlled drama in England but to an enlightened church leader. Just as importantly, an atmosphere was provided for the revival of the mystery plays which was neither commercial nor academic but religious. When Browne set out to produce, for the first time in four hundred years, the 'Marian cycle' from the *Ludus Coventriae* at Chichester, it was not for the sake of profit or out of antiquarian curiosity, but as an 'act of worship.'

Browne's adaptation of the Marian sequence from the *Ludus Coventriae* took place in the garden of the Bishop's Palace in Chichester in August 1931. It consisted of a condensed version of four plays dealing with the early life of Mary, which Browne entitled 'The Play of the Maid Mary.' Two 'mansion' platforms were erected, modelled after Giotto's frescoes of the Biblical stories in Padua. One served as the house of Joachim and Anne, Mary's parents, and later as the house of Mary and Joseph; the other represented the altar of the Temple. Costumes were similarly Giotto-esque. The action of the play passed between the two platforms, and also made use of natural surroundings: a door in the garden wall, the gate of the Palace, and a flat roof from which the message of the Annunciation was delivered. When the play was moved to nearby parish churches, Browne made a diffeent use of his surroundings. At the beginning of the play a messenger ran up and down the aisles crying out his summons to all the members of the House of David to assemble. In the 'Parliament of Heaven' scene, the Four Daughters of God – Truth, Justice, Mercy, and Peace – set out to search through the audience for the one sinless man, coming back empty-handed. Music was an important part of the production, chosen from plain-song, early polyphony, and the Oxford Carol Book, while a freely composed recitative was used for the offstage voice of God, in the manner of William Poel's production of *Everyman*.[36]

'The Play of the Maid Mary' began with the conception of the Virgin and ended with the Annunciation. Soon after the success of the Chichester production, Browne expanded the series to include the episodes of the Visit to Elizabeth, the Nativity, the Visits of the Shepherds and the Magi, and the Purification in the Temple, under the title 'The Play of Mary the Mother.'[37] Later a third play, 'the Assumption of the Blessed Virgin' from the York Cycle, performed at Tewkesbury Abbey in 1937, completed the Marian cycle. In choosing these subjects Browne was taking on some of the most controversial material in the mystery cycles, scenes which had long been considered by Protestants to be apocryphal and idolatrous. At the time, however, it was the one extended sequence of episodes available to a producer who wanted to show something of the epic scope and continuity of the cycles. The only other possibility was the Passion sequence, which, as Browne knew, was still off limits. Even in the Marian plays it was necessary for him to make some prudent changes in the text. The episode of the Cherry Tree miracle, for example, despite its charm and its familiarity to modern audiences through the Oxford Carol Book, was an apocryphal incident that Browne felt obliged to omit.

The style of the production was similarly influenced by rules of decorum which Browne had developed in response to Bishop Bell's request for a drama that would be an 'offering of worship.' These rules were set forth in Browne's books, *The Production of Religious Plays*, published in 1932, and *Putting on a Play*, published in 1936. 'All religious drama,' he wrote, 'should strive to attain participation in a common experience, vicariously suffered, whose perfect model is The Eucharist.' Because of this, religious plays should not be realistic representations of human life, but 'avenues of worship.' A play performed in a church, he declared, must treat its subject in a manner conducive to worship, and use language 'of a style not too far below that customarily heard in the building.' Scenery should not be changed in view of the audience unless a proscenium arch could be constructed, for 'it is even more important in religious than in secular drama that all should be done decently and in order.' To attain the dignified effect proper to the setting, 'the pace of a religious play should usually be slow.' Finally, all acting, Browne felt, stemmed from the original impersonation in religious ritual of a god. 'No one can act a part, even the smallest, unless he sees it as instinct with divine life. The actor must enter so deeply and sincerely into the feelings of his character as to convey to us its relation to the divine order of things.'[38]

In conformity with these principles, Browne introduced a number of practices while preparing his Chichester production that he was later to follow at York. To instil the proper spirit in the cast, for example, rehearsals often, though not invariably, began with prayers. Browne also followed Nugent Monck's practice of enforcing anonymity on his actors, on the grounds that 'the rule of anonymity among actors of religious drama is one which has the best effect in impressing on both company and audience the nature of the play as an offering to God without personal recognition.'[39] Acting the mystery plays, he felt, required no special histrionic skills and might safely be kept free from false theatricality: 'the original actors were amateurs, and the range of emotion written into the parts is accordingly no wider than that experienced by any spiritually-minded person in any age.'[40]

Despite the deliberately untheatrical nature of his productions at Chichester, Browne made considerable use of some modern stage techniques in them, particularly lighting. The famous, and enigmatic, stage direction in the *Ludus Coventriae* Annunciation play, 'Here the Holy Ghost descends with three beams to our lady, the son of the godhead next with three beams to the Holy Ghost, the Father Godly with three beams to the son, and so enter all three to her bosom,' which was presumably accomplished in the middle ages by a contrivance of gilded wires, became in Browne's production simply: 'three beams shine down upon Mary' with the aid of spotlights. Similarly the birth of Christ in the York Nativity (another play he performed at Chichester, and the only one of the medieval Nativity plays requiring the divine delivery to take place on stage before the audience) was accomplished under cover of a momentary blackout. Browne later devised a more stylized and effective solution to this difficulty for outdoor daylight performances, involving a symbolic sweeping of Mary's cloak over the crib.

Lighting, Browne felt, was the main resource which the producer of church plays had to compensate for the lack of scenery and props. Browne used lighting chiefly for atmospheric effect, particularly the technique of isolating individual actors against a dark background. 'In church,' he wrote, 'I have found "spots" by far the most useful lights, and have worked usually to make the actors appear as visions in surrounding darkness.'[41] Some of the effects gained in this way were later to be repeated in Browne's productions of the mystery cycles at York. He might already have been planning his productions there when he wrote: 'To see, for instance, the Archangel Gabriel appear out of the darkness of a great building, move in a glow of light, and fade into the darkness again, is to experience the seeing of a vision.'[42]

Martin Browne's tenure at Chichester gave the most extended publicity to the medieval mystery plays that they had yet received. In addition to the Marian plays, he produced and published his acting versions of the York Nativity Play and the Brome Sacrifice of Isaac, as well as the York Assumption of the Blessed Virgin at the Tewkesbury Festival. In 1934, however, the experiment at Chichester having been successfully accomplished, Browne began an association with T.S. Eliot which led him increasingly away from church drama into the professional theatre. It was Browne and Bishop Bell who, during a week-end at Chichester, persuaded Eliot, a recent Anglican convert, to turn to religious drama. The association between author and producer was close, as Browne has related in his book on *The Making of T.S. Eliot's Plays* (1969). Browne wrote the scenario for Eliot's *The Rock* and produced it at Sadler's Wells in 1934. In the following year he produced Eliot's greatest success, *Murder in the Cathedral*, at the Canterbury Festival, and later directed the play on the professional stage. In 1939 he assisted Eliot in forming the final text of *The Family Reunion*. After the war he was to continue his association with Eliot by directing both the New York and London productions of *The Cocktail Party*.

Browne's collaboration with T.S. Eliot was one of the most important episodes in the history of modern English drama. Between them the two made religious drama both respectable and professional. Never again would it be the province solely of well-intentioned amateurs. During the Second World War Browne formed his own company, the Pilgrim Players. Sponsored by the Religious Drama Society, of which he was now director, the company toured England performing religious plays, including the Wakefield Second Shepherds Play, *The Way of the Cross*, *Murder in the Cathedral*, and Yeats' *Resurrection*. When the war was over Browne became director of the Mercury Theatre in London, a company devoted to the production of verse plays. There he proceeded to justify Christopher Fry's praise as the man who 'has driven more poets to drama than any man living.' Not surprisingly, a number of the Mercury's plays were on religious themes, most notably Fry's *A Phoenix Too Frequent*. When the call to produce the first full-scale modern version of the York Cycle eventually came in 1951, Browne was more than ready.

SHEPHERDS, CENSORS, AND NUGENT MONCK AGAIN

Apart from Martin Browne's contributions, productions of the mystery plays between the wars did little to advance their cause. Still hampered by the Lord Chamberlain's restrictions, producers were limited to plays about the birth of Christ or to the better-known Old Testament subjects. To the average theatre goer of the 1920s and 1930s the term 'mystery play' was virtually synonymous with nativity pageants at Christmas time. Specifically, it was likely to mean the Wakefield Second Shepherds Play, which, like *Everyman*, became the standard example of its genre in all the textbooks and the most frequently seen on the stage. Like *Everyman*, which compresses its action into a more classically unified plot than any other English morality play, the Second Shepherds Play is also atypical of its genre, and was singled out for qualities more modern than medieval: its unusually protracted comic scenes, its concern with secular social issues, and its pungent colloquial dialogue. As a supposed precursor of Shakespeare's rustic comedies, it became a favourite of theatre historians, who took an active hand in assisting it back to the stage. As early as 1904, a University of California Professor, Charles Mills Gayley, prepared an acting version of the play for Ben Greet's touring company as a companion-piece to *Everyman*, Greet having acquired the rights to Poel's original production. Gayley's version ran the First and Second Shepherds Plays from the Wakefield Cycle together, taking the best of the comic business from each, and inserting the Journey of the Magi episode into the middle, with the help of speeches from several other cycles and some 'original dialogue.'[43] A similar composite play was prepared by Gayley for the Christmas repertoire of the Old Vic in 1915, the text of whch was issued two years later in a hand-lettered collector's edition.[44] A more practical edition of the Second Shepherd's Play was published in the 1930s by the Religious Drama Society, which translated the peasant scenes into modern dialect prose ('Lord, how cold it be! My clothes be too thin for these weathers. So long have I slept I am near-hand gone silly with it'), but retained verse for the adoration at the manger.[45]

Shepherds plays from the other cycles were no less popular. In 1909 the York Shepherds Play was performed on a reproduction of a medieval pageant wagon during a celebration of the city's history.[46] In 1923 the Old Vic coupled the Chester Nativity Play on a holiday bill with Dickens' 'Christmas Carol.' The following year it was combined with Hauptmann's *Hannele*, now rescued from the Lord Chamberlain's wrath (see above, chapter 1). Comparing the two works, one critic found Hauptmann's piece to be 'a sentimental, rather tawdry affair, beside the old Chester play, with its simple beauty and superb dignity.'[47] A notable performance of the York Nativity Play was given in the Guildhall in York in 1925 by Edith Craig, sister of Gordon Craig and daughter of Ellen Terry, with a text prepared by R.W. Chambers and costumes lent for the occasion by Dame Ellen herself from her Shakespearean wardrobe.[48] Less elegant productions of Shepherds plays throughout the period are too numerous to mention.

The case was necessarily different with the Passion episodes. Despite the occasional, though infrequent, appearance of Christ in some plays written for church performance, such as those of B.C. Boulter and Dorothy Sayers, there is no evidence of a single public performance of a medieval Passion Play anywhere in England during this period. In 1932 Martin Browne summarized the existing state of the law on the matter as follows:

The Lord Chamberlain has ruled that 'neither God nor Jesus may appear on the stage or take a speaking part.' A voice heard off-stage does not constitute a 'speaking part.' Peformances in church where no charge is made for admission fall outside the scope of this ruling; but for these the permission of the Diocesan Bishop or analogous authority must be obtained ... It is at present axiomatic in England that the person of Christ shall not be shown even in church.[49]

Public performances of the Passion sequences in the mysteries could avoid the censor's regulations only if they were given unaltered, in the original Middle English – something no producer of the time was willing to do.

Passion plays were not the only portions of the cycles affected by this rule, however. In 1930 an attempt to stage the Chester Noah's Flood at a village fête ran into trouble with the Lord Chamberlain. Despite the fact that the purpose of the production was to raise funds for the repair of the parish church, the censor insisted that the usual regulations be followed. A local press report gave details of the controversy:

The Deluge is a modernised version of one of the Chester Miracle Plays, similar to those performed in the fourteenth and fifteenth centuries, and a controversy has raged recently over the introduction of God as a character in the play. Under the Censorship Act of 1737 this must necessarily have been deleted, but as the Chester Miracle Play was written prior to the introduction of the Act no objection could have been raised had it been presented in the original form.

In modernising the play, Mr. O. Bolton King, the producer, deleted the objectionable passages, and rewrote a considerable portion, bringing it, inadvertently, into a category of new plays. The character of 'The Deus' was deleted by the Lord Chamberlain, but after further inquiry it was admitted that a 'voice off' was not a speaking part. Mr. Bolton King recited the part of God from behind a screen, but did not appear on the stage.[50]

Even in print the modern reader might find himself protected from what was considered to be the grossness of medieval plays. A bowdlerized version of the Wakefield Crucifixion Play was issued, for example, in 1920 under the title *A Little Drama of the Crucifixion*. In his Preface the editor, Ernest J.B. Kirtlan, explained that 'our ancestors were less sensitive than moderns, and, no doubt, took a strange pleasure in contemplating the physical agonies of the Crucifixion. I have, therefore, omitted lines 100 to 232 [i.e., the nailing to the cross] as being unsuitable and almost revolting in their realism.' In place of the offending passage Kirtlan inserted the following stage direction: 'Behind the scene and unseen of the audience Christ is crucified, and is henceforth invisible.'[51] Nativity plays, too, occasionally received similar treatment. In 1926 an edition of the York Nativity noted that the play contained 'passages in which the language is perhaps too bluntly plain-spoken to be acceptable in the ears of an audience of today, necessitating the use of the blue pencil for the excision of such passages as might prove offensive.'[52] With such texts to guide them, it is little wonder that most producers still considered the mystery cycle as a whole inappropriate for modern production.

One exception was Nugent Monck, the veteran antagonist of the Lord Chamberlain. Despite his setback in 1909, Monck had not forgotten medieval drama. Still less had he abandoned his devotion to the resurrection of neglected or persecuted plays. Following the dissolution of the English Drama Society in 1909 Monck took up residence in the East Anglian city of Norwich, where he was to spend the rest of a long theatrical life. In 1910 he founded a small group of amateur actors called the Norwich Players whose announced purpose was to 'devote their leisure time to the performance of dramatic works of art, the tendency of which was to show the beauty of truth and goodness and the ugliness of vice.' The repertoire of the Norwich Players, like their credo, was a throwback to older times: mystery plays, morality plays, and Shakespeare formed the staple of their programs and continued to do so for the next forty years. At first even their theatre was genuinely Elizabethan, if not Shakespearean, consisting of a drawing room in the Tudor mansion that Monck had bought. In this room during the first four years of their existence the Norwich Players produced a number of English plays, many of them for the first time since the Middle Ages, including *The World and the Child*, *The Interlude of Youth*, the Norwich *Grocer's Play*, *Everyman*, the Second Shepherds Play, and the Chester Nativity sequence. The casts were anonymous, because of the religious nature of the plays, and all profits went to improving the resources of the company.

In 1912 Monck, at Yeats' invitation, took time off from Norwich to direct the Abbey Theatre in Dublin while Yeats himself went on tour to America. There he produced three of the Wakefield plays – The Annunciation, The Second Shepherds Play, and The Flight into Egypt.[53] In 1914, back in Norwich, he moved the company to something more closely resembling a theatre, a medieval banqueting hall attached to an inn called the Old Music House, which had once been the home of Sir John Paston in the fifteenth century. On Twelfth Night, 1914, a group of Nativity plays from the Chester Cycle inaugurated the new theatre. Under these more auspicious conditions, and despite the interruption of the First World War, the repertoire and the finances of the company grew until in 1921 it was able to purchase the building, originally erected as a Catholic church, that is now known as the Maddermarket Theatre. Monck designed the Maddermarket, in consultation with William Poel, as an Elizabethan theatre, modelled on the dimensions given in the contract for the Fortune Theatre in London. It had a forty-foot-square apron, entrances on either side of the stage, a rear balcony with portable steps leading to the stage, and a curtained inner stage. There were no scenery and no footlights. In 1921 the Maddermarket was officially opened by W.B. Yeats. Ten years before, Monck had owned the smallest licensed theatre in England. Now he had the only theatre of its kind in the world.

Monck's productions for the Norwich Players were matters of controversy from the beginning. At their best they were disciplined and subtle; at their worst they were, in the words of one critic, 'lifeless and anaemic.'[54] There was a touch of dandyism in the producer and more than a touch of snobbishness in his aims for his company. 'I have always tried,' Monck said, 'to make the Maddermarket a "gentlemanly entertainment," without fuss, with a maximum of taste and a minimum of vulgarity. It is very difficult not to be vulgar in a theatre, and even the fear of it makes one suburban.'[55] If contemporary reviews can be believed, fear of vulgarity sometimes made Monck's productions dull as well. An account of his production of the Wakefield Nativity sequence in 1919 by a critic prepared to be sympathetic found little to commend:

The Wakefield Mysteries were interesting, but they lacked conviction. This may have been the actors' fault. Mysteries and Moralities must be acted with passion and sincerity. One felt that actors and audience were out of touch with the spirit of the things – the Old Musick House was a house of mourning – there was no reality and no joy. Perhaps I am altogether wrong; maybe these things ought to be done in a spirit of reverence. But the lugubrious gloom which infected the stage and the audience was about as truly reverential as the uncomfortable silence which follows the Benediction, when the stiff-kneed congregation hold on tensely while the minister affects a private colloquy with his Maker. Even that sparkling comedy 'The Shepherds Play,' suffered from too much gloom.[56]

Excessive solemnity seems to have marred some of Monck's other productions of the mystery plays as well. Yet this was perhaps the only approach to the plays that could have succeeded at the time. 'Anaemic' as they may sometimes have been, Monck's productions succeeded in allaying the doubts which many of his audience felt as to whether the mystery plays should be produced at all. Norwich was a remote provincial city with no recent tradition of theatre, though it had had a rich one in the Middle Ages and again in the eighteenth century. Reviewers of Monck's production in 1910 of the Norwich Paradise Play, the only surviving play from the city's medieval past, arrived apprehensively to witness the novel spectacle of God on the stage. 'There may be some who will think that it cannot be possible under such conditions,' one of them wrote, 'to obtain the reverence necessary for a representation of the Supreme Being.' But the tastefulness of Monck's performance led him to assure his readers that they might safely attend the performance without the 'least suspicion of irreverence.'[57]

Even *Everyman* carried no guarantee of safe passage for a religious production, in Norwich or anywhere else. When Monck opened the Canterbury
Festival in 1929 with a production of that play outside the Cathedral (using
costumes and sets that he had purchased from William Poel), a local vicar
publicly accused Dean Bell of violating the word of God in approving what
he called 'this scandal.'[58] Critics from both the *Church Times* and the *Daily
Chronicle* agreed that the impersonation of God in the production was an
unfortunate mistake. ('One felt that one was getting an undesired glimpse
of another world, and one which it was impossible to regard without feelings
of thankfulness that it had ceased to exist.')[59] As late as the 1930s local
reviewers in Norwich were still sceptical whether the things depicted in
mystery plays were not 'better left to the imagination.'[60] In such circumstances Monck had little choice but to adopt the style he did and to
save his sense of humour for his program notes:

There is a common belief that Adam and Eve played in the nude. In this particular
Norwich play, as both Adam and Eve are ordered to wear gloves, it may be presumed
that they were in ordinary Tudor costume, as they were not likely to wear gloves
and nothing else.[61]

Whatever Nugent Monck may have lacked in theatrical vigour he made
up in courage. In 1938, nearly thirty years after his first skirmish, Monck
prepared to do battle with the Lord Chamberlain once again. This time he
made sure of his ground beforehand. With the help of lawyers, he set up a
private society called the Maddermarket Theatre Society, legally separate
from the Norwich Players, whose purpose was 'the presentation of plays
which have only a limited appeal, or which for political, social, or religious
reasons cannot be given publicly.' Members were enrolled in advance, and
prospectuses issued containing the warning that 'these performances will be
entirely private, admission being to members only.' Thus having skirted the
Lord Chamberlain's jurisdiction, Monck announced the first, and as it turned
out the only, production of the new Society: *The Norwich Passion Play*.

The 'Norwich' Passion Play was in reality the passion sequence from the
Ludus Coventriae cycle, the same one he had tried thirty years before.
Monck labelled it 'Norwich' out of local pride and because the plays were
written in the East Anglian dialect. For the performance, Monck prepared
an expanded version of the script that he had written for the ill-fated 1909
production. This was a 'slightly modernized' text of the plays from the
Conspiracy to the Resurrection (but omitting the Harrowing of Hell). Some

scenes in the original cycle, which had, of course, been written for outdoor performance, were 'rearranged so that they can be performed more smoothly upon the limited stage of the Maddermarket.' Given this limitation, the staging requirements of the original text were met with as much fidelity as possible. The *Ludus Coventriae* plays call for 'mansion and place' staging, a series of localized scaffolds or houses giving onto a neutral area or 'place.' Monck let his curtained inner and upper stages serve as the mansions, using the forestage for entrances and exits while the next 'mansion' was being prepared. Use of the upper and lower stages together permitted the simultaneous staging of different actions – such as the Scourging and the Denial of Peter – as called for in the original text. The two curtained stages were also put to the use of framing pictorial tableaux, particularly those of the Crucifixion and *Pietà*, each of which was revealed as a set-picture by drawing the curtain, in the manner of Oberammergau, rather than forming a single continuous action as in the original. (At a lecture previewing the production for members of the Society, Monck had shown slides of the 1930 Oberammergau performance.)

As might be expected, it was the pictorial rather than the dramatic quality of Monck's production that stood out. Monck still clung to his idea that these were luturgical plays, and his stage décor accordingly sought to transform the theatre into a church, much as he had done earlier in the 1909 production. 'The set is on the lines of a very old, darkly magnificent church screen,' wrote a reviewer, 'just the design and colouring that might be encountered in a quiet Norfolk church, with deep blues and reds predominating and a general air of restfulness and dignity.'[62] Attention was focused on the more hieratic moments in the story, such as the 'symbolic, almost static scenes of the Last Supper, the procession to Calvary, the Crucifixion, and the lifting of the lid of the tomb by two angels.' 'In these still scenes,' noted one critic, 'the brilliant colour, the falling lines of the draperies and the beautiful grouping of the figures are noticeably influenced by the great tradition of Christian painting. As in the paintings there is a spiritual aspect which triumphs over physical violence. In the last scene, where figures on two levels raise their arms upwards and proclaim that Christ is risen, the lines soar upward expressing aspiration to heaven like those of a Gothic Cathedral.'[63] (See plate 3.)

In such an atmosphere the Saviour took his place naturally enough as a pre-Raphaelite figure. The actor who played Christ was bearded, long-haired and long-robed, speaking his lines with dignity and 'a minimum of emotion.' Throughout the play he was followed by a pencil-beamed spot providing a halo effect. Comparisons with Oberammergau were frequent and seldom odious, though the *Catholic Herald* complained that the medieval play 'lacked the more psychological embroiderings' of the German one. When Monck revived the production in 1952, the pictorial effects were equally elaborate. The stage was decorated to resemble a medieval triptych with the curtained inner stage as the central panel, and the actors positioned to form 'a succession of tableaux in the style of fifteenth-century altar-pieces.' Each scene developed into a set picture and then 'dissolved until, by subtle handling of the stage, the next picture began to take shape.'[64]

Reactions to Monck's medieval Passion Play were varied. The performance was praised by the Bishop of Norwich as a 'heart-rending inspiration, effected in a spirit of utmost reverence,' and condemned as blasphemous by anonymous correspondents in the press.[65] Critics were impressed by the scenic effects but unsure whether what they had seen could be called a drama. 'As one picture flows into another,' wrote the *Theatre* critic, 'the impression left by the whole production is of a beautifully staged religious ritual which appeals to the eye and ear but leaves the emotions comparatively untouched. Even the devil is restrained to a point where a medieval audience would probably have had difficulty in recognizing him.'[66] But at least one critic found in the play itself, emasculated as it may have been on the Maddermarket stage, a revelation of a kind of drama that had been missing from the English theatre for too long:

The performance of the savage and beautiful fifteenth-century Passion play at the Maddermarket Theatre last week had something of the effect of telling the story for the first time. The play must indeed seem savage to the many of us for whom the story is so embedded in sentimental Victorian hymns and a mild humanitarian tradition that we have long ceased to think of it as dramatic ... The highest drama of the conflict of good and evil, written in terms of five hundred years ago, was brought freshly on to the stage to edify our generation ... It is like us, that until recently we have refused to license such a play for public performance.[67]

In 1952 there was no longer any need to dodge the Lord Chamberlain through private societies. The ban on medieval Passion plays had finally been relaxed and the great precedent at York the year before had been set.[68] Nugent Monck had formed his ideas about the mystery plays more than forty years previously. The public performance of the *Norwich Passion Play* at the Maddermarket in 1952 was, in fact, the long-delayed fruition of plans that had originally been drawn up in 1909. If there was something strangely outdated about the Maddermarket production, it is not to be wondered at. Monck was to live another six years, dying at the age of eighty-one in 1958.

By that time he was to have the opportunity of seeing at least parts of all the extant English mystery cycles performed in their original locations under more authentic conditions than he could ever have provided at the Madder-market. If history was to pass him by, he could still feel the satisfaction of knowing that that history might never have started without his own lonely efforts.

4

The York Festival

Because we are drawn in certain ways to the medieval drama, we have to be aware of the gulf which still separates us from those who wrote and played it, and to look for the right bridge across which to take our audiences if the medieval drama is to renew its appeal to them.

E. Martin Browne (1963)

York in 1951 was, to the eye of the visitor, much the same city that it had been in the fifteenth century. Unlike Wakefield, Coventry, and other English towns that had once possessed mystery cycles, York had escaped the worst ravages of industrialism, city planning, and German bombers. One could still walk nearly the whole circumference of its ancient city walls and see the spires of its thirty medieval churches, rising above the narrow, crooked streets through which had passed, more than four hundred years before, the gaily-coloured wagons of the Corpus Christi procession. Looming over all were the mammoth limestone towers of the Minster, permanent witnesses to the energy and prosperity that had once made York the most important, and still kept it the most beautiful, city in the north of England.

The towers of the Minster, however, also tolled the passing of time, and time had brought more changes to life within the walls of York than one could read in the cold stone monuments that it had left behind. Factories, breweries, and railway yards had slowly encircled the city, replacing the wool merchants' companies and craftsmen's guilds of the Middle Ages as sources of livelihood. In the nineteenth century, rows of workers' cottages had sprung up beside the quiet river that flowed through the city, and later amorphous council-tenements in the suburbs beyond. By 1951 nearly 90 per cent of the population of York had moved outside the city walls, leaving the Minster and its once-teeming parishes behind to rot.

The change in the religious life of York from the Middle Ages to the twentieth century had been as radical as the movement of its population. If the city offered a uniquely authentic physical setting for the modern revival of its ancient mystery plays, the spirit of the audiences who would come to see these plays would necessarily be very different from that of their medieval predecessors. The sociologist B. Seebohm Rowntree determined in 1941, after studying the social and economic life of modern York, that fewer than one out of every five persons living in the city was a regular church-goer. Ten years later he found that the figure was even lower. Rowntree, born of the wealthiest family in York, had begun his statistical surveys of life in the city at the turn of the century in order to identify the causes of its poverty. As the years went by he became progressively more alarmed at the even greater spiritual poverty of his subjects. Drunkenness, divorce, crime, gambling, fornication, boredom, despair, and suicide, he reported, were the life-staples of York's industrial classes, seeming to increase in magnitude even as the last vestiges of actual poverty were being eliminated by the welfare state. Turning his attention to how York's citizens were spending their newly won leisure, Rowntree discovered that there was nothing among their entertainments that remotely corresponded to the annual celebrations of the city's spiritual heritage that had once occupied the people of York. 'The survey we have made,' he observed ruefully, 'of the ways in which people spend their leisure reminds us how much greater today than in the past is the temptation to seek fullness of life by indulging too largely in forms of recreation which make no demands on physical, mental, or spiritual powers.' The Minster was empty, the pubs were full. The influence of the Church, Rowntree added almost parenthetically, was 'weaker than at any time in the memory of those now living.'[1]

What Rowntree perceived about the spiritual life of York was widely felt to be true on a larger scale of Britain as a whole. A nation which had devoted nearly all its energies over the past century to alleviating the material needs of its people was discovering that it had been living on what Rowntree called the 'moral capital of the past.' More important than raising the material standard of living, Rowntree urged, was the raising of the 'mental and spiritual life of the whole nation – an infinitely harder task, yet one on whose accomplishment depends the lasting greatness of the State.' Remarkably enough, the State itself agreed with Rowntree's diagnosis. In 1951 the Labour Government set out to inject a new infusion of 'moral capital' into the national bloodstream. The method it chose was a nation-wide revival of the glories of Britain's cultural and spiritual past, to be called the Festival

of Britain. It was as a part of this revival that the medieval mystery plays
at last found an officially sanctioned place in modern English life.

For the Festival of Britain each city was invited to devise its own contribution, with priority to be given to celebrations of local antiquities and cultural
traditions. Inevitably, many of the events of the Festival fell short of the
planners' goals. Cricket matches and exhibitions of parachute-jumping
proved more popular in some cities than symphony concerts and historical
pageants. Liverpool boasted as its principal contribution to the festivities 'a
firework display to end all firework displays.'[2] But religion, and especially
religious drama, played a large and calculated part in the festivities. The
Religious Drama Society was appointed by the Arts Council to supervise
this aspect of the Festival, and under its sponsorship productions were
planned of classics like *Everyman* and *Samson Agonistes*, as well as of newly
commissioned plays like Christopher Fry's *Sleep of Prisoners*. Bishop Bell
of Chichester, in endorsing these productions, noted the progress which
religious drama had made in England since the beginning of the century:

Religious drama is an essential part of the Festival of Britain. It had almost vanished
for 350 years, till the beginning of this century. Then some of the old plays were
revived by William Poel and others, and a few new plays were written. But it was
uncertain going, and the very notion of a play in church was regarded with horror.
By degrees, when the first world war was over, a change took place in the public
mind. And now religious drama is coming into its own in quite a new fashion. There
is a movement in the Church. The doors are no longer closed. The play and the
players are welcome.[3]

Despite such encouragement, the decision to put on a full-scale production
of the mystery plays at York was not reached hastily. The original plans for
York's contribution to the Festival were modelled on the first Edinburgh
Festival of 1947, with emphasis on local colour and pageantry rather than
on any single event. The main attraction was to have been a guild procession
through the streets of the city, led by the Lord Mayor in full ceremonial
regalia, in imitation of the old Corpus Christi processions of the Middle
Ages. Performances of one or two of the mystery pageants were contemplated
in the Minster and other churches following the procession. The Museum
Gardens appeared in these early plans only as a possible setting for a Shakespearean play – either *A Midsummer Night's Dream* or one of the histories.
Only gradually did a more ambitious plan take shape, centred on the mystery
plays. The theatrical viability of the plays, however, was still an unknown
quantity. Could they be staged intelligibly for a modern audience in anything

like their original form? Nugent Monck's experiment at Norwich in 1939 formed virtually the only precedent, and that had involved only a small portion of one of the cycles, staged for a private audience. What the response of a mass public audience would be to a full-scale production no one could predict.

A more recent experiment, closer to home, offered greater encouragement. At Edinburgh in 1948 Tyrone Guthrie had staged the early sixteenth-century Scottish morality play, *Ane Satire of the Three Estates*, to unexpected critical and popular acclaim. In that production Guthrie had rediscovered for the professional theatre the principle of medieval open staging, converting the austere Church of Scotland Assembly Hall into a three-sided arena, without a proscenium arch, which drew the audience into the world of the play. The 'heavy, antique, scholarly rhyming verse' was converted into modern Scots dialect, the 'shockingly broad' scatalogical jokes were tactfully pruned (though enough were left 'to make old ladies sit up and blink'), and the text was trimmed by two-thirds. Characteristically, Guthrie himself had no personal interest at all in the religious content of the play, having chosen the headquarters of the church of John Knox as the setting for the production for purely theatrical reasons:

The general air of solid, smug, well-fed respectability, the sage-green upholstery, the stained glass, the corridors lined with sanitary tiling, the strong odour of sanctity, and the faint odour of gas, were all so sharply opposed to the whole spirit and feeling of the play, so gloriously wrong, that, perversely, I was convinced of their rightness.[4]

The critics agreed and came away feeling that they had witnessed a new and exhilarating brand of theatre. 'Success was in the very shape of the building and the way the play and the place were one,' they reported. 'Sometimes one felt almost like an actor in the play, or rather a person existing in the life of the play, such was the effect of no proscenium arch, of an arena stage, and the exciting invasion of the aisles by travellers who had come far to bring us arresting news.'[5] Audiences filled the house to see this revival of a genuine Scottish drama, and continued to do so when the production was repeated at the 1949 and 1951 festivals. In *Ane Satire of the Three Estates* the Edinburgh Festival had found the local dramatic tradition that it had been looking for, and discovered at the same time that medieval drama could be a commercial success.

It was largely the success of *Ane Satire of the Three Estates* that persuaded the York Festival Committee to undertake a full-scale performance of the mystery plays. The first suggestion came in the summer of 1949, from the Reverend J.S. Purvis, who offered to prepare a modernized text of the plays for the production. In April of that year a committee had been formed to plan the upcoming festival, headed by Keith Thomson, secretary of the York University Planning Committee. The committee had already drawn up a preliminary design for the Festival along other lines, but was instantly attracted to Purvis' idea – more, as Thomson later confessed, by the potential 'draw' of the plays than by any specific religious motive.[6] Religion, however, soon became the chief factor in securing official approval of the production and remained the overriding concern of those who planned it. The Arts Council in London, which had overall supervision of the Festival of Britain, was the first to be persuaded, but the Church of England and the Lord Chamberlain threatened to be more formidable obstacles. Unlike Bishop Bell in faraway Chichester, the Archbishop of York was less than enthusiastic about the idea of religious drama. As for the Lord Chamberlain's office, it had an almost unblemished record extending over two centuries of protecting the Deity from the tarnish of the stage.

Luckily for the committee, both time and family connections were on their side. The Lord Chamberlain in 1949, Lord Scarborough, happened to be chairman of the Festival of Britain Committee. Better still, he was also a Yorkshireman. By an even happier stroke of luck, Keith Thomson's grandfather had been, in his time, the Archbishop of York. Purity of motives being assumed on all sides, an informal meeting was arranged at the Archbishop's palace between Thomson, Archbishop Cyril Garbett of York, and the Archbishop of Canterbury. There the archbishops gave their blessing to the production, in exchange for two guarantees: first, that the plays would be performed on sacred ground, as a religious rather than as a purely theatrical event; and second, that Martin Browne would be appointed to direct them. The Lord Chamberlain was content to accept the archbishops' decision, obligingly ruling that since the mystery plays had been written prior to the Theatres Act of 1737, they therefore fell outside his jurisdiction and need not be submitted for licence. He stipulated only that the cycle be given 'in its traditional form,' and that any modernization of the text consist solely of 'word for word substitution of modern for archaic English.'[7] On the first of October, 1949, a public announcement was made by the York Festival Planning Committee that the plays would be performed against the ruins of the former Benedictine Abbey of St Mary, now a part of the gardens of the Yorkshire Philosophical Society Museum. On the 18th of January 1950, the board formally appointed Martin Browne as producer. The stage was set.

THE PERFORMANCE OF 1951

Martin Browne faced a perplexing problem. His task, as he saw it, was how to stage an act of worship that would be entertaining to the sceptical, while at the same time creating an act of theatre that would be palatable to the devout. Reviewing the state of religious drama in England a few years before, Browne had noted the difficulty of reconciling these two aims on the modern stage:

We can all remember plays which were unexceptionably pious, but which were despicable as plays. We can all remember others in which artists prostituted religious emotions to obtain success with the undiscerning. We know that both these types have done harm to drama and to religion alike.

The future, he felt, was equally uncertain:

Religious drama is attempting to combine two human activities, each strong in its own right and set in its own ways. It is trying to express in terms of the art of the theatre the experience of religion. Thus it will be suspect, on the one hand, by the theatre-men as an attempt to use their art for propagandist ends; on the other hand by the religious men because it presents the profundities in terms of limited human personalities and emotions. ... A perpetual watch needs to be kept against these dangers.[8]

At York it was the believers rather than the 'theatre-men' who presented Browne with his greatest problems. Militant Protestant organizations like the Lord's Day Observance Society seized the occasion to denounce Biblical drama and to complain against Sunday performances. Archbishop Garbett, despite his acquiescence in the plans for the production, remained worried. Before rehearsals began, he wrote to the Festival Committee, expressing his uneasiness over the staging of the Crucifixion and asking that it be omitted from the performance. The Last Supper, he felt, was an equally touchy subject, owing to the long-standing controversy over the nature of the sacrament of communion. (Although the Last Supper play was missing from the York text, Browne wished to insert the scene into the production.) Even Father Purvis, who had been responsible for the original proposal to put on the plays, grew apprehensive as he prepared the acting script. 'There is an enormous and impassable gulf between us and the people who wrote, performed, and watched these plays,' he declared in an interview several months before the opening. 'The scourging and crucifixion scenes are too realistic for us today. Nobody would dare to put on some of these plays today. They are too shocking.'[9]

The precautions that Browne was forced to take in response to these fears largely determined the tone of his production. In casting the mystery plays, Browne announced that 'only persons who sincerely believed in Christian doctrine' would be welcome to try out.[10] When auditions of local amateurs proved disappointing, the Festival Committee authorized the director to seek professional actors for the leading roles. Browne stipulated that the actors who took on the parts of God and Jesus 'would have to accept anonymity as part of their engagement.' 'We do not want people,' he explained, 'to get away from the fact, so vitally important to the original writers, that these two divine beings are fundamentally different from the other people in the play.' It was, he also felt, 'wrong for anyone to profit by playing such a role.'[11] The part of the Virgin Mary he decided to assign to a seventeen-year-old schoolgirl, a tradition that he continued to follow in future festivals. (Ironically, at least two of Browne's schoolgirl discoveries later used the role of the Virgin Mary as a stepping-stone to distinctly non-virginal roles in the professional theatre: Mary Ure, who played the part in 1951, and Judi Dench in 1957.) As to the script, the Last Supper, out of deference to the Archbishop, was confined to an exit through the door in the house where the event was presumed to have taken place. On the sensitive issue of the Crucifixion, Browne went to see the Archbishop and arranged a compromise, in the style of Oberammergau. The scourging scene he agreed to place offstage, to be conveyed to the audience by sound effects only. The nailing to the cross, which could not be done offstage, was to be tactfully masked by the grouped banners of the Roman soldiers. By this device Browne pacified not only the Archbishop but, as it turned out, the critics as well, one of whom called it on opening night 'an alleviation of settings that might have led to the harrowing of others besides the inhabitants of Hell.'[12]

With these precautions, the production began to take form. The text prepared by Father Purvis pared the cycle down to about three hours' playing time. Beginning with the Creation and Fall of Man, it skipped over the rest of the Old Testament plays directly to the Nativity. The plays on the life of Christ were then dovetailed together into a continuous narrative. No single play was given entire, and many, such as the Massacre of the Innocents, the Purification of Mary, Jesus and the Doctors, the Transfiguration, and Jesus before Herod, were omitted altogether. From the Resurrection and Ascension, Purvis proceeded directly to the Last Judgment, omitting the plays on the Assumption and Coronation of Mary which take up the latter part of the York Cycle. The resulting script was thus essentially a Passion Play with a Prologue and Epilogue. The official Festival brochure referred to it as 'The ancient York Plays of the Creation and Redemption of Man and the Life of Christ.' This cutting fulfilled two purposes, one aesthetic and the other doctrinal. It reduced the sprawling, episodic cycle to something like classical unity with a central figure on stage at nearly all times. And it purged the cycle of some of its more controversial legendary and apocryphal accretions, especially the Mariolatrous matter, retaining only the Harrowing of Hell from the non-Biblical material of the original. As Archbishop Garbett noted with approval, after opening night, 'The text of the plays was thoroughly scriptural, and far more impressive than that used at Oberammergau.'[13] Both the comparison and the praise were appropriate.

If the text for the 1951 performance was more modern than medieval, the setting for the production was as medieval as it could be, though it was not the one that the plays had originally known. The Abbey ruins formed a huge stone arcade, enclosing on three sides a grassy lawn 144 feet wide. The acting space it provided was more than three times the width of an Elizabethan stage, and immeasurably larger than that of any pageant wagon that might have rumbled through the streets of medieval York. To fill this space Browne and his designer, Norah Lambourne, turned to a continental model, the famous mystery-play stage used at Valenciennes in northern France in 1547. The Valenciennes setting had consisted of a series of 'mansions' arranged linearly along a rear wall. To the spectator's left was Heaven, raised high on a platform, beneath which was a 'room' used for interior scenes. Three other lower mansions stretched to the right: the Temple, with an altar at the back topped by a tabernacle surrounded with curtains, was used chiefly for the Annas and Caiaphas scenes; the Palace, with its central property, the throne, formed the domain of Pilate and Herod; and finally, jutting forward closest to the medieval spectators, was a gigantic Hell-Mouth, spouting fire and smoke, within which appeared a cauldron boiling the souls of the damned. Attached to the Hell-Mouth was a half-ruined fortress containing Limbo, above which Satan rode on a fire-breathing dragon. Between the mansions and extending outward toward the spectators was the neutral playing area, or 'place,' furnished with its own impressive properties, including a 'lake' made of stretched dried sheepskins and two 'mountains' for the Sermon on the Mount and the Temptation.[14]

From the manuscript miniatures by Hubert Cailleau preserving the details of the Valenciennes set, Browne and Lambourne took their inspiration. At York in 1951 five mansions were ranged against the Abbey ruins (see plate

4). On the left was an open platform for Paradise, underneath it a sepulchre for the Resurrection. Then, stretching from left to right, came Pilate's Palace; a Stable for the Nativity at centre-stage, directly under God's Throne; Caiaphas' Temple; and lastly a wooden Hell-Mouth, wheeled into place on a wagon – the one reminder of the presumed original staging of these plays.[15] Above, in the empty clerestory vaults, was Heaven, connected by a staircase to the Paradise platform, which in turn had a ramp leading to the 'Place' below. Seats at ground level accommodating sixteen hundred spectators faced the stage.

The resemblance between the 1951 York performance and that at Valenciennes in 1547 was largely confined to the setting. The Valenciennes plays had been 'miracle' plays in the literal sense of that word. Their stage was designed to take advantage of every opportunity in the text for illusion, trickery, and theatrical *frissons*. Machinery hidden behind the Limbo fortress permitted devils to fly back and forth on cables to Pilate's palace. Similar contraptions sent angels descending on clouds to earth and re-ascending to Heaven. The jaws of Hell-Mouth opened and closed, its cauldron boiled, its racks and wheels pulled lifelike stuffed dummies apart. Boats, moved by hidden windlasses, scuttled across the lake of Galilee. Jesus popped up and down through trap doors, befuddling his apostles and scaring the devils.[16] Though the original text of the York Cycle called in many places for similar theatrical devices,[17] the actors at York in 1951 behaved more decorously. In place of the *diableries* of Valenciennes, Browne gave his audience what Archbishop Garbett praised as 'a solemn exposition of the contrast between righteousness and sin, between light and darkness.'[18] Spectacle was largely confined to the crowd scenes – necessitated by the large number of local amateurs who wanted to take part in the show and by the need to fill the vast stage area. It was also present in the colourful medieval costumes modeled on quattrocento paintings, and in the Abbey ruins themselves, which rose in mute majesty over the players below.

In 1948 Browne had stated his belief that the 'theatrical technique of the Mystery Plays is simple and misses many of the chances for effect that we should seize upon nowadays.'[19] In keeping with this conception, Browne's effects were, like Nugent Monck's before him, chiefly pictorial: mute tableaux of God and his angels in the Abbey arches and of such events as the Deposition and Resurrection. The actor who played Jesus, conscious that he was the first to do so in a public performance in the history of the modern British stage, was commended for 'wisely relying on an evocative repose of face and figure.'[20] Clean-shaven and white-robed, he showed his physical kinship to God the Father, handsomely regal in a Pre-Raphaelite headdress reminiscent of William Poel's *Everyman*. ('Burne-Jones might have conceived such a God in nylon,' complained Herbert Read, 'and only the Church of England (or Holman Hunt) could have groomed this curly-headed, beardless Nordic Jesus.'[21] Disdaining flying-machines, Jesus accomplished the Ascension by a dignified walk up the staircase until he was out of sight behind the arches. The rest of the cast behaved with equal decorum. Adam and Eve appeared modestly in ample leather tights and 'warm Wolsey underwear.'[22] Few critics shared Read's disapproval of these decisions. 'It was not so much the dialogue that held the audience,' one reviewer concluded, 'it was the sublime artistry of it all ... People declared that it was something they would remember all their lives for its beauty, the beauty of an old oil painting come to life.'[23]

Not all of the precautions taken to ensure the reverent tones of this old 'oil painting' succeeded, however. As fate would have it, a member of the opening-night audience recognized the actor playing Jesus as Joseph O'Connor, an Irishman who had appeared with the Windsor Repertory Theatre and had also acted Shakespeare in Regent's Park. Judas-like, he informed the press of his discovery, and Jesus' anonymity was gone. (In subsequent years of the Festival the actors playing Christ and God the Father were duly named in the program.)[24] Mary Ure, the seventeen-year-old schoolgirl whose role as the Mother of God required her to age thirty-three years during the interval, unexpectedly proved more effective as the Mater Dolorosa than as the agent of the Virgin Birth: 'Grief she could feign, innocence was beyond her,' Mrs Martin Browne remembered wryly afterward.[25] More significantly, Canon Purvis' text, far from sticking to a 'word for word substitution of modern for archaic English' (an impossible task), turned out to be a conglomerate of Middle and Modern English, often sounding like neither. ('Hey: Spar our gates! Ill might thou speed, / And set forth watches on the wall.') Despite the editor's attempt to retain the characteristic inflexions of modern Yorkshire dialect ('Oppen uppe, ye princes,' 'Make him go his gate'), the script was spoken by almost the entire cast in BBC English, much to the annoyance of the most distinguished native Yorkshire critic in the audience, Herbert Read, who objected that only Satan should have been given a southern accent. Read excused the three shepherds and Caiaphas' Portress from his censure, praising them for 'adding a new dimension of reality to the scene' whenever they spoke. But 'many more of the local actors might have been encouraged to leave their vowels broad,' he urged.[26]

Despite these difficulties, the 1951 York production was a breath-taking success. Browne had hit upon exactly the right combination of spectacle and reverence to move his audience to unreserved enthusiasm. In spite of the program warning that 'in view of the nature of the subject of these plays, it is expected that the audience will not wish to applaud,' the applause was soon heard all over England. *The Times* wrote:

To have witnessed the recovery last night of a great part of the York Mysteries from four centuries of practical oblivion was to have had an experience. There was no telling beforehand what would be the effect on an audience of today of this cycle of medieval devotional plays that set out to rehearse the whole ecclesiastical history of the world. But from the moment God the Father, crowned and in white raiment, was revealed at a high window of the ruined Abbey of St. Mary, there to declare his purpose in creation, it was evident that we were to hear a text of great interest and to see the plays revived in full imaginative splendour ... Perhaps we cannot see these plays, so freshly direct in their language and their approach, so astonishingly sure-footed in their drama, as their own people saw them, since they saw with the eye of unconsidering faith. But Mr. Browne has left no other reason why we should not.[27]

As word spread, tickets were grabbed up and every performance was quickly sold out. A scalpers' market arose in London, offering entry to eager tourists at exorbitant prices. The BBC hurried to arrange a national broadcast of the script. What Martin Browne had predicted beforehand would be only a 'very local and devotional performance'[28] had become an overnight sensation. Other reviewers added their praises. 'An experience one can never possibly forget,' enthused the usually imperturbable *Punch*. 'What might have been no more than an interesting pageant turned out to be utterly gripping, in places almost intolerably dramatic.'[29] *Sphere* discovered that 'contrary to some expectations, these Mystery Plays have tremendous power to move a modern audience.'[30] 'Something startlingly different from the devout little religious dramas so often done in church,' noted the *Church Times*, which at the same time found the plays 'thoroughly religious.'[31] Comparisons with Oberammmergau were frequent, one critic remarking that 'the suggestion that York should become a kind of English Oberammergau seems to me to have everything to be said for it.'[32] Even Herbert Read, despite his distaste for the nylon deities and their Oxbridge accents, gave full credit to the production for having rediscovered a masterpiece of English literature:

The York Mystery Plays are poetry of the highest order – plain, perspicuous and powerful. They are on the level of our medieval architecture, our medieval illuminations and stained glass. But what a strange nation we are! Who but for a few scholars has read them? How many of us, before this present season, knew but dimly of their existence? ... The whole cycle should be a common possession, and the York performance an annual event.[33]

When the production came to an end after playing for two weeks to packed audiences, the Archbishop of York made a curious statement. 'The mystery plays,' he declared, 'were undeniably the most remarkable feature of the Festival.' 'I had,' he recalled, 'some doubts about the advisability of their revival during the Festival, but my misgivings were completely removed. The plays were produced with great reverence and skill, and the audience, by their own reverence, co-operated with the performers.' He concluded, however, with a new outburst of worry: 'Nevertheless, I recommend that they not be revived again until after a considerable interval – at least five years.'[34] Figures, though, spoke louder than words, even the Archbishop's. During the two weeks of the plays' run, 26,486 people bought tickets to see the fifteen performances that were given. The plays made a profit of £2400, and were the only event in the Festival to finish in the black (the Festival as a whole lost £10,000). More important, York had found an identity, one which marked it as different from every other city in England and which was profitable at the same time. Purvis' text sold out its first edition by the end of the summer and the editor quickly renegotiated his royalty agreements for a second printing.[35] The elated Festival Committee announced plans for a repeat performance in the following year. Though this was later changed to a three-year interval to allow for proper planning, there could be no doubt that the mystery plays had returned to the English stage for good. 'The success of the Festival,' wrote Keith Thomson in his final report, 'was due to the greatness of its design, the exclusion of amateurishness, the consistency of the artistic standards and the unity of its spiritual theme. Unlike all other Festivals in Britain, the York Festival was a unified conception like a work of art.'[36] The preliminary report of the committee that was now set up to plan the next festival echoed the same civic pride: 'Only if the citizens of York themselves with something like unanimity wish to think of their City as the centre for such an experience and sincerely wish to establish the York Festival as a tradition, counting not only the material gains of tourism but the moral gains of joy and self-respect, can the plans we make find their fruition. If this is the true feeling of the citizens we need fear no failure and can think ahead with confidence.'[37]

The mystery plays had been written to stir their audience to a desire for the city of God. The twentieth century was beginning to prove that they could also do something to ennoble the city of Man.

THE PERFORMANCE OF 1954

In 1954 York set out to repeat its triumph of three years before. To do this it decided to keep as many of the ingredients as possible that had made for success in 1951. Martin Browne was again hired to direct, and Norah Lambourne to recreate her Valenciennes mansion-stage beneath the ruins. The actors who had played God the Father, Adam, Joseph, Judas, Caiaphas, Annas, Pilate, and Mary Magdalen all returned to their original roles, while Joseph O'Conor repeated his 'serene and patient' portrayal of Christ, this time duly credited in the program.[38] A fresh actress had to be found to replace Mary Ure as the Mother of God, but the words she spoke from Canon Purvis' script were identical to those heard three years before.

Such changes as there were in the 1954 production all went in the direction of making it bigger and more spectacular. Browne was encouraged by the Festival Board to make the crowd scenes as large as possible, so that as many local people as wanted to could participate.[39] The budget was increased by four thousand pounds to provide twenty-three performances in place of the fifteen of 1951, while the dates of the performances were pushed back to late June and early July in order to accommodate the influx of American tourists with their un-devalued dollars. A ninety-minute recorded version of the spoken text was prepared for playing in the Minster on rainy evenings so that tickets would not have to be refunded. New music was written for the production by the prominent musicologist Denis Stevens, based on medieval sources. And in addition to the main production, a free performance of Noah's Flood was staged each evening on a pageant wagon in front of the Minster and again in King's Square as a prologue to the main show, a practice that proved popular enough to be repeated regularly in subsequent festivals.

Once again the critics were entralled. A chance to see the plays for a second time only confirmed their original judgment and sharpened their sense of the ironies of history. 'It is strange,' wrote *The Times*, 'to think that these plays, which make so immediate and so deep an impression on a modern audience, should 400 years ago have been discarded as obsolete. In its desire for change, in its response to the ambiguous voice of progress, what a treasure the sixteenth century threw away. As the plays go their vigorous way, at the feet of God Almighty as he sits enthroned among his angels high up within the frame of a great broken window, we may feel that the wheel has at last come full circle.'[40]

The chance to see the mystery plays in production was already leading to a re-evaluation of their literary worth, in the light of which much modern religious drama came to seem pale and lifeless. As one critic wrote after experiencing the 1954 performance:

Only supreme genius can write religious drama: anybody can write plays *about religion*, and anybody does. Once a man has read a book about 'play producing for amateurs' or has taken a few classes in it, he passes in the churches as an expert. One of the lamentable results is a great plenitude of plays suitable for production in church halls. Most of them are published by church publishing houses, to their eternal discredit. It would be unkind to mention particular cases, but it needs no imagination to identify them. This disgraceful stuff, on which the taste and judgment of so many of our young people is [sic] being corrupted, is never about real men and women but about automatons, mechanical stand-ins for the good and the not so good. The characters in the Mysteries are also types but they are drawn not as mere vehicles for abstract virtue or vice but as fleshly creatures who *are* people of this or that order. The writers wrote about their neighbours, not about remote Biblical characters ... They were not concocted to meet a case and confined within the bounds of what is 'suitable' for church halls (there is a certain blasphemous comedy in trying to be more respectable than the Bible!)[41]

But if the critics remained captivated, all was not well at York. Despite the increased attendance and rising profits, internal disagreements over the artistic goals of the Festival began to develop among its organizers. In his report on the 1954 production, the new artistic director of the Festival, Hans Hess, who had replaced Keith Thomson, complained that 'the 1951 production appeared fresher, truer, and more dramatic. The 1954 performance, on the other hand, suffered from a good deal of sentimentality.' Hess went on to urge 'thinking afresh and bringing a fresh mind with new thoughts to work out the style of production,' rather than 'repeating an established pattern until it is outmoded.' 'The principal actors,' he argued, 'by their art and personality have established a pattern which will not be easy to remodel.' Nevertheless there should be, Hess concluded, 'no firm pattern of production and no continuity of the same people, because the Plays are greater than the men.'[42] A quarrel grew up between Hans Hess and Martin Browne that was to continue intermittently for the next ten years. While some of their disputes were of a personal nature, many were over basic principles. Browne, while thoroughly committed to achieving professional quality in his productions, believed that the tone of the plays must be kept 'local and devotional' if they were to reflect the original impulse that had created them. Hess, on the other hand, had his eye on an international festival of the arts, on the models of Edinburgh, Salzburg, and Spoleto, in which the mystery plays would take their place, free from provincialism and sentimentality, beside

Mozart, Beethoven, Ibsen, and Brecht. The problem of reconciling religious and theatrical goals that had first presented itself in 1951 had not, after all, been solved. It was to continue to raise its head in every successive production at York.

THE PERFORMANCE OF 1957

In 1957 the York Festival, despite its internal dissensions, reached the height of its success. For the plays it was a year of both consolidation and innovation. Bolstered by the sales of his *Shorter Version*, which had now sold out its first two printings, Father Purvis prepared a totally new translation of the entire cycle, permitting additional scenes to be added to the production. From this *Complete Version* Martin Browne selected the Abraham and Isaac play, the prophecy of Isaiah, the Denial of Peter, and the dipping of the Roman soldiers' banners at the trial of Christ to add to his acting script, lengthening the production to nearly four hours. Purvis' new version stuck somewhat closer to the original than had his first translation, providing fewer paraphrases and retaining dialect words, much to the delight of professional Yorkshiremen like Herbert Read, if not to the delight of the actors, who had persistent trouble in pronouncing it.

The set for the production was also remodelled. The Valenciennes mansion-stage was scrapped as too costly and replaced by a more flexible, less localized combination of open scaffolds. At the left angle of the ruins stood a 'hill,' as it had in the two previous productions, on which Eden and Calvary shared a single symbolic location (the Sacrifice of Isaac was also performed here, to emphasize its typological connection with the Crucifixion). Surrounding it, however, painted scenery deliberately clashed rather than blended with the stonework of the ruins, to indicate a protected area out of time and space, beyond ordinary human experience. Stairways, as before, connected the 'hill' above to Heaven in the clerestory arches and below to Middle Earth. There an open, multi-levelled platform served as a rostrum for the scenes of Christ's ministry, props and furniture being changed in a frankly theatrical manner. Hell was now a Miltonic rocky cavern rather than a dragon's mouth, though it continued as before to issue forth its comic and frightening devils.

An almost entirely new cast was engaged for the 1957 performance. Of the veterans of the first two festivals, only John Westbrook as Michael returned to a principal role in 1957. The part of Jesus was taken over by Brian Spink, who did his best to preserve the dignity and repose of his predecessor, Joseph O'Conor. Judi Dench, graduating from minor angelic

roles, was a notable addition to the principals as Mary. (See plate 5.) The
Times reviewer remembered her 'unforgettably lovely gesture, drooping her
blue cloak over the cradle to signify that Jesus had been born.' The cloak
gesture was devised by Henzie Raeburn, Martin Browne's wife and production assistant, to replace the old Gordon Craig light-in-the-straw device
used in 1951 and 1954, and proved so successful as a symbol of the virgin
birth that it became enshrined as a tradition in the York Nativity. John
White and Sheila Barker as Adam and Eve, rising up through trap doors in
the soil of Paradise, Robert Rietty as a vigorous, sardonic Satan, and Norman
Tyrrell as a racy St Joseph, ashamed of having been cuckolded by an angel,
all performed memorably.

The popularity of the mystery plays at York remained undimmed for all
the innovating. The *Times* reviewer declared that Browne's production had
'lost nothing of its first bold, imaginative expertness' and that the director
had 'never made better use of the space beneath the long abbey wall.'[43]
Robert Speaight, writing with memories of William Poel, whose biography
he had written, and of Browne's productions of T.S. Eliot's plays, in which
he had acted, felt that 'Mr. Browne's production, like Reinhardt's *Jeder-
mann*, is likely to take rank among the classics of the modern stage. Visually,
it is continually taking your breath away.'[44] A crowning compliment of sorts
came shortly after the close of the show, when Cecil B. DeMille called on
the director of the Festival and offered to take over the management of a
'York International Festival of Mystery Plays,' a temptation which the board
declined, though not without taking due note of its flattering nature.[45]

But if praise continued to pour in, complaints also mounted. The very
success of Martin Browne's productions now made them susceptible to a
kind of professional criticism that no one would have been impolite enough
to apply to the earlier performances. 'The agreeable little shock of surprise
upon discovering the dramatic power of plays so long ignored was apt to
wear itself out,' confessed the *Times* reviewer, who found himself bored in
1957 by the slower-moving scenes. He urged Browne to 'whittle down' such
verbose and expendable episodes as Abraham and Isaac, the 'various prophetic utterances,' and the 'tedious reasons for the reluctance of Simon of Cyrene
to bear the cross.'[46] In vain did Robert Speaight come to Browne's defence
with the argument that 'if a man cannot listen for three and a half hours to
the story of his Redemption, he had better not come to the Mysteries at
all.'[47] Speaight was a believer, but more and more of the audiences who came
to the mystery plays, especially the American tourists and academics, were
interested not in their religion but in their drama. Hans Hess felt that he
was speaking for them when he issued a criticism of the production that

was far more scathing than that of any of the critics. 'Theatrically speaking,' he declared in his report to the board, 'the Mystery Plays have reached a dead end. The third "Martin Browne" production should be the last.' There was, Hess felt, 'too much third-rate acting amongst the professionals and a complete absence of coherence in the style of acting.' For this Hess held Browne responsible, and with a backhanded compliment to the producer's integrity Hess insisted that he be replaced. 'It is impossible for a man, if he has any stature, to change his views, and in spite of many outward changes, some of which were improvements, the production was a repetition of former years.' With an eye on future greatness, Hess urged the board to accept his verdict: 'the plays are still a great attraction, but they must be thought out afresh or they will wear out in the not too distant future.'[48] For the moment it was Hess who carried the day. In the fall of 1957 the board accepted the director's report and agreed to seek a new producer. The reign of Martin Browne over York was, temporarily, ended.

THE PERFORMANCE OF 1960

If 1957 had been a year of innovation at York, 1960 was a year of revolution. With the 'sentimentality' of the Martin Browne productions put aside, the race was on to see who could bring the York mysteries into the vanguard of the modern professional theatre. Ironically, it was not long before the Festival planners discovered that they had created a Frankenstein's monster which they neither understood nor wanted.

As soon as Martin Browne's work on the 1957 Festival was finished, the board turned its attention to finding a new producer. Hans Hess proposed two names: Tyrone Guthrie and Richard Southern. Guthrie was the *enfant terrible* of festival theatre, fresh from his triumphs at Edinburgh and Stratford, Ontario. Southern was a well-known theatre-historian who had recently written a study of the staging techniques of medieval round theatres. Of the two, Hess favoured Guthrie, on the grounds that it was better to have professional showmanship than 'a mediocre production full of good intentions.'[49] The job was accordingly offered to Guthrie, and in July, 1958, Guthrie agreed to take it on, at a salary far higher than Martin Browne's.

York's troubles began as soon as Guthrie arrived in the city for a visit. Guthrie, who had never seen the mystery plays performed, took one look at the Abbey ruins and declared that he could not do his production there. The ruins were, he felt, too 'romantic,' and would tend to enclose the plays in a petrified past. During the next six months Guthrie came back to York twice with his designer, Tanya Moiseiwitsch, to inspect alternative sites, which included the Minster gardens and the square in front of the mayor's mansion, finally offering the bewildered board a compromise setting in the northwest corner of the Museum gardens, away from the ruins, with semi-circular seating for the audience. This, however, was an innovation the board was unwilling to accept. It was to be the Abbey ruins or nothing, and in January, 1959, Guthrie resigned.

With Guthrie gone, Hess suggested three alternatives. First, the board could seek out another experienced, 'name' producer: Hess proposed Peter Brook or Peter Ustinov. Second, it could invite recommendations on young but promising directors. Third, in a pinch, it could offer the job to Joseph O'Conor, the Christ of the first two Martin Browne productions. The board, still eager for a name, decided on the first proposal. Inquiries were sent off to both Brook and Ustinov. Brook, at Stratford-upon-Avon, never replied. Ustinov, in America, reported that he was unavailable. As time grew short, the board sought out names of younger producers who might be available. Finally they settled on David Giles, a director at the Royal Academy of Dramatic Art in London, chiefly known for his productions of Brecht, but with experience in York going back to 1951, when he had played the Archangel Gabriel for Martin Browne. Giles accepted. Even with this decision made, though, the thirst for fame died hard. The board now sought out 'name' actors for the lead roles, offering the part of Christ to Paul Scofield and the role of God to Paul Robeson.[50] Neither was interested, and David Giles arrived in York to fend for himself.

Giles, as it turned out, was a man with ideas of his own, and when they were known they appeared remarkably similar to Tyrone Guthrie's. Saddled with the Abbey ruins as a condition of his contract, Giles proceeded to ignore them in every way that he could. In front of the arches, effectively hiding them from view, he decided to build a series of five timbered siege towers, inspired by Durer's drawings, with twenty-foot-long wooden ladders reaching to the ground. (See plate 6.) A sixty-foot-wide, two-storey rostrum in the centre served as the main acting area, while the grassy lawn beneath was covered with stone paving. Hell was a concentration-camp guard-tower with an iron portcullis. Pilate, Giles explained, called Jerusalem (i.e. York) '"this tower-builded town," so we built towers.'[51] His purpose, he declared, was to counteract the romantic atmosphere of the ruins and to suggest instead a battleground, the city of man under siege by the forces of good and evil.

If Pilate inspired the set, Bertolt Brecht inspired the acting style of the play. It was perhaps no accident that the *Good Woman of Setzuan* ran concurrently with the mystery plays at the York Theatre Royal during the

1960 festival. The mysteries, Giles believed, as did Brecht himself, were a perfect example of epic drama, or in Giles' phrase, 'total theatre.' Such theatre depended on distancing the audience from the play, and Giles' direction was full of the 'alienation' techniques used by Brecht. Giles' God entered, not in the picturesque central arch as he always had before, but casually at audience level, proceeding to climb up to his place on top of one of the siege towers. He then turned his back to Adam and Eve during the temptation scene. Similarly, Mary turned her back to the audience to give birth to Jesus (no sweeping cloaks here), and Jesus was crucified backwards, the thirty-foot cross being hauled into place by ropes and pulleys and stationed closer to the audience than to the rest of the characters. During the Crucifixion the audience was thus forced to watch not the face of the Saviour but the crowd of common men and women who were crucifying him.

Giles' crowds were consistently used for dramatic rather than pictorial effect. The splendid quattrocento costumes in which even the lowliest of their members had been clad in past productions were replaced by ones modelled on Bosch and Breughel – 'clothes rather than costumes,' as Giles called them. The point was not lost on the audience: 'We are the crowd,' one of them wrote after the production. 'Where would we have been when they crucified our Lord?'[52] Some of the other visual effects created by Giles were even more startling. Like Blake when he read *Paradise Lost*, Giles found Satan the most interesting and sympathetic character in the cycle, a poignant alter ego of Christ. He accordingly cast the two as look-alikes, an effect that came out most strikingly in the Temptation in the Wilderness scene.

Giles' production of the mystery plays in 1960 was in many respects the most imaginative that they had yet received. Reviewers were generally favourable, if cautious in their praise. The Archbishop of York felt the production had a 'deeper spiritual impact' than the 1957 play had, though he disliked the set and the costumes.[53] A. Alvarez, writing in the *New Statesman*, objected only that the production was too solemn and humourless, while the *Guardian* trumpeted its traditional paean to 'a vision of a whole community celebrating its common faith in the arts and idiom of its people.'[54] The response of local audiences, however, to Giles' assault upon their cherished traditions can only be described as one of outrage. Newspapers were flooded with letters to the editor protesting against the ugliness and irreverence of the production. An outsider, they felt, had been allowed to meddle with a hallowed custom. A 'sanctified setting' had been desecrated, and by 'soulless' Londoners at that. The York *Evening Press* reported a 14 per cent drop in attendance, and attributed it to 'native cautiousness' in the face of radical innovation.[55] Many correspondents urged a return to an all-local, all-amateur performance that would restore piety and good taste to the mystery plays. The natural distrust of northerners for invaders from below the Humber flared anew, and the drive to restore the original purity of the mystery plays gathered head. Tyrone Guthrie was vindicated. He had been right: Brecht and the Abbey ruins did not mix.

THE PERFORMANCE OF 1963

In 1963 York had one more fling with Brecht and 'total theatre.' This one began no more auspiciously than the first. After much deliberation and delay, the job of producer was offered to Michael Croft, director of the National Youth Theatre. In November 1962, however, barely six months before the opening, Croft was forced to resign because of ill health, and William Gaskill was appointed in his place. Gaskill at that time was an associate director of the National Theatre in London. Like Giles, he was best known for his productions of Brecht. He brought to the mystery plays a conviction, well-founded historically but ill-designed to suit the prevailing opinions in York, that they should be: 1/ didactic and non-realistic in style, and 2/ completely modern in spirit, as they had been in the Middle Ages. They should, he felt, make the audience uncomfortable rather than quiescent, and, like Brecht's plays, aim not at emotional involvement but at intellectual scrutiny and moral commitment. For this purpose he felt, like Guthrie and Giles, that the Abbey ruins gave too 'inflated' an effect, and determined to mask them as best he could, to prevent the mysteries from looking like a 'Hollywood epic.'

Together with his designer, John Bury, Gaskill set about creating the alienation effects proper to a Brechtian rendition of the mystery plays. The romantic medieval arches were again hidden by a central wooden platform flanked by two thatched towers. There was no localization and no attempt at scenic splendour. Crowds were kept small, and costumes simple. God and his angels were identified by Oriental masks, the angels carrying Chinese handbells. Satan was a cynical modern 'tough,' dressed like a Teddy-boy. Adam and Eve wore full-flowing peasant gowns over which was pasted a placard with a drawing of a naked body. Christ was not the traditional long-robed, bearded, dark-haired figure but a clean-shaven, fair-haired Englishman, played by a young West End actor, Alan Dobie. At every point in Gaskill's production the artificial and the theatrical were emphasized. Lucifer, on being expelled from Heaven, was lowered to earth on a winch operated by the victorious angels in full view of the audience. (See plate 5.)

His entrance for the Temptation in the Wilderness scene was made through the audience, whence he bounded onto the stage and changed into a friar's costume in full view of the spectators.

The preliminary scenes in Gaskill's drama were marked by underplaying, throwaway lines, and a wry humour. The central scenes, by contrast, were played with unrelenting brutality. The Massacre of the Innocents was staged for the first time. The nailing to the cross was unmasked and given in its full text. The soldiers grunted and sweated grotesquely as they stretched Christ's limbs to make them fit the wrongly bored holes:

> Yea, sundered are sinews and veins
> On every side. So have we sought.
> Now any man may tell the least bone of this lad.

For the first time also the two thieves joined Christ on Calvary, producing a triple horror for the audience.

Reaction by the press to Gaskill's innovations was almost unanimously hostile. Among critics only Bamber Gascoigne in the *Spectator* found the production 'authentic and solid.'[56] For most others it was little more than a perverse parody of what they considered the original plays to have been like. 'A Chinese Festival, perhaps, but not the York Cycle,' declared one reviewer, who compared the angelic masks to 'hair-dryers' and complained that he could not get a good view of the ruins.[57] Local critics were even more aghast at the 'alien conventions' of Gaskill's production. For the first time the York *Evening Press* panned the mystery plays. Devices by which Gaskill had intended to endow the mysteries with modern relevance were treated with scorn: Satan, for instance, was criticized for not being suffi-ciently 'Biblical.' Whatever that meant (Satan, of course, is not mentioned in the Bible), it was clear what the reviewer was objecting to: 'a brash, not over-intelligent smart-alec corner-boy, his manner that of today's more corrupt teenage "pop" idols.' The underplaying, the same reviewer felt, had been carried to 'insensitive extremes,' while the opportunities for violence had been seized on with 'hideous brutality and ghastly competence.'[58]

As for the local public, the feelings of outrage that had been vented three years previously grew even more intense. One spectator poured his contempt on what he called 'this non-emotional, non-acting, all-teaching, symbolic nonsense,' and laid the blame on Brecht. Another objected to the fact that the part of Jesus had been played by a 'left-wing agnostic.'[59] Despite the fact that the plays once again made a handsome profit, there were renewed cries for an all-York, all-amateur production, or 'People's Festival.' Against these demands, the festival Director, Hans Hess, stood firm. 'May I point out,' he replied acidly, 'that an event is popular when it is sold out and unpopular when it is not,' a remark, of course, that he might equally well have made about the Martin Browne productions. As for the possibility of enlisting more local talent, he was just as contemptuous: 'The answer to this is equally simple: there is none, nor can it be expected to exist. Local artists were last seen alive in the eighteenth century.'[60] Pressures were nevertheless mounting. Two critical failures in a row, even if they were box office successes (the 1963 production played to an 80 per cent house), were two too many. Hess had to give in, and for the next performance, in 1966, Martin Browne was brought back with a mandate to restore the mystery plays to their original purity. York was itself again.

THE PERFORMANCE OF 1966

Preparations for the 1966 performance were marred by continuing friction among the Festival planners. In recommending Martin Browne's reappointment, Hess acknowledged that 'the general consensus of opinion is for a return to the original simplicity of the early productions which made full use of the architectural and scenic possibilities of the Abbey.' But more conservative suggestions than that awaited their turn. As soon as Browne's appointment had been approved, the board decided to confer with him on the possibility of a completely amateur performance, with the different plays in the cycle each being given by a separate local drama society, under the overall supervision of a single producer. At the same time, the board was being pressured by the Junior Chamber of Commerce to provide 'alternative entertainment' for those who were 'not attracted by the artistic side of the Festival.' The days of firework displays and parachute-jumping seemed imminent again. The quarrel drew to a head on the very eve of the Festival. On the 9th of June, 1966, Hess charged that other members of the Festival Board had been organizing 'fringe events' behind his back and threatened to resign if they were not replaced. While he was persuaded to remain at his post for the duration, two weeks after the Festival ended Hess handed in his resignation.[61]

Martin Browne navigated these swirling currents as best he could. To the idea of placing the performance in the hands of local drama societies he turned a deaf ear, insisting on reserving the right to cast the principal roles with professionals, though agreeing to hold auditions for local actors first. To the plea for a return to simplicity he was more sympathetic. The ruins and the grass would be prominent, he assured the board, and there were to be no siege towers or paving stones. Low, unobtrusive, wooden platforms were to be built instead. Recorded medieval music, used in the first three productions, would replace the modern music commissioned by Giles and Gaskill. A return to Father Purvis' original 'Shorter Version' text, with its freer paraphrase and greater modernization of the verse, would aid the audience's comprehension and the actors' pronunciation, though a fully actable translation was still a major *desideratum*.

Only two innovations appeared in Browne's plans for the performance. One was original, the other borrowed. First, in the spirit of the current ecumenical movement, the old requirement that members of the cast be professing Christians was quietly dropped, the danger of a 'left-wing agnostic' again capturing a lead role being apparently small. The same spirit was perhaps to be detected in the fact that Pilate at the Last Judgment this year joined the souls of the saved in Paradise. Second, William Gaskill's idea of doubling the parts of God and Jesus, tried out in the 1963 production, was retained. 'This becomes a statement in acting,' Browne explained, 'that these two are one: it states the central tenet of the Christian faith, that God made the world and mankind because of love, and because of love came Himself to be a man and share man's life and death.' Browne stoutly denied that any disbelief in the Incarnation lurked behind the device: 'This does not at all take away from His humanity. I think it is fair to say that there will be no doubt of the human sympathy of this Jesus, and no feeling that He isn't fully sharing the life of the people around him.'[62]

Browne's choice for the double role of God and Jesus was John Westbrook, an imposingly tall actor with a deep, resonant voice, who fulfilled Browne's prediction by giving a strong, moving performance. As always in Browne's productions, the crowd scenes were prominent. 'The crowd plays a large part in the plays,' he announced, 'and each person has his own significance. The movement devised for the scenes is based on the creation of little groups within the crowd, each with its own relationships – and these are playing with one another as well as being swept along by the main events of the story.' In this way the production attempted to give 'a single vision of the world and its meaning, a great sweep of history as viewed by the eye of God.'[63]

For the people of York this was the view that was wanted. Reviewers praised the combination of reverence and spectacle in the production, and spectators came back for more. Even Hans Hess, prior to his departure, acknowledged the production to be 'the most beautiful that had taken place.' For Martin Browne it was a triumphant return, made even more so by the success of the three 'gravely beautiful' medieval liturgical music-dramas – *The Lament of Mary, The Visit to the Sepulchre,* and *The Journey to*

Emmaus – which he staged concurrently with the mystery plays with the aid of W.L. Smolden, in St Michael-le-Belfrey Church. In addition, there was Noah's Flood, performed twice nightly on a pageant wagon before the Minster. In 1966 the city was saturated with medieval plays. An examination of the Festival program revealed no Brecht being performed anywhere in York.

THE PERFORMANCE OF 1969

In 1969 the champions of a 'People's Festival' at last had their day. Their victory was helped along by a financial crisis, but was ultimately rooted in the cultural atmosphere of York. In 1966 the Festival had suffered its largest financial loss in history. While the mystery plays continued to make money, other events ran consistently in the red. A reorganization of the entire Festival became necessary, and in 1967 the independent York Festival Society Ltd was liquidated and the organization of the Festival was taken over directly by the City Corporation. Plans for the upcoming production of the mystery plays were immediately coloured by this arrangement. Agreement in principle was quickly reached by the council that 'there should be more participation by amateur players, and, if possible, the cast to be entirely amateur, with as large a crowd as possible.'[64] Townspeople, it was felt, had become progressively alienated from previous festivals. This time York would return to 'the medieval tradition of community participation.'[65]

In keeping with these resolves, Martin Browne was passed over, despite his past services, and the job of producing the mystery plays was bestowed on Edward Taylor, a clerk in a solicitor's office who had been active for many years in local theatrical societies. He in turn chose as his designer Patrick Olsen, a young artist employed as a window-dresser in a York department store.

The resulting performance, as might be expected, was a conglomerate of theatrical traditions that had grown up in York since 1951, though it had a few of its own innovations too. A mammoth architectural set, built out of styrofoam and ingeniously coloured to blend in with the medieval stonework, outdid in splendour and realism anything that had gone before, while keeping the Abbey itself the focus of attention in the play. (See plates 7 and 8.) The effect was so convincing that one reviewer even suggested that the Minster, gradually collapsing from dry-rot, might be replaced by one built of styrofoam by Mr Olsen. In the costumes there was little to be seen of Bosch or Breughel. Italian finery prevailed, even among supposedly impoverished characters like Joseph and Mary. Annas and Caiaphas appeared resplendent in medieval copes and bishop's mitres, copied from fourteenth-century alabaster carvings and monumental brasses. Herod made his entrance in an opulent sedan chair; the Three Kings had their trains borne by three elegantly clad page boys. Crowd scenes displayed similar splendour, all but blinding the audience to the principals, especially in the Baptism and Woman Taken in Adultery scenes.

If the actors in 1969 suffered the stigma of amateur status, there were only intermittent signs of such a handicap in the production. Not all of them were, in fact, amateurs, though all were from York. To distribute the strain of the principal role, three different actors were cast as Jesus, rotating the part on successive nights. When they were not playing Jesus, the other two were cast as either God the Father or Judas, a curious but practical trinity. On opening night the three drew lots to see who would play Christ. While all gave creditable performances, the favourite with local reviewers tended to be Peter Blanshard, principally because he was clean-shaven, thus avoiding any unwanted comparisons between Jesus and the contemporary 'hippies' who were occasionally to be seen among the audience. 'Mr. Blanshard's clean-shaven face,' declared the York *Evening Press*, 'added rather then detracted from the dignity demanded of the role; it stressed further the simplicity of the Saviour's way of life, of His dress, in contrast to other elegantly robed and bearded leading characters who, as a result, seemed all the more vulnerable to the false values of life.'[66]

Adam and Eve both volunteered to play in the nude, but the suggestion was turned down by the producer on the grounds that 'it might offend an awful lot of people.' Even the fact that it was considered, though, indicated how far religious attitudes had changed in England since 1951. When the Last Judgment had been enacted for the last time, the 1969 production brought to a close nearly twenty years of performing the mystery plays for modern audiences in York. What had begun as a gamble had become a guaranteed success. Unlike most other theatrical events in modern times, it had taken place, not in a social vacuum for the entertainment of the few, but as part of the larger social and spiritual life of the community. The dilemma facing Martin Browne in 1951 – how to resolve the conflicting claims of religion and theatre – had not yet been fully solved. Complete historical fidelity to the dramatic style of the original was out of the question as long as there was a danger that it might strike the wrong religious response in a modern audience. In 1969 the Archbishop of York was still worrying about this. 'As we watch the Mystery Plays in this lovely city,' he declared, 'we may smile at the very vividness with which God's dealings with Man are represented: at the crudity of the smoke which belches from the internal regions, and at the language of anthropomorphism whch the Plays constantly need.' For the Middle Ages the drama had been an embodiment of what had seemed most real in life, but the Archbishop, like T.S. Eliot, still feared that for modern spectators it might serve only as a distraction from reality. 'Our greatest danger,' he went on, 'is the danger of regarding the facts of Christianity as matters of mere interest, to be dismissed as academically as we might points of architecture, poetry or pottery.'[67] The history of the Festival had already shown how well founded his fears were. Yet as the 'modernized' productions of David Giles and William Gaskill also proved, attempts to get the plays out of their stained-glass frames ran an equal danger of seeming irreverent and blasphemous to an audience for whom Christianity was incomplete without a halo around it. The York Festival's past had been a triumphant one; its future was an open question.

THE PERFORMANCE OF 1973

The gap of four years rather than the traditional three that intervened before the next York production reflected the uncertainty of the City Corporation as to the proper direction the Festival should take in the 1970s. There were other causes as well. With the death of Father Purvis in 1969, the question of preparing a new acting translation of the text arose again, and a committee was formed to investigate the problem. After considerable discussion the task was allotted to Howard Davies, a former cast member and a producer with experience in performing medieval plays in London churches (not to be confused with the Royal Shakespeare Company director of the same name).

When the production finally took shape in 1973, however, there was little, even in the text, that was new. Edward Taylor was again the director and the Abbey ruins once more furnished the setting. (See plate 11.) A professional actor, John Stuart Anderson, was engaged to play Christ. As a specialist in church drama, Anderson brought a chant-like intonation to his reading of the part that was in keeping with the essentially Pre-Raphaelite design of the production. Even more than in the Martin Browne years, this York production seemed intended to remind the audience that they were assisting at a religious ceremony rather than watching a dramatic performance. A program note by the Archbishop of York once again spoke apologetically of the 'charming naivety' of the plays and of the fact that they were 'not without touches of humour,' but expressed the hope that the audience would concentrate on the 'eternal realities' and 'the great facts of Christian revelation' which the plays embodied.[68]

In the choice of scenes, the new version made only slight changes in the parts of the cycle that had been shown at York since 1951. The Baptism and the Massacre of the Innocents were cut; the Last Supper was added. In addition, a scene from the Wakefield cycle was interpolated 'to bring Mary Magdalene happily to the disciples at the Resurrection, on the assumption that the borrowing of a line or two can cause no offence to a town who borrowed five of York's plays whole.'[69] As in the past, there was still not a single one of the original plays given intact, the cycle having been adapted, in producer Taylor's words, 'to tell a swiftly moving story.'[70]

While the mystery plays in 1973 remained a popular attraction, the artistic level of the production drew little praise, or even attention. For the first time since 1951, *The Times* failed to review the performance, presumably on the grounds that there was nothing new to be said. The resemblances to Oberammergau, now in some disrepute itself after charges of anti-Semitism in the 1970 performance, appeared to be growing even stronger, as much in the style of the production and in its script as in its casting (the part of God the Father was given to a local vicar), and even in its press releases (for the first time the role of Jesus was habitually referred to as 'The Christus'). Since the last production, York had been outrun by new competitors in the performance of the mysteries, and it now seemed in considerable danger of becoming ossified in its own traditions.

THE PERFORMANCES OF 1976 AND 1980

In 1976 the pendulum at York swung once again toward innovation. The City Corporation made the first move in this direction by hiring a woman director for the production, Jane Howell. She, like David Giles and William Gaskill, had had her previous directing experience principally with modern plays at the Royal Court Theatre in London and at the BBC. Perhaps in reaction to the overly pious atmosphere of the previous production, Howell decided to make the plays into a medieval carnival. Huge crowds of extras (the program listed 175 actors) roamed the vast stage – even in such intimate scenes as the Nativity – ostensibly pursuing the daily business of medieval life, which under Howell's direction became an almost steady diet of what one reviewer called 'plebeian fun.'[71] Giant puppets, a forty-foot-long Chinese dragon, and banners painted and carried by York schoolchildren adorned the Creation. Livestock from local farms brought an aura of medieval agricultural reality to other scenes: the three Kings made their entrance on horseback, while real heifers, donkeys, and sheep witnessed the birth of Christ. (See plate 12.) Two pageant wagons rolled noisily on and off the permanent stage, providing comically ceremonious entrances for Herod and Pilate. The wagons suggested the original medieval staging of the plays, and suggested as well that a 'staging' was what indeed the audience was watching – 'York families and working people acting the life of Christ.'[72]

In this re-enactment, the acting styles for all the characters except the divine ones were kept rough and boisterous, in keeping with the notion that the style of the original performances must have been amateurish and naive. 'Miss Howell will have no perfectly spoken voice except for the angels,' a perceptive local critic noted.[73] The audience was thus given a play-within-a-play, much like Bottom the Weaver's in *A Midsummer Night's Dream*, in which the manner of performance rivalled the actual subject of the play for attention. If Howell's actors were less bumptiously inept than Bottom, they nevertheless invited a similar kind of condescension. Her interpretation of the cycle was less overtly Marxist than Giles' and Gaskill's had been, but the busy, noisy jollity had much the same effect of obscuring the plays' text through a smothering overlay of technique. While a polite local reviewer commended the 'earthiness' of her vision, others were less impressed. The *Daily Telegraph* critic wrote that the production

is amusing when jaunty, and beautiful when spectacular, but secular in tone. It communicates no burning conviction in the Bible stories. In her anxiety to avoid dullness, Miss Howell has diminished the drama. The emphasis is on charm rather than meaning.[74]

The last York production within the scope of this book, in 1980, directed by Patrick Garland, took the play-acting metaphor one step further by assigning specific fictional identities to the actors themselves. Two prologues, one for each half of the show, were delivered in 'additional dialogue' created by David Buck. The first was spoken by the actor who was later to play Christ, who identified himself as 'Nick the Carpenter'; the second was spoken by a minor actor who called himself 'Lambert the Joiner.' The result was to prepare the audience for a clownish version of the mystery plays, along the lines of Shakespeare's 'Pyramus and Thisbe':

But how (you'll ask) may Cook or Baker
In hoary beard, portray our Maker?
Or cross-eyed Jackie from the dairy
Be our Lord's Mother, blessed Mary? ...

If Joseph should forget his cue,
Don't mock the man – give him his due;
He brews and sells a tasty beer,
And that alone deserves a cheer ...

Unpractised in the Players' arts
Are these our actors, stammering their parts.
Clumsy of gesture, rough and rude of voice;
Forgive their faults; indeed you have no choice.[75]

Needless to say, the actors at York in 1980, and especially 'Nick the Carpenter,' ignored this condescending view of their abilities as best they could and tried, as all actors must, to play their parts as convincingly as possible. The overall direction of the production, however, minimized the religious content of the plays in favour of spectacle, humour, and a general ambience of 'medieval high-jinks,' much as in 1976. This rejection of the religiosity which had once characterized the Festival struck some critics as charming but others as an overly strenuous effort at crowd-pleasing.[76] In 1976 Robin Thornber wrote a critique in the *Guardian* which passed in review the whole history of the York Festival and assessed the point to which it had come:

The York Cycle of Medieval Mystery Plays was first revived 25 years ago for York's contribution to the Festival of Britain. Since then it has been regularly ritually restaged, as a socially, culturally, and religiously respectable way of spending a pleasant summer's evening in the Museum Gardens, and attracting visitors to the city. Perhaps the time has come for a radical reconsideration of why and how it should be done.

This year's director, Jane Howell, has deliberately concentrated on visual impact ... She crams the huge acting area with wagons, canopies, horses, sheep, pigeons, balloons, smoke, and a cast of, well, hundreds of angels, devils, washer women, and spear bearers. There's a brass band and choir ... and community carol singing during the nativity scene ...

If the story is swamped by the spectacle, it is no fault of the company ... The show's dramatic weakness lies rather with the translation by J.S. Purvis of the medieval plays, which has more of the nineteenth century's notions of cardboard pageantry than fourteenth-century vitality or twentieth-century lucidity.

If the York Mystery Plays are to be seen as an international event worthy of the pilgrimage from Toronto or Tokyo the festival authorities might start wondering how to recapture some of their original life, purpose and meaning. They could well begin with a commission for a fresh interpretation of the text. They might consider farming out each episode to a different company, either fringe theatre groups, students or local amateur societies. Or they could contemplate trying to revive trade union sponsorship (after all, the cycle began with the crafts guilds). Unless something is done, there is a very present danger of the system ossifying into an atavistic amateur dramatic jamboree or a county set social occasion, and it's too good to waste.[77]

In point of fact, experiments in producing the mystery plays much more radical than any of Thornber's suggestions had already been tried out in many other places in England since 1951 in search of the plays' 'original life and meaning.' To these we now turn our attention.

5

The Cycle Complete

So long as we simply re-act the medieval plays, whether with meticulous attention to historical accuracy, or with extraneous trappings to emphasize their medievalism, to make a pretty show, or even in modern dress, we shall not be getting the full value out of them. ... We get a very pretty piece of pageantry, at the expense of the essential emotion of religious drama or of any drama. If we want a living religious drama we must be prepared to accept something less sedative, and perhaps something which may cause us some discomfort and embarrassment in the process of getting used to it.

T.S. Eliot (1937)

In the years that followed 1951, the York Festival became the best-known venue for mystery play productions in England. But other productions soon took place, many of them quite different in style and spirit from the York model. Over the next two decades all four of the other extant cycles were attempted on the stage, at least in partial versions, until by the end of the 1960s the mystery plays could be said to have come full circle. Beginning as local antiquarian ventures, acted largely by amateurs in an atmosphere of 'church drama,' the plays soon made their way into regional repertory companies, academic drama departments, and the London professional theatre itself. In the different styles adopted for these productions we can trace the search for a successful modern equivalent to the original spirit of the plays, as well as the changing meaning of the Christian myth for modern audiences.

THE CHESTER FESTIVAL

While York gained international fame from its mystery play production in

1951, it was not the only city in England to revive its medieval cycle for the Festival of Britain. On 18 June 1951, the city of Chester, some one-hundred miles southwest of York, presented an equally ambitious selection of plays from its cycle, though with less publicity and critical attention. Fifty years before, a single play from the Chester Cycle, the Sacrifice of Isaac, had been presented in London by William Poel in the first modern performance of any medieval Biblical play in England. In 1951 a close replica of the entire cycle was staged in Chester Cathedral, drawing on the dramatic resources of the entire city.

The Chester Cycle, though only half the length of the York Cycle (twenty-five plays), was originally presented over the course of three days. The modern production in 1951 followed this procedure, dividing the cycle into three parts called 'In the Beginning,' 'The Nativity,' and 'The Passion.' The first comprised the Old Testament plays from Adam and Eve to Abraham and Isaac; the second, the Annunciation through the Flight into Egypt; and the third, the Last Supper through the Resurrection. (The manuscripts do not tell us precisely how the cycle was divided in the Middle Ages.) The three plays were acted on successive days, each by a different cast drawn from local drama societies, the city having been divided into three parts for this purpose. Each lasted about two hours. The acting version used in 1951, prepared by Betty and Joseph McCulloch, omitted several important plays from the original cycle, notably the Fall of Lucifer, the Massacre of the Innocents, the Harrowing of Hell, and the Last Judgment. All of these, however, except the Harrowing, were restored, at least in shortened versions, in subsequent years. By 1962, when the Last Judgment finally made its appearance, Chester could boast that it had done fuller justice to the scope of its cycle than had York.

Despite its good intentions, the staging of the Chester production in 1951 failed to create the same excitement among critics and the public at large that had been generated at York two weeks before. One reason for this was the deliberate amateur quality of its acting. At Chester this quality was even more resolutely cultivated than at York, both for social reasons (the desire to involve the entire community) and for artistic ones (the belief that the plays had originally been written for non-professionals). The director, Christopher Ede, was less experienced with medieval plays than Martin Browne and more sceptical about their relevance to the present. 'We cannot push aside,' he wrote in a program note, 'the 600 years that separate us from the author.'[1] Even more important in limiting the plays' effect was the choice of a setting, a small room that was once the refectory of St Werburgh's Abbey, now Chester Cathedral. A stage some thirty feet wide was set up at one end of the room, leaving space for about three hundred spectators. With the audience seated in front of the stage, the effect was more that of a traditional proscenium-arch theatre than of the theatre-in-the-round of medieval practice. Contact between actors and audience was kept to a minimum, and some of the most important action was hidden from the audience, presumably out of fears similar to those of the Archbishop of York that too much realism might offend them. The Crucifixion took place off stage ('in the Greek manner,' as Ede put it), and was indicated visually only by a shadow in the shape of a cross projected onto a back curtain.[2] Similar caution was exercised with Adam and Eve. As one critic described them,

the supposedly naked Adam and Eve acted on a small inner stage which was converted by a chest-high screen into something like a bathing cubicle until, decently fig-leaved, they opened the folding doors and tripped forth onto the stony beach of this fallen world.[3]

The same 'cubicle' was also used to mask the Virgin Birth.

In such a setting, pictorial effects inevitably took precedence over dramatic ones, though less spectacularly than at York. Painted scenery, copied from medieval manuscript illuminations, and artificial lighting created a colourful picture-frame for the action, much as in Nugent Monck's productions at Norwich. Martin Browne described the Chester production as 'a series of ornamental illuminations in a Gothic frame which encloses the very simple and limited action possible in the small space.'[4] For added effect, God the Father was stationed as a permanent silent observer throughout all three plays in the high stone wall-pulpit used by the medieval monks for sacred readings during meals. Wearing a golden crown, he was tastefully screened from the audience by a lighted gauze curtain.

The Chester production thus showed many of the same concerns as at York: a concentration on visual effect, a care for the tasteful presentation of sacred figures, and a quest for dignity and reverence in the tone of the drama as a whole. An even more basic goal of the translators was to make the story itself intelligible to an audience which had had no previous acquaintance with medieval drama. As was the case with Father Purvis' translation at York in the same year, the text prepared by the McCullochs pared away much of the original verse that was deemed too difficult for modern ears, and freely modernized what remained. A comparison of the opening lines of God's speech in the Chester Creation Play with the McCullochs' version demonstrates the amount of both cutting and modernization.

Manuscript text:

> I am greate god gracious which never had beginninge.
> The wholle foode of parente is set in my essencion;
> I am the tryall of the trynitie that neuer shall be twynninge;
> Peareles Patron Imperiall and Patris Sapentia.   4
> My beames be all beatytude; all blisse is in my buyldinge;
> All myrthe is in my Mansuetude Cum Dei Potentia.
> Bothe Visible and eke Invisible, all is my Weldinge;
> as god greatest and glorious, all lyeth in mea licentia.   8
> For all the mighte of the maiestye is magnified in me,
> Prince principall proved in my perpetuall prudens.
> I was never but one and ever one in three,
> set in substantiall sothenes within Caelestiall sapience.   12
> These three tryalls in a Trone and true Trynitie
> Be grounded in my godhead, exalted by my exellence;
> the mighte of my making is marked all in me,
> dissolved under a Dyademe by my divyne experyence.   16

1951 Chester version:

> I am God, great and glorious, which never had beginning,
> I never was but One, and ever One in Three,
> the Person of the Trinity that knoweth no dividing
> for all the might of majesty is magnified in Me: 4
> My beams be all beatitude, all bliss is of my building:
> thus grounded in my Godhead, I Am, and have been ever!
> Both visible and invisible, all is of my making
> the Father, great and glorious, as I bid, thus it be!⁵   8

Here the sixteen lines of the original have been reduced to eight, largely by the elimination of Latin phrases and scholastic terminology; a few lines of the original (line 7) have been kept more or less intact; and some lines (line 8 of the translation) are free inventions paraphrasing the general sense of the original.

Reviewers, in so far as they paid any attention to the Chester production at all, were content to praise the plays' 'pastoral simplicity' as opposed to the 'involved richness' of the York performance. The production was successful enough locally, however, that it continued to be performed at intervals, though somewhat less frequently than at York. It was repeated in 1952, then regularly at five-year intervals thereafter. Its evolution over this period, moreover, showed a more serious attempt to come to terms with the performance possibilities of the original texts than was ever ventured at York. The history of the Chester performances is, in fact, a paradigm of the fortunes of the mystery plays in England as a whole during the next twenty years.

The 1952 performance at Chester was largely a revival of the performance of the year before. It included, however, considerably more of the plays in the cycle, a trend that was to continue in subsequent years. The first day was now introduced by the Fall of Lucifer and concluded with the Prophets play, foretelling the coming of Christ. The second day made room for the Massacre of the Innocents, and the third included the Doubting Thomas episode. Five years later in 1957, the group of plays dealing with Christ's ministry, from the Woman Taken in Adultery to the Cleansing of the Temple, was restored to the cycle, in a translation prepared by Donald Hughes, who also played the part of Christ.

Clearly, the Chester production was outgrowing its rather cramped setting, in much the same way that theatre historians had long ago conjectured that the original mysteries had gradually outgrown their church homes and moved into the marketplace. In 1957 all performances in the Refectory had been sold out. In 1962 it was therefore decided to move the plays outside to the Cathedral green, with the exterior of the Cathedral serving as a backdrop to a multi-level stage. At the same time, a wholly new version of the text was prepared by John Lawlor and Rosemary Anne Sisson, closer to the original, in the belief that the intelligibility of the text depended less on its modernity than on the way in which it was presented on the stage.

Lawlor and Sisson were less fearful than other tanslators that modern audiences would be baffled by these texts. They agreed with T.S. Eliot that peotry can communicate through sound before it is understood, and for that reason sought to preserve the rhyme and rhythm of the original. They also believed, unlike most producers hitherto, that the mystery plays communicated mainly through stage movement and action, and therefore sought to create a script that would avoid the hieratic and statuesque style of earlier productions, permitting instead a bold, large-scale presentation of the story with a variety of pace. The 1962 production, taking advantage of its setting, consequently formed a considerable contrast to the one five years before, which had been praised by the local media for avoiding the 'too fast moving methods of the modern stage.'[6] Lawlor was especially anxious to avoid what Eliot describes as the modern audience's expectation of being meritoriously bored by religious plays, an expectation Lawlor felt was particularly catered to by the religiosity of the York productions. Rather, he agreed with Eliot that the creation of 'a living religious drama' requires the audience 'to accept ... some discomfort and embarrassment in the process of getting used to it.'' It is noteworthy that in 1962, for the first time at Chester, the Crucifixion was presented on stage.

In 1967 something like the crisis that had occurred the year before at York over the tainting of the mysteries by Marx and Brecht appears to have taken place in Chester. The movement in the direction of greater authenticity paradoxically seemed to some to be a move toward secularization. They criticized the 1962 performance for 'coldness and lack of spontaneity,' though this effect may well have been the accidental result of the cast's difficulty in projecting the text on the large stage (one cast mimed the action while a duplicate cast read the words into microphones).[8] As a result of the dissatisfaction, a new director, Peter Dornford-May, was hired for the 1967 production, and the more modernized text of the McCullochs was reverted to. In a program note the new director, after calling attention to the spectacular and entertaining qualities of the plays, assured the audience that the performance would be 'pervaded with a spirit of sincerity and belief, the impact these plays have had on the casts who have performed in the previous revivals.'

If this decision proved a setback for those interested in the dramatic possibilities of the original text, the next production at Chester in 1973 took an unexpectedly novel approach to the plays, one which was intent on finding a thoroughly modern equivalent for the theatrical style of the original. Directed by James Roose-Evans, it took place inside a circus tent erected on the Cathedral green. This unconventional setting was used as a festive magic circle within which the actors bounced, sang, and danced like clowns and acrobats. While similar in concept to Jane Howell's production at York three years later, Chester's evocation of 'proletarian fun' was totally modern in design: the actors wore simple rehearsal clothes and the tent auditorium was devoid of any suggestion of medievalism or indeed of any historical period whatsoever.

After a prelude of blaring rock music, the play began with the entrance of the entire cast strewing the stage with bundles of newspapers, which were then used, with the aid of tape, to fashion a paper robe and crown for the actor who was to play God. When the costuming was finished, the anonymous actor announced 'I am Alpha and Omega,' at which point he was carried to the back of the platform and just as ceremoniously disrobed by his fellows, resuming his place once again in the crowd.

Roose-Evans' approach to the Chester plays owed much to Brechtian concepts of 'alienation.' There was also, perhaps, a trace of the influence of

Peter Brook's circus-version of *A Midsummer Night's Dream*, which had taken place in London the year before, and more than a touch of *Godspell*. Bizarre as it seemed, the approach had the merit of sweeping away many of the presuppositions about the mystery plays that had encrusted their performance in previous years. It attempted to demystify and deromanticize them by showing the plays to be the artificial creations of ordinary human actors, not illusions of celestial reality. Moreover, despite the ingenuity of the production's style, the technique ultimately called attention away from itself and toward the subject matter of the drama by showing the audience the impossibility of 'playing God' in any realistic sense. By avoiding historical localization in setting and costume, it sought to emphasize instead the timelessness and universality of the story in a way that previous productions, both at York and at Chester, had not succeeded in doing.

In many respects the Roose-Evans production was not a performance of the Chester Cycle at all. The original text was pared to a bare minimum, with liberal additions of Biblical passages not to be found in the original, such as the Lord's Prayer and the Sermon on the Mount, not to mention the inserted hymns and local pub songs that alternately delighted and embarrassed the audience. By ending with the Pentecost play rather than with the Last Judgment, the production radically altered the theological emphasis of the original, replacing the terrors of the damned with a wave of sweetness and light at the descent of the Holy Spirit. Hell itself was entirely banished from the dramatic world of the circus tent.

Purists could hardly have been happy with the result, but the performance did show how the mystery plays could be reshaped in a modern idiom to provide both entertaining and spiritually moving theatre. A large part of the success of the production stemmed from the director's accurate assessment of the needs of an audience of the 1970s, more accurate, perhaps, than had hitherto been made at York. Instead of catering to spectators who were imagined to want their religious sensibilities protected, the Chester production was aimed frankly at a generation of unbelievers who needed imaginative help in order to 're-create the great truths and insights of the Mystery Plays,' as a program note suggested. The difference reflected the changes in public attitudes toward religion that had occurred since the end of World War II, changes which Chester had proved more adept than its more famous rival at understanding.[9]

CENSORS' END

For the first seventeen years after the York and Chester revivals of 1951, it remained necessary for producers of the mystery plays to apply for special permission from the Lord Chamberlain for an exception to his general policy of refusing licences to plays in which the persons of God or Christ were represented on the stage. This permission was regularly given to performances of the mysteries on the same principle that had been invoked during the Festival of Britain in 1951, namely that since the plays were written before the 1737 and 1843 Theatre Acts which gave the Lord Chamberlain his powers, they were technically outside his jurisdiction as long as they were given 'in their original form.' (In modern plays, as late as 1966, Christ could be represented only by 'a bright light or a voice off stage.')[10] As it was generally considered impossible to present the mysteries 'in their original form' so far as their language was concerned, a rule was devised which stipulated that a 'word-for-word' substitution of modern language for the original Middle English constituted giving the plays 'in their original form.'[11] This too, of course, was impossible: such scripts existed only as legal fictions. Nor, even if it had been possible, would the rule have been sufficient in all cases to protect the scripts against the censor's interference. In 1968 the phrase 'kiss my arse' was stricken by the Lord Chamberlain from an acting version of the Wakefield plays, despite the fact that the offending phrase was in fact a literal translation of the original (Cain's insult to Abel in the Killing of Abel).[12]

To be fair to the Lord Chamberlain, it must be conceded that his tastes generally coincided with those of the public, and that producers did not always feel unduly restricted by his policies. As late as 1956 Martin Browne could write that 'the cruelty of the grim scenes of the passion is so terrible that we could probably not endure to see portrayed what the folk of York and Chester watched each year as the pageant-wagons moved round their streets.'[13] Nevertheless, there can be little doubt that the conservative nature of most English productions of the mysteries was encouraged by the producers' realization that the plays dealt with a subject that was still felt to be controversial on the stage, and by their reluctance, in effect, to bite the hand that fed them.

By the mid-1960s, however, the long history of theatre censorship in England was drawing to a close. In 1966 a Joint Select Committee of the two houses of Parliament was appointed to investigate the desirability of retaining the Lord Chamberlain's powers. Half a century earlier, testimony before a similar committee had been evenly weighted on both sides of the question. Now the only body that could be found to testify in favour of the retention of censorship was the Society of West End Theatre Managers, who, as before, wanted the continued protection of the Lord Chamberlain's licence against the threat of Common Law prosecution. For everyone else in the England of 1966, theatre censorship had become obsolete. The Church, which in 1909 had deplored the prospect of opening the stage to religious subjects, now took an opposite position, based at least in part on the success of the revival of medieval plays since 1951. Testifying before the committee three days before Christmas, 1966, the Archbishop of Canterbury stated that the Lord Chamberlain's traditional refusal to permit a portrayal of the Deity on the stage 'reflected the Church's thinking at that time on what is seemly and reverent.' Now, he went on, 'people's feelings on this subject have changed,' and it was the Church's position that 'encouragement to face unfamiliar and temporarily distressing images of God is probably more help today than censorship designed to protect from the confrontation.' In support of this position he pointed out that 'recent productions of mystery plays and other relgious dramatic works in churches and cathedrals has [sic] demonstrated their value and provided experience in handling the subject matter reverently.'[14]

The long struggle of the mystery plays against ecclesiastical and civic censorship, begun in the days of Henry VIII, was over. The committee's recommendation that theatre censorship be abolished was passed into law unanimously by the Commons on 26 July 1968, and the Lord Chamberlain's functions ceased on the first of September. Interestingly, one of the last plays to run afoul of the censor's rules was *A Man Dies*, a modern version of the Passion set in working-class London. At first refused a licence by the Lord Chamberlain, who publicly admitted that he was 'biased against any satirical attack on Christianity,'[15] it was finally granted one in the summer of 1966, thus becoming the first post-medieval English play in which the figure of Christ was permitted to appear on the public stage. Acceptance of Biblical subjects in the drama – even those that were 'distressing' – was now complete, and in this acceptance the mystery plays had clearly played an important part.

FROM SACRED GROUND TO THE WEST END

The difference between the Chester circus production of 1973 and the more traditional versions of that cycle that had preceded it is illustrative of what may be called the pre- and post-censorship attitudes toward these plays. Certainly a boisterous carnival atmosphere would have seemed blasphemous for such a play in 1951. With the growing popularity of the plays, however, as well as the change in attitudes toward religious drama as a whole, productions of the mysteries soon came to break the shackles which traditional concepts of what 'church drama' ought to be had imposed upon them. A brief look at some of the more important productions from 1951 to the present time, outside of York and Chester, will serve to indicate the directions they have taken.

(In the pages that follow I make no attempt to mention all of the performances of mystery plays that have taken place in England since 1951. I include only those which I have been able to see personally or which have had clear historical importance. Only performances of complete cycles or close approximations of them are treated. A study of the hundreds of performances of individual plays, such as the Shepherds plays given in so many churches and professional theatres each Christmas, would be beyond the capacity of a single author to recount, and probably pointless for the reader. A chronological list of principal productions of the mysteries from 1901 to 1980 appears at the end of this book.)

Aside from the York and Chester festivals and Nugent Monck's *Ludus Coventriae* Passion at Norwich, two other productions during the 1950s, both involving the Wakefield Cycle, stand out as attempts to explore historical methods of producing the mystery plays. In the summer of 1951 the Surrey Community Players made the first modern effort to perform the plays on a pageant wagon. Selecting three plays from the Wakefield Cycle – the Annunciation, the Salutation, and the First Shepherds Play – the group gave ten performances at different stations in the borough of Reigate, south of London. The wagon, pulled by two horses borrowed from the Whitbread brewery, was equipped with a two-level stage, with God's throne on the upper level and a Hell-Mouth on the lower. Since this method of performance had never been tried since the late sixteenth century, the purpose of the venture was experimental. 'We wished to take a Corpus Christi play into the streets simply to see what happened when it got there ... we wanted to learn something of the public's reaction to it when set free from the study, the text-book, the proscenium opening and the box office, together with the whole variety of "attitudes" connected with these things.' Audiences responded warmly to the production, and the following summer it was presented again, this time in London, with stops at such picturesque places as the George Inn in Southwark, Tower Hill, and St Paul's Cathedral. The reactions of spectators, sometimes as many as three thousand of them, were reported by the producers as follows: 'the feelings evoked were more complex and perhaps more deeply rooted than reverence. One felt an audience shorn of contemporary sophistications and absorbed in an eternal irony in which both religion and theatre are rooted. As so many people were heard to say, after two minutes one forgot that the thing was taking place on a cart.'[16]

In 1958 a larger selection of plays from the Wakefield Cycle was given a different type of medieval staging by Martial Rose at Bretton Hall College in Wakefield. Rejecting the usual assumption that this cycle had originally been staged on pageant wagons, Rose sought to demonstrate its suitability for performance on a fixed, multi-level stage using several localized 'mansions,' an arrangement that we know was used for the *Ludus Coventriae* cycle as well as for the Valenciennes Passion in France. In 1954 Rose had directed three of the plays from the cycle in an outdoor performance given in the original Middle English. For the 1958 performance, which presented twenty of the thirty-two plays in the cycle over the course of the church year, Rose prepared a translation into modern English. Heaven was set high in a large archway, the roof of a stable-block served for 'Middle Earth,' and underneath was the traditional medieval Hell-Mouth. Two farm wagons were employed to increase the stage area and for such mobile sets as Noah's Ark.[17]

These, like all the other productions of the mystery plays during the 1950s, were amateur performances. This was due partly to economic considerations and partly to the continuing belief that amateur performance was suited to the simplicity and naivety of the plays themselves. The fact that in the Middle Ages the leading roles were generally undertaken by professional actors, or at least by actors skilled enough to be paid for their work, and that considerable pains were taken to ensure high quality in the other roles, was usually overlooked.[18] The success of the productions at York, Chester, and elsewhere, however, inevitably called them to the attention of commercial producers. The adoption of the mysteries by the English professional theatre beginning in the early 1960s was a major new departure in their fortunes, bringing them a different kind of audience and a different kind of critical attention than they had known before.

It is perhaps no accident that the emergence of the mysteries on the commerical stage coincided with a turning point in the history of English theatre as a whole, the moment when a theatre 'in need of a fix' was discovering a new generation of playwrights, such as John Osborne and Harold Pinter, and new possibilities of both style and subject matter in the drama of the past. The first professional performance of the mystery plays took place at the Mermaid Theatre in London, an experimental theatre founded in 1959 by Bernard Miles, in which the traditional proscenium arch was replaced by an open stage. The availability of the Martial Rose translation prompted directors Colin Ellis and Sally Miles to choose the Wakefield Cycle for their production, which opened during Easter Week in 1961. The eighteen plays they chose were selected for their appropriateness to the Easter season and omitted most of the Old Testament plays and the Last Judgment. A public announcement made before the opening explained the legal status of the production:

In the Mermaid production Christ and God himself will appear on the stage. This is not normally permitted by the Lord Chamberlain but because the Wakefield plays precede the 1843 Theatre Act they do not fall within his jurisdiction providing they are given in their original form. As they have not been translated they require no license.[19]

The last sentence was, of course, completely untrue, but the legal fiction prevailed. The stage-design was reminiscent of that in the Bretton Hall production three years earlier. God sat on a high scaffold, against a white background. Below him were Middle Earth and Hell. The action was spaced according to stage-symbolism, 'all unkindess ... enacted on the left of the stage, all good on the right.'[20] The chief effect of the Mermaid performance on most critics was not symbolic, however, but visceral, produced by the shock of its violence. For the first time in England the Crucifixion was performed in full view of the audience and with all the sadistic glee of the executioners written into the original text by the 'Wakefield Master.' The plays, observed one reviewer, 'do not shroud the Cross in romantic mist. They show you the ruthless details of just how you crucify a man.'[21] *The Times* noted the production's 'stark momentum and startling violence,' while another critic remarked on its 'sense of divine purpose' and 'amazing sense of inevitability.'[22]

In addition to its violence, the epic style and sweep of the production struck the critics, and the name of Brecht was frequently invoked, as it was to be in York and Chester a few years later. Martial Rose himself remarked after the first Mermaid performance: 'I see Brecht in it. It's epic drama. It sweeps in location and in time and cuts across all the classical rules.'[23] The mysteries could consequently be seen as a validating example of one of the most important modern theories of drama. Reviewing the revival of the Mermaid production in 1965, Alan Simpson found them to be a vehicle through which the contemporary stage, hitherto eclipsed by film and television as a mass medium and reduced to entertaining elite audiences, could return to the theatre's traditional function of 'making big, timeless, simple, epic statements about humanity to as large an audience as logisitics permit.' The Wakefield Cycle, he felt, had 'far more dramatic excitement than the best film epic.'[24]

Not all such comparisons were as flattering. Philip Hope-Wallace preferred Pasolini's real Italian peasants, in the film of *The Gospel According to Saint*

Matthew, to the 'mummerset soldiery and actressy mothers,' in the Massacre of the Innocents, carrying 'bundles which dropped with the wrong sort of thud.'[25] But the very mention of medieval plays in the same breath with current films and the interpretation of them in terms of the most advanced dramatic theories demonstrated how far they had come from the condescension with which most critics had regarded them only ten years before.

The Mermaid productions of 1961 and 1965 were instrumental in bringing the mystery plays into the forefront of contemporary English theatre. The Edwardian notions of 'church drama' which had been applied to the plays in their first revivals now seemed as obsolete as the culture that had produced them. Reverence and good taste seemed less important goals than emotional realism and intellectual challenge. Smoothness of narrative and consistency of tone ceased to be artistic virtues; sudden contrasts and Gothic mixtures of levity and sublimity, cruelty and tenderness, took their place.

From the London stage the plays made their way into the repertories of provincial professional companies, where they continued to receive innovative performances. The Derby Playhouse in 1968 and the Lincoln Theatre Royal in the following year each presented substantial segments of, respectively, the Wakefield and *Ludus Coventriae* cyles, the first adapting the plays to the intimacy of a small playhouse stage and repertory cast, the second (in Lincoln Cathedral) demonstrating how the ingenious use of pantomime, dance, and lighting could overcome the notorious acoustical difficulties and poor sight-lines of a church performance. At Lincoln, the slow, silent progress of the skeleton of Death, making his way up the length of the nave and lit only by a single following spot, taking by surprise the unwary Herod as he sat on a fur-lined throne idly gorging himself with grapes, made a memorable scene, though it was performed with scarcely a word of text.[26]

It was perhaps inevitable that with the increased sense of the modernity of the mysteries, attempts at relevance would eventually reach the point of wrenching the plays totally out of their medieval frame of reference. Such was certainly the case with an adaption of the cycles called *I Am*, produced at the Hampstead Theatre Club at the height of the Viet Nam war in 1971. The theatre's publicity posters announced that the play had converted the mysteries into a 'blatant attack on cherished Christian beliefs,' calculated to leave 'any receptive audience shattered.' Concentration-camp decor suggested the topicality of the story, beer bottles littered the Last Supper, and the Crucifixion was presented so brutally that it reportedly provoked, at an earlier performance in Yorkshire, 'an attack from an onlooker on a member of the cast.'[27]

Such deliberate cultivation of shock value was far from the conspicuous piety of the first revivals of the mysteries two decades before, and perhaps equally as far from the spirit of the originals. A distraught reviewer who predicted that 'not many people will like it' undoubtedly caught the intentions of the producer exactly. The latter, in turn, seems to have taken the Archbishop of Canterbury's invitation to present 'unfamiliar and distressing images of God' on the stage somewhat more literally than that prelate must have meant it. *I Am* was clearly more interested in making a contemporary political statement than in reproducing medieval theatre with historical fidelity. Even so, it may have served to shake off some of the encrusted attitudes which had grown up around its subject matter and to expose something, at least, of what must have been the plays' shock value for their original audiences. The use of modern dress and props, the unflinching identification of the contemporary equivalents of the Scribes and Pharisees, the unsqueamish depiction of the brutality of evil – all these were important parts of the original plays, and their effects cannot be easily reproduced by period staging. While there are no historical records of spectators physically attacking medieval actors, similar transferences of play-action into the real worlds of the spectators were common enough in the Elizabethan period, Claudius' response to Hamlet's 'Mousetrap' being only the best-known dramatization of this real-life phenomenon.[28] The actors of *I Am* were, one hopes, physically prepared for the consequences of their work; if so, they may have felt it worthwhile to provoke, for once, an audience reaction that was neither bored nor complacent.

Similar ingenuity and innovation, though of a less stridently political sort, has marked the most recent professional production of the mysteries, the National Theatre's York *Passion* in 1977. Here within the confines of an indoor theatre (the smallest of the three new National Theatre houses, the Cottesloe), an attempt was made to reproduce, in modern terms, the milieu of a medieval craft-guild performance. The audience stood or moved about in a seatless arena whose walls were decorated with objects associated with the contemporary agricultural and industrial working-classes: oil heaters, lanterns, hoes, brooms, pitchforks, dart-boards. The cast, costumed as miners, bus-conductors, firemen, mingled and talked with the audience before assuming their roles in the play, whose scenes were spread over the whole of the auditorium. The script, adapted from the Purvis version of the York Cycle, covered the events in Christ's life from the Entrance to Jerusalem through the Crucifixion. Another dimension of contemporary reality was added by means of a translation, by Tony Harrison, of the Purvis text into modern Yorkshire slang. The Knights trying to fix Jesus to the Cross, for example, express their exasperation in such lines as

This bargain buggers me,
I'm proper out of puff,

and

Him as made mortice made it too wide,
That's why it waves. Young gormless get!

– lines which led one critic to conclude that 'only the lack of a teabreak between hammering sessions distinguishes the 14th century from the 20th.'[29]

The goal of producers of *The Passion* was to recreate a 'people's theatre,' one which would 'marshall the spirit of the whole community.' The difficulty of accomplishing this in a modern pluralistic society was noted by several reviewers, one of whom remarked on the impossibility of 'building a sense of community from scratch.'[30] The actors were told to play medieval craftsmen playing Biblical characters, a device that struck another critic as producing an effect 'two steps away from reality.'[31] But in spite of that reviewer's conclusion that the audience was 'not being moved, it was being milked,' the popular success of the production indicates that something in this conception of the plays has struck a responsive chord in current audiences. It has already been revived more often than any show in the history of the National Theatre and promises to become the first commercially successful production of a medieval play outside a festival setting since William Poel and Ben Greet made a profit from *Everyman* in the early years of this century. Benedict Nightingale has called it the most 'absorbing' production ever mounted by the National Theatre, and John Walker found in it a revelation of what medieval religious drama might have been like:

In the audience's close encounter with the actors and participation in the events ... it was possible to believe that some sort of community, however illusory or evanescent, had been created in that emotionally charged space, and that we all, and perhaps drama as well, were the better for it.[32]

THE CORNISH 'ORDINALIA'

While the professional theatre was exploring ways of relating the mystery plays to contemporary life, another segment of English theatre – college and university drama – was taking the opposite approach of bringing scholarship to bear on the recreation of authentically medieval productions. The realization of this goal was slow in coming about. In 1951 the historical study of medieval staging was virtually a non-existent field. Aside from the data collected in E.K. Chambers' *The Medieval Stage* (1903), little information had been gathered on the subject and none of it had been systematically studied with an eye to applying it to actual production. Editions of the texts of the cycles printed by the Early English Text Society furnished analyses of the philological features of the scripts, but showed little if any interest in them as plays.[33] Since scholars had had little personal opportunity to judge the theatrical qualities of the plays in performance, they tended to assume that they had been crude and artless, worth studying only for linguistic reasons, or as historical 'influences' on the later drama of Shakespeare's time. The judgment of Hardin Craig, delivered in 1951, was widely accepted: 'this drama had no theory and aimed consciously at no dramatic effects.'[34]

With the revival of the cycles on the stage, however, such attitudes began to change, and the focus of medieval drama studies shifted from the purely literary to the theatrical. The first major contribution to our knowledge of medieval staging practice was Richard Southern's *The Medieval Theatre in the Round* (1957), a detailed analysis of the fifteenth-century morality play *The Castle of Perseverance*, based on the staging plan contained in the manuscript of that play. Here, for the first time, a scholar concerned himself with the kinds of questions which would need to be answered if an accurate reconstruction of the play were to be undertaken in practice – the size and siting of the scaffolds or 'mansions'; the dimensions and use of the Place; the placement of the audience; as well as scores of smaller details involved in bringing the action of the play to life, including costumes, props, and music. Southern's book was soon followed by two others of major importance – Martial Rose's translation of the *Wakefield Cycle* (1961), with an extensive commentary on the staging problems of each play, and the first volume of Glynne Wickham's *Early English Stages* (1959), an extensive study of medieval and Elizabethan theatre design and performance conditions. It was significant that all three of these writers were scholar-producers, with teaching posts in college or university drama departments. While not all subsequent books on medieval drama have been written by authors with practical theatre experience, it is rare to find a book published since 1960 which does not acknowledge the experience of seeing one or more of the revivals of the mysteries as a formative influence on the author's thinking.

It was a logical step for such writers to test their theories with actual performance, and it is to their experiments that we owe some of the most illuminating modern poductions of the mysteries. Martial Rose was, as we have already seen, the first to do this, in his productions of the Wakefield Cycle at Bretton Hall College in 1954 and 1958. In 1967 Rose's successor at Bretton Hall, John Hodgson, extended Rose's production to include all thirty-two plays of the the cycle, performed on Corpus Christi Day, the first complete performance of a cycle in modern times. By far the most ambitious such venture, however, and the most painstakingly researched, was the presentation in 1969 of the complete Cornish Cycle at Perranporth, Cornwall, by the Bristol University Drama Department. This production achieved both a dramatic intensity and an historical accuracy unmatched in productions of the mysteries before or since, and an account of its discoveries is essential to any understanding of the present state of our knowledge of medieval theatre.

The production of the Cornish Cycle was the climax of a project unique in the history of British university theatre – an entire academic year devoted solely to the production of medieval plays. The Bristol University Drama Department, headed by Glynne Wickham and including such other medieval drama scholars as Richard Southern and Neville Denny, scheduled a variety of plays, sacred and secular, to acquaint its students with the techniques of medieval stagecraft. That this could be done with students whose pressing professional needs centred on the modern repertoire and the techniques of film and television was itself an indication of the enhanced prestige of medieval drama. The schedule of plays represented virtually every European country and contained many works which had seldom or never received modern performance – Calderón's *Gran Teatro del Mundo*, Bodel's *Jeu de Saint Nicolas*, Han Sachs' *Fahrende Schuler in Paradies*, the Dutch miracle-farce *Het Esbatement Van Den Appelboom* ('The Play of the Appletree'), and, from the British Isles, John Bale's *God's Promises*, the Cornish saint's play *The Life of St. Meriasek*, and the Cornish *Ordinalia*.

The Latin word *ordinalia*, found at the head of the manuscript, means simply 'order of events.' Adopted in the nineteenth century for want of any other title for the plays, it has sensibly given way in recent years to the simpler and more uniform title, the Cornish Cycle. This cycle survives in a fifteenth-century manuscript now in the Bodleian Library in Oxford. It is divided into three parts for performance on consecutive days. Day 1 treats the Creation of the World and a number of Old Testament stories; day 2 is a Passion play, apparently influence by French rather than English models, since it lacks the Nativity episodes; day 3 is a Resurrection play ending with the Ascension rather than the Last Judgment. Two other elements not to be found in any English cycle add to its interest. One is the motif of the Cross-Tree, or Legend of the Rood, which runs throughout the first two days, tracing the journey of the wood of the cross from its parent stem in Paradise (Eve's fatal apple-tree), to its felling for the roof-beam of Solomon's Temple, to its employment as a bridge at Cedron, to its use by the torturers of Christ. The second is the Death of Pilate, a long, farcical anti-saint's play, again based on legendary sources, about the retribution meted out to the murderer of Christ, inserted into the Resurrection Play of day 3.

As the cycle was written in Cornish, a Celtic language no longer spoken, it was understandably the last of the extant cycles to receive serious attention. A translation into English prose by Markham Harris, adapted for performance by Neville Denny, overcame this linguistic hurdle and enabled the plays to be seen on the stage and judged in the same light as their English equivalents.[35]

By historical accident, we know more about the staging of the Cornish Cycle than about any of the English mysteries, despite the linguistic difference. From Cornwall, for example, comes the only surviving verbal description of a medieval outdoor round theatre. According to the antiquarian John Scawen, writing in the seventeenth century, the Cornish mysteries took place in a '*plan-an-gwarry*,' or 'playing-place,' which he described as comprising 'open and spacious downs of great capacity, encompassed about with earthen banks, and in some part stone work of largeness to contain thousands, the shapes of which remain in many places at this day.'[36] The Cornish 'rounds' are also mentioned by Richard Carew, writing in 1602:

The Guary miracle, in English, a miracle-play, is a kind of interlude compiled in Cornish out of some scripture history. ... For representing it, they raise an earthen amphitheatre, in some open field, having the diameter of his [i.e. its] enclosed playne some 40 or 50 foot. The country people flock from all sides, many miles off, to hear and see it, for they have therein devils and devices to delight as well the eye as the ear.[37]

The exact layout of such a theatre is indicated in the manuscript of the Cornish Cycle by three sketches, one for each day, showing eight mansions disposed equidistantly around the circumference of a circle, labelled with the names of the principal characters who occupy them. Some of these, such as Heaven and Hell, retain the same inhabitants throughout the three parts of the drama; others change occupancy to meet the requirements of each day's action.

The similarity of this design to that depicted in the manuscript of *The Castle of Perseverance* permitted Richard Southern to apply his discoveries concerning that play to a reconstruction of the Cornish theatre for the Bristol performance. (See plate 9.) Even more fortunately, the original sites of the Cornish productions, which Scawen noted as remaining 'in many places at this day,' are still in evidence now, and the largest and most impressive of them, Piran Round near present-day Perranporth, was made available by the local authorities for the revival.

Piran Round is an earthwork enclosure, some 120 feet in diameter, originally constructed as a neolithic farmstead. Archaeological evidence indicates that it was renovated in the fourteenth century, almost certainly for use as a theatre. At that time, terraced seating was added, a second entrance provided, and the interior levelled. It remained only for twentieth-century workmen to restore the labours of their medieval predecessors in order to resurrect an actual medieval playing-place.

At Piran Round it was thus possible to reproduce with considerable accuracy the physical milieu of a medieval cycle-play performance. Other details of the original performance were also known and copied faithfully. An idea of the colour symbolism used in the costuming could be gleaned from a 1539 inventory of church goods at Bodmin, which included 'three Jesus coats, two red worsted and one of red buckram'; 'three Tormentors' coats of satin, yellow and blue' [yellow was evidently a 'bad' colour and so was also used in the Bristol production for Judas]; and 'two Devil's coats and a crown of black.'[38] Although stage directions in the cycle manuscript itself are scarce, a similar manuscript of a Cornish Creation play furnished some significant ones, in English, which could be applied to the corresponding scenes in the *Ordinalia*. Among these, perhaps the most intriguing is the stipulation that the serpent in Paradise shall have 'a virgin face and yellow hair upon her head'[39] – i.e. the bare-bosomed female temptress with snaky tail depicted in so many medieval paintings and sculptures of the Temptation of Eve.

Production details not specified by documents relating to the cycle itself were filled in by reference to medieval visual material. The shape and dimensions of the mansions were derived from the Fouquet miniature of 'The Martyrdom of St. Apollonia,' already studied in detail in Southern's *Medieval Theatre in the Round*. Hell-Mouth, in the medieval tradition, was 'an enormous monster's head, the Leviathan of Isaiah 27.1: a lividly painted, nightmare creation of fanged and gaping jaws, glaring eyes and smoking nostrils,' from which smoke-bombs signalled the exits and entrances of the devils.[40] Costumes, designed by Iris Brooke, were modelled after contemporary paintings and carvings. The attention to historical accuracy was most noticeable in the outfitting of the devils, who were authentic medieval harpies, with bird-beaks, outsized wings, and claws.

Scenic units demanded by the script were similarly based on medieval models. The principal units needed over the course of the three days were Paradise, with its all-important tree; an Altar, for the various sacrifices; the

Ark; a 'Mountain' (for the Temptation of Christ); a Temple; a House; and a Boat (for the disposal of Pilate's polluted body). These were positioned at one of three points in the Place, plotted as an equilateral triangle in the middle of the circular theatre. Some of these scenic units were capable of being transformed into each other – that is, of 'doubling' – for both practical and symbolic reasons. The mortise that held the Tree of Paradise in place, for example, also held the cross, and the two were placed on the same spot in order to bring out the theological significance of Christ as the second Adam, atoning for original sin. The Jewish Temple on day 2 was the same structure that on day 1, differently assembed, had formed the Ark, while on day 3 it became the Sepulchre of Christ – the old church thus literally giving way to the new. Behind this device lay the medieval iconographical tradition which depicted the Ark as a prefiguration of the Church. Director Neville Denny explained the historical basis for his design as follows:

Iconographic representation of the Ark seems to have gone through three more or less distinct phases: a primary stage when the Ark was conceived of simply as a house or box floating hull-less on the waters; a secondary (and to the theatre historian most interesting) stage where the Ark was still seen as a building of some kind but suggestive of a church, because of the typological significance of the vessel (the sanctuary and refuge of the saved) but contained within the ship's hull; and finally the most sophisticated, late medieval projection, simply a contemporary sailing vessel. … In the second of the stages the building within the hull, though sometimes a single-storied one, and sometimes a two-storied structure, most frequently was a three-storied one, bearing a marked resemblance to another conventionalized medieval edifice, the Temple of Jerusalem (and by extension the Church, or simply churches anywhere), and also to the Holy Sepulchre. … This phenomenon suggested a convenient and efficient way of dealing with our decor problem: why not have just the *one* principal unit, a Temple, on the medieval artist's model, which could also serve as the Sepulchre and, by the mere wrapping of a hull around it, the Ark as well.[41]

This device thus brought dramatic as well as doctrinal coherence to the play, linking together visually three different episodes likely to seem unrelated to a modern audience.

The cohesion of the separate parts of the cycle was perhaps the most notable discovery of the Cornish production. Unlike the distinct pageants of the Chester and York plays, the Cornish text is a continuous one that skilfully takes advantage of the opportunities for multiple, simultaneous, and interlocking action afforded by performance in a round theatre. In the

Bristol version, the entire action of the play was placed in a cosmic perspective by the continued presence of God in his 'mansion' overseeing his creation, while from Hell-Mouth the devils constantly threatened to emerge to thwart his plans. Individual scenes offered further examples of such contrasts and perspectives. Satan, 'invisible,' hovered around Christ during the Sermon on the Mount, offering cynical commentary to the audience. In large scenes like the Entrace to Jerusalem, the Trial, and the Crucifixion, the audience was offered a variety of simultaneous impressions. At the beginning of this sequence Jesus sends John and Peter to fetch an ass while he preaches to a crowd of disciples. Simultaneously, a bazaar is being set up in the Temple, which Jesus soon enters and denounces. All the while the principal occupants of the mansions have emerged to watch the scene in which they will presently take their different parts: Caiaphas with his attendants; Annas with his; the Doctors; Herod and his court; Pilate and his officials; the four Torturers, eager for employment. The audience saw, as it were, a theatre within a theatre, the world as a stage with each actor waiting to play his appointed part in the drama of salvation.

As the scene progressed, the worried officials, secular and ecclesiastic, descended to the Place to confer about Jesus, while the latter ministered to the sick and the citizens chose the sides they were to take in the drama to follow. Caiaphas and Annas schemed together while Jesus conducted the ceremony of the Last Supper. Judas' posse made a sneaking circuit of the arena to launch its ambush while the Angel was presenting the cup of sorrow to Christ. Jesus was buffeted by the Torturers in front of Caiaphas' mansion while the disciples huddled miserably by an inn-yard fire and Peter hotly denied knowing his saviour. The two separate events were suddenly united by the crow of the cock, as Christ, seen by the audience but not by Peter, slumped unconscious to the ground. (See plate 10.)

Even more complex simultaneous action took place at the Crucifixion. While Jesus hung on the cross in stoic silence, several different groups, each with their own interests and hopes, looked on and commented: the two thieves on flanking crosses, repentant and defiant; Caiaphas and Annas, smug and victorious; the Torturers, proud of their craft, mocking the dying man with sadistic satisfaction; Pilate, worried and fretful after his wife's warning; the disciples, grieving; the three Maries, lamenting; the devils, expectantly awaiting their cue to clear the bodies from the arena; the Centurion, increasingly agitated, nearing conversion; knots of common citizens, some appalled by the event, others going about their ordinary business. As Denny observed of this scene:

it makes for an extraordinarily unsettling balance and contrast of impressions, a stretching and bending of the mind, a controlled complexity of response, in which perceptions of basic human realities (man's inhumanity to man, the quarantined remoteness of Them, suggestible and malleable Us) are presented side-by-side with implications of a cosmic order: the accomplishment of God's purposes by means of the very nestfeathering and pragmatism ('It's better that one man should die than that all the faithful should be lost') of rulers and officialdom, and the malice and casual brutality of an easily-led and entertained populace. ... Not even cinema, even in its 'epic,' wide-screen form, has been able to match, never mind excel, the dramatic possibilities, the intensities of contrast and irony and emphasis, made possible by such simultaneity of action.[42]

The Passion Play of day 2 was thus revealed by the Bristol performance to be a tightly written tragic drama, full of subtleties and ironies, all serving the ultimate theological purpose of demonstrating the validity of the Centurion's concluding line: 'Truly this was the son of God.' The Cornish Resurrection Play of day 3 changes its tone to the joyful and the triumphant, and it was here that the epic possibilities of the medieval round theatre could be most fully demonstrated. The Harrowing of Hell episode that opens the day's action is pure spectacle – Christ's victory over Satan portrayed in sheerly physical terms as the triumph of a medieval warrior-knight over a fabulous monster-enemy. The whole round came into use as Christ advanced across the Place toward Hell, dressed in white and carrying a red banner shaped as a lance with which he was to joust with Satan. The dialogue, adapted from the apocryphal Gospel of Nicodemus, combines Old Testament gravity with medieval chivalric boasting:

JESUS
Open your gates, you lords of Hell,
At once! If you do not
There shall be woes indeed
Before I pass from here!
For the everlasting gates
Shall be flung wide, so that
The King of Glory can come in!
LUCIFER
Tell me now, who is this
King of Glory?

JESUS
The Lord strong and mighty,
The Lord marvellous in battle!
Therefore open on the instant
     You Lords of Darkness
     Knights of Hell![43]

At this, Christ lowered his standard, the gates of Hell burst open with explosions, and the devils emerged through the smoke, terrified and defeated. Behind them, released from their prison, came Adam and Eve and all the patriarchs whose fates the audience had watched on day 1, greeting their deliverer. From Hell they were escorted by the Archangel Michael across the Place to the Heaven scaffold, where they were welcomed to bliss by God and his angels, while in another part of the Place Christ returned to the Sepulchre to await his Resurrection.

Equally broad visual effects were achieved in the farcical Death of Pilate play, which celebrates Christ's victory over his chief human rival as energetically as the Harrowing of Hell celebrates his victory over Satan. The play, which had commonly been regarded as an irrelevant interpolation into the cycle and had often been printed in anthologies as a self-contained piece, took on new meaning when seen as the festive climax to a celebration of the triumph of Christianity over its enemies. Pilate – irredeemable villain, not a 'troubled colonial governor' – here becomes a sort of ritual scapegoat, drummed out of the society of the faithful. Isolated from even the remaining pagan characters, he is driven into frenzy and then death by divine vengeance. At the climax of the play, when both the earth and the sea refuse to accept his polluted body, the four Torturers, now turned burial-detail, had their finest comic moment as they attempted to deal with the inexplicable supernatural events. The fact that they were played by the same actors the audience previously saw tormenting Christ was a comforting signal of the complete turn-around that had occurred in world history. Under orders from Tiberius, who has been miraculously cured of leprosy by St Veronica's veil, they now turn their ghoulish talents to work on the condemner of Christ. Through the sadistic fun, the major theme of the cycle appeared clearly: Christ is the rightful ruler of the world, not bishops, kings, or governors, however temporarily powerful they may seem or claim to be.[44] The Ascension of the crowned Christ to his place in Heaven, amidst the joyful singing of the angels and the fanning out of his apostles upon all the other scaffolds in the theatre, overlooking the world they are about to convert, formed the triumphant finale of the drama.

For those involved in the performance and for those who saw it, the Cornish production offered empirical answers to some of the questions which had long occupied students of medieval drama. Those who doubted that an enclosure the size of Piran Round could possibly have served as a theatre – including, initially, Richard Southern – were now satisfied. Not only were the acoustics adequate, despite the inexperienced voices of some of the actors, but the size of the theatre was in itself an asset in conveying the epic quality of the action. The presentation of the cycle without cuts, far from deterring audiences, attracted them. Many came from long distances, including the other side of the Atlantic Ocean, to stay the three days required to see the whole play, and some cheerfully endured one of the Sunday performances when the three parts of the drama were given consecutively – morning, afternoon, and evening, a total of some twelve hours of playing time. (The production gained an entry in the *Guinness Book of Records* as the longest single play-performance ever given.) Of the forty-seven different episodes which comprise the story of the cycle (using E.K. Chambers' divisions), only the Doubting Thomas episode was generally regarded by spectators as tediously written and expendable. Above all, the production demonstrated that the more faithful they are to their original theology, the more dramatic the plays become. A striking example, among many that might be cited, is the stage business that is called for at the moment when Cain kills Abel. The devils emerge snarling from Hell, and the instinctive response of a modern audience is to look for them to punish the murderer. Instead they carry off Abel's body to Hell, forcing us to remember the doctrine that only after Christ's atonement will men, however innocent, find entrance to Heaven. Similar fates befall all who die in the Cornish Old Testament plays. The medieval playwright here found, in one stroke, both an economical way of ridding his stage of bodies and a dramatic device by which to inculcate a crucial theological belief. He displayed, in short, a professionalism of technique beside which Hamlet's 'I'll lug the guts into the neighbour room' seems almost like hack-work.

The very ingredients that made for the success of the Bristol experiment also ensured that it would seldom be repeated. The amount of planning and manpower, the expense of renovating and maintaining the theatre, the cost of housing the cast and building the sets and costumes, the co-ordination with local officials, all were daunting, and have since 1969 discouraged any attempts at a revival. Even with some sixty student participants, the cast and stage-crew were felt to be too few, and a budget of £2500 (at that time $6000) proved so inadequate that such important elements in the drama as music had to be eliminated almost entirely. Moreover, the educational function of a university drama department being to teach a diversity of skills to its students, it is doubtful that even if the production could be independently underwritten it could be regularly undertaken by the same group. In 1970 the Cornwall County Council approached the University of Manchester Drama Department about the possibility of their reviving the cycle, but without success. To date, the only such revival has been a much shortened and modernized adaptation of the Passion sequence, presented at the Northcott Theatre in Exeter at Easter, 1972, and later in London, involving some of the original participants in the Perranporth venture.[45]

Those fortunate enough to see the Cornish Cycle in its entirety were therefore few, a tiny fraction of those who have attended the York Festival since 1951. They were also a far less heterogeneous segment of the population: some local Cornish folk, some surprised tourists, and a disproportionate number of dons and American academics. Perhaps because it was only an 'academic' production, or perhaps because it took place so far away from London, there were no reviews in any of the national newspapers. In many ways this was the most important production so far of the mystery cycles in England, yet paradoxically its influence has been negligible. For those who experienced it, however, the Bristol production made all the years of trial and error in the revival of medieval drama, from the days of William Poel and Nugent Monck to those of Martin Browne and his now multiplying successors, worthwhile.[46]

6

Mystery Plays for Modern Audiences

'If the *Wakefield Mysteries* are still running when you read this, see them. You will be seeing the theatre of today and tomorrow as well as the theatre of yesterday.'

Alan Simpson reviewing the Mermaid Theatre *Wakefield Mysteries* (1965)

All of the performances of the mystery plays described so far have reflected, consciously or unconsciously, the value which their producers felt the plays held for modern audiences. With the changes in religious beliefs and literary taste which have taken place in our century, it is not surprising that most current productions of medieval plays look little like those of twenty or thirty years ago, even though the same play-texts are involved. The same, of course, may be said of Shakespeare, and for the same reasons.

T.S. Eliot noted over forty years ago that the renewed interest in medieval drama reflected the absence of contemporary plays which could perform the same function for our society that the mysteries did for theirs, the definition and celebration of a common culture. It is little wonder, then, that the mysteries, like Shakespeare, have been pressed into service on behalf of so many different causes, and there seems little doubt that if they are to be performed at all they will continue to be treated in this way in the future.

In such a situation it would be presumptuous to pass judgement on particular approaches to staging these plays. Today's illumination easily becomes tomorrow's cliché, and today's profundity tomorrow's irrelevance. Nevertheless, it may be useful here to summarize what the past three decades have taught us about mystery-play staging, and then to try to assess the importance of the revival of the mysteries for contemporary English culture.

We may begin with a look at some lessons and some still unsolved problems.

STAGES

The English mystery cycles are what we have now come to call presentational rather than realistic dramas. That is, the illusion of scenic verisimilitude plays no essential part in their meaning. If if is difficult to imagine a play of Chekhov being performed other than in a nineteenth-century proscenium-arch theatre, it is entirely possible to imagine the mystery plays being performed virtually anywhere. The York and Chester plays may have been performed on pageant wagons, but they do not have to be performed on them. The plays still have the same meaning, if not precisely the same flavour, if performed anywhere else; in fact some cycles, such as the *Ludus Coventriae*, seem to have changed their original manner of performance radically over the course of the fourteenth and fifteenth centuries.

The current situation is thus much the same as with Shakespeare. We find the mystery plays today being performed in theatres, auditoriums, and classrooms, indoors and outdoors, in the round and in the square, in castles, abbeys, marketplaces, concert-bowls – in short, nearly anywhere that a play can be put on. In the early days of the mystery-play revival, as we have seen, churches were the preferred location for performance. Sometimes it was the interior of the church, sometimes a nearby outdoor precinct. The assumption that the mysteries should be treated as church dramas and performed on 'sacred ground' determined the selection of a site for the York Festival. In recent years this assumption has gone out of fashion, if not entirely out of practice, for both scholarly and practical reasons. In point of fact, the mysteries were never performed in churches during the Middle Ages, and were not conceived by their authors with either the acoustics, the sight-lines, or the atmosphere of a church in mind. T.S. Eliot's observation that most twentieth-century audiences attend church dramas in the expectation of being virtuously bored forms a further, purely practical reason why most current producers tend to avoid staging the mysteries in church. Liturgical dramas like *The Play of Daniel*, of course, which rely on music and formal processional movement, are a totally different kind of play and can only be successfully performed in a church. It is instructive to observe that the most successful of the recent church productions of the mysteries, that of the *Ludus Coventriae* at Lincoln Cathedral in 1969, cut the dialogue of the plays severely and replaced it with music, dance and mime.

Of the remaining possible sites for the plays, the remarks above about the flexibility of their scenic requirements indicates that many different staging arrangements may be successful. In the past twenty years the mysteries have received numerous productions by professional theatre companies, though conventional theatres do not always provide the right kind of space for the plays. An experimental production of the York Cycle on pageant wagons at Leeds University in 1975, followed by a complete production of the same cycle in that manner at the University of Toronto in 1977, gave added impetus to the movement to adopt strictly medieval forms of staging for the cycles. Jane Oakshott, director of the Leeds performance, noted that 'the demand for acting space becomes enormously exciting when the actor is literally thrusting people out of his way,' and that the 'closeness of the audience members to each other speeds the communication of emotion so that the drama becomes more alive' when performed in this manner.[1]

Such effects are more easily accomplished outdoors than in, but a theatre of Elizabethan type, or of completely flexible design like the Cottesloe, may create a similar ambience. Outdoor performance, however, has the added value of removing the audience's customary expectations of mere entertainment upon entering a conventional theater – a Victorian argument that still has some validity. In such a setting, too, the audience can more readily appreciate the relationship between the 'real' world of the play and the illusory world of daily life visibly going on outside its confines – a medieval paradox basic to our appreciation of the plays' artifice.

COSTUMES

About costuming it is possible to be somewhat more dogmatic. There are four possible costuming styles that may be used for the mysteries: 1 / Biblical; 2 / medieval; 3 / modern; 4 / neutral ('rehearsal clothes').

This is, of course, the same range of choices available to the producer of Shakespeare, if we substitute the terms 'Roman' for 'Biblical' and 'Elizabethan' for 'Medieval.' As with Shakespeare, the choice in the great majority of modern productions of the mysteries has been for the second, the contemporary costumes in which the plays were originally presented. Biblical costuming, as in the Oberammergau Passion Play and modern film versions of the life of Christ, has been unanimously rejected as ill suiting the medieval perspective of the plays. Medieval writers were not interested in portraying the fashions or customs of Biblical Palestine, but rather in translating what they considered a timeless myth into terms of their own present-day reality. Shakespeare's Roman plays may be profitably given in togas, since Shakespeare shows some historical sense of the difference between Julius Caesar and King James. For the medieval playwright all Kaisers were the same.

Since medieval costuming was, for its time, 'modern dress,' theoretically a current producer wishing to duplicate the original effect of the plays would be forced to adopt twentieth-century dress. Unfortunately, however, there are no equivalents in modern fashions for the class differences which were so vividly expressed in medieval clothing and which formed such an important part of the gospel story, as medieval writers interpreted it. Our political leaders no longer wear crowns and ermine robes, our bishops are less ostentatious than were the successors of Annas and Caiaphas, and even our farmworkers are less visibly destitute than Mak and Gill. Much of the revolutionary meaning, spiritually speaking, of the plays is thus inevitably lost in modern dress, though it may be roughly approximated, as it was in the National Theatre's York *Passion*. Rehearsal clothes are clearly even more hopeless in this respect and have, to my knowledge, been tried only twice, by John Bowen in 1968 (see below, p 138) and in the Chester 'circus' production in 1973.

The use of medieval costuming is thus both historically correct and clearly preferable to the alternatives. It does, however, bring with it a serious aesthetic difficulty in present-day performances. A modern audience watching such a performance becomes, of necessity, much more concious than was the original medieval audience of the historicity of these plays, of their being products of their particular time and place rather than expressions of eternal truths. The plays become, as one spectator at York has put it, 'expressions of a former belief.'[2]

Costuming is not alone responsible for this difficulty, of course. The ideas of the plays are equally remote from most modern beliefs, and so the distance between the world of the play and the world of the audience is likely to exist in any case. We can probably say to the costume designer that it is his job simply to make sure that the distance is not made greater than it has to be. Productions which dress Joseph and Mary in aristocratic Florentine finery are likely to seem merely quaint and pretty; those which take the peasants of Bosch or Breughel for their models are likely to seem more real, as well as more truthful to the original characterization.

ACTING STYLE

Perhaps no aspect of mystery play production has changed more radically in recent years than the conception of the acting style, or styles, that they require. The conception of the plays as church dramas in the early years of their revival brought with it a set of preconceived attitudes about the tone deemed suitable for such works. The terms we encountered so often in chapters 2 and 3 were taken to be self-evident prescriptions: 'solemnity,' 'simplicity,' 'sincerity.' Actors were expected to behave in much the same way that people ordinarily do in church. It was assumed, moreover, that the plays had originally been written for unskilled amateur actors and that modern performances should aim at reproducing this 'artlessness.' In extreme but not infrequent instances, it was further assumed that the actors should even *be* artless, in real life, like the pious peasants of Oberammergau. As recently as 1963 one translator of an acting version wrote that 'the acting itself was, no doubt, rough and crude, but what it lacked in skill and subtlety was perhaps compensated for by enthusiasm.'[3]

In the 1960s these received notions began to be challenged both by scholars and by actors themselves. Scholars pointed out that the plays as a whole call for a variety of styles – serious and farcical, grave and colloquial, lyrical and dramatic – and that it is this combination and contrast of styles, rather than any single one, that gives the plays their vigour and interest, much as in Shakespeare. Many of the leading actors in medieval performances, moreover, we know were skilful enough to be paid for their services, and received high praise for them. Modern professional actors coming to the plays could hardly be expected to forget their training, nor would commercial theatre audiences, as opposed perhaps to the church audiences of the 1930s, want them to do so. The new atmospheres in which the plays came to be performed – particularly the large outdoor productions – demanded a more robust style of speaking and more vigorous physical action than had hitherto been customary. Changing tastes encouraged, rather than just tolerated, the humour and the violence in the plays. The result was occasionally a production, like the Mermaid *Wakefield Mysteries*, that emphasized those elements of the plays to the exclusion of their lyricism and tenderness. By the mid-1960s what had once seemed self-evident had come to seem aberrant: one editor of an acting version urged that 'a reverential approach to the subject need not be uppermost,' and that what he wanted was not 'the effect of a Victorian stained-glass window, but of a painting by Bosch or Breughel,' full of 'excitement and a sense of spontaneity.'[4]

How much this shift in taste is a transient phenomenon and how much it reflects an increased perception of the dramatic qualities of the original is not easy to assess. Historically, we know little about medieval acting style, aside from the inferences we may make from the play-texts themselves, and from a handful of eye-witness accounts. We do not know how medieval actors were trained (assuming that some of them were), what effects they strove for, or what theory, if any, they had about their craft. The publication of the complete *Records of Early English Drama*, now in progress, may fill some of the gaps in our knowledge.[5] To date, the only modern experiment in the reproduction of possible medieval acting methods has been that undertaken in a series of productions at Oxford for the *Joculatores Oxonienses* in the early 1970s by Meg Twycross. Working backwards from seventeenth-century materials on the art of elocution, Twycross taught her actors a set of stylized hand-gestures, each expressing a different feeling or action, which they used to illustrate the phrases in their dialogue. The technique brought a visual rhythm to the speeches (given in the original Middle English), not the least benefit of which was to greatly increase their intelligibility. The resulting style struck some spectators as more oriental than western. It may be that the mysteries, or at least some of them, were acted more like Noh and Kabuki than we have suspected.[6]

Possibly the only conclusion we can reach at this point is that the mysteries, if given in anything like their original form, demand from modern actors a style quite different from that which most of them have been trained in. However medieval actors created their characters, we may be sure that it was not by means of the Stanislavskian methods which dominate our drama schools and actors studios today. The characters in the mysteries are types, not individuals, and the actions they perform are mythic and larger than life. The mirror they hold up reflects not only nature but the supernatural as well. It would be pointless to ask an actor to 'internalize' the character of God or the risen Christ, though the method might have slightly more success with Satan, and a good deal more with Judas and Peter. The actor's time would probably be better spent, however, developing an ear for the rhythm of the verse, and a voice powerful enough to be heard and gestures broad enough to be seen in the open air by a large, easily distracted audience.

This is not to suggest, of course, that actors in the mysteries did, or should, vie with each other to out-Herod Herod. Herod, after all, was in the business of out-tyranting other tyrants, and there is only one way to play such a character. Hamlet's remark, we should remember, is not about bad roles but about bad actors, and in particular about the bad actor's habit of transferring the traits of one character, an easy one, to all the other roles he is asked to play. There is no reason to think that this happened any more or less frequently in the medieval theatre than it did in Shakespeare's.

Bertram Joseph has shown that in the case of Elizabethan acting, a style that we have tended to assume was conventional, artificial, and even bombastic was always praised in its time, when it was practised by experts like Burbage, for its realistic effects. Then, as now, the actor's ability to make the audience imagine that he actually *was* the character he presented – 'as if the personator were the man personated,' in Thomas Heywood's words –

was the chief goal of his craft.[7] It is unlikely that the medieval actor's goals differed in any way from those of actors in other periods. His concept of what was 'real,' however, must have differed considerably from ours, as must the acting conventions that his audience accepted as being 'realistic' when skilfully used. Medieval playwrights employed a repertory of conventional techniques, now long abandoned but many of them identical to those used by Shakespeare, to give meaning to their characters. Direct addresses to the audience, self-identifying speeches, prophecies, laments, and curses, litanies of praise, anachronistic foresight, total recall in hindsight – all these are less techniques of characterization in the modern sense than of exposition and thematic commentary, though in medieval drama they become qualities of the character as well. The creation of a character capable of saying such things and still seeming natural is one of the main challenges the mysteries offer to the actor.

In contrast to Elizabethan ideals, though, we may assume that the medieval actor, however skilfully he created his character, could not have expected, in all instances, to persuade his audience that he *was* the character he was portraying in any literal sense. 'Playing God' is just that, 'playing,' and there must have been a visible, undisguised artifice in the undertaking for which simplicity and sincerity cannot have been adequate substitutes. Just what this artifice consisted of in practice we do not know. It may be that William Poel was correct in having God's lines chanted. At any rate, the modern actor may take comfort in one certain fact: an actor cannot *be* God, he can only suggest Him and hope that his audience goes along with the game.

The element of playfulness in medieval acting has perhaps been underrated. It has come out, almost by accident, in some modern productions unhampered by too conventional an atmosphere. In the Cornish Cycle at Perranporth, for example, the actors' own evident delight in the audacity, not to say impossibility, of their undertaking to re-enact the history of the world was a chief source of the play's impact on the audience, though it did not diminish the 'seriousness' of its theme. In addition, a large amount of improvisation was found to be necessary in order to make the dialogue fit the timing of the many crossings and recrossings of the huge arena. The script was often treated more like a sketch or scenario than like a sacred text to be memorized and recited. The task of improvising was made easier by the fact that the play was given in a modern English translation, thus putting the actors in the same situation with regard to the language they were speaking as the original medieval actors. The improvisation was often recognized as such by the audience and applauded for its ingenuity and appropriateness. The actors in this production had, in a very literal sense, 'created' their parts, and in doing so proved once again that important historical discoveries may be made in the laboratory of the modern theatre.

TRANSLATIONS

With the exception of a few school and university productions which have managed to give the plays in their original linguistic forms, it has been assumed, plausibly, that the only feasible way to present the mysteries to modern audiences is in some type of modernized version of the text. The question of what kind of translation or adaptation this should be is obviously an important one, as the sound of the language does much to condition the response of both actors and audiences to the plays. By the same token, a translator cannot begin his work without first making a decision about the kind of appeal he feels the plays to have and the kind of production style he imagines as appropriate to them. Every translation is, in this sense, an interpretation.

We may better understand the choices facing a translator of the mysteries by looking at a particular example from one of the texts. The following passage contains the opening lines, in their original version, of play 5 of the York Cycle, the Fall of Man. In it Satan is explaining to the audience the reason for his hostility to Adam and Eve.

> For woo my witte es in a were
>   That moffes me mykill in my mynde,
> The godhede that I sawe so cleere,
>   And parsayued that he shuld take kynde,   4
>   of a degree
> That he had wrought, and I denyed that aungell kynde
>   shuld it noght be;
> And we were faire and bright,   8
>   Therfore me thoght that he
>   The kynde of us tane myght,
>   And ther-at dedeyned me.[8]

We notice to begin with that about half of the lines in this passage cause little difficulty for the modern reader or listener, if given some slight modernization of spelling or rearrangement of word order (for example, lines 1, 3, 8, 9). The rest, on the other hand, make little sense at all without a knowledge of Middle English (especially 4, 6–7, 11). This proportion is fairly typical for all the cycle texts. In addition, we may note a further difficulty in this passage, that of the grammatical structure of the stanza, which is hopelessly loose by modern standards. A literal prose translation might be as follows:

For woe my wits are in a whirr! This moves me greatly in my mind: when I perceived that the Deity which I saw so radiant intended to take on the nature of a creature he had made, I protested that he did not choose the race of angels. For we were fair and bright; therefore I thought that he might choose our race; and about this I grew indignant.

The literal translation, of course, fails to capture the emotions expressed in the passage: envy (of Adam and Eve), wounded vanity, anger, and general mental agitation. Like Herod and Pilate after him, Satan is a tyrant in a frustrated rage. The repetition of the same idea in lines 6–7 and 9–11 may be a sign of this mental turmoil, or merely a characteristic device of medieval oral poetry: the speech is the first one in the play and the audience may not be paying attention; therefore the same thing is said twice, in different words.

In 1951 J.S. Purvis translated these lines as follows for the opening production of the York Festival:

> For woe my wit is troubled here,
> Which moves me mightily in mind.
> The godhead that I saw so clear,
> And saw he would some creature find   4
>   For dignity;
> And of them all, our angel kind
>   Should it not be,
> Since we were fair and bright?   8
> Therefore me thought to be
> Shown favour in his sight –
> Yet he disdained me.[9]

In this version the passage is modernized to an extent even greater than we might feel is strictly necessary. Not only are the obscure words replaced ('kynde,' 'degree'), but perfectly intelligible ones like 'whirr' and 'mickle' (the latter still current in Yorkshire English) are given more ordinary equivalents. (Purvis in 1951 greatly feared the strangeness of a language 'so unlike anything to which "theatre-goers" were accustomed.')[10] Paradoxically, though, we notice that what Purvis takes away with one hand he restores with the other. Archaisms not present in the original are made up and introduced in order to preserve the antique tone of the language. To reduce the obscurity of line 10, for example, a phrase from the King James Bible (Esther 5:8) is thrown in, sounding oddly pious on the lips of Satan. In other places the grammar is made even more confusing than in the original (the noun 'godhead' is left dangling without a predicate, and a rhetorical question is gratuitously inserted at line 8). The result is that while the literal meaning of the passage is made somewhat clearer for the audience, its sound is kept deliberately old-fashioned and 'medieval,' a term which for Purvis seems to have included the sense of 'obscure.'[11]

In 1957, prompted by the commercial success of the York Festival and Martin Browne's desire to have more of the text available for use in the production, Purvis brought out his translation of the complete York Cycle. In this our lines appear as follows:

> For woe my wit works wildly here,
> Which moves me mickle in my mind.
> The Godhead that I saw so clear,
> And perceived that he would take kind   4
>   Of a degree,
> That he had wrought, and I denied that angel kind
>   Should it not be.
> For we were fair and bright;   8
> Therefore methought that he,
> Take one of us he might,
> Yet he disdained me.[12]

Clearly this version is closer to the original than the first, the fear of unfamiliarity having decreased since 1951. 'Mickle' is reinstated, and even the formidable 'take kind of a degree,' intelligible perhaps to those who know Shakespeare well but probably not to the bulk of a modern audience. The passage is, in fact, scarcely a translation at all, only lines 2 and 10 containing any significant alteration. Rather, it is a transliteration in which, in most cases, all that has been changed is the spelling and punctuation. Obviously more satisfactory to the scholar, this version nevertheless introduces by its very conservatism some new problems. The words 'denied' and 'disdained' do not mean the same thing in the original text thay they do in modern English, both verbs having changed their meaning since the fifteenth century.[13] If the speech is to be given in modern pronunciation, these words must be translated in order to get their correct meaning across to the audience. Nor can one expect even the most sensitive ears to comprehend at a first hearing the tangled syntax of lines 3–7, though the repetition later on of the idea they contain shows that the original author may have anticipated the same difficulty in his medieval hearers.

Yet a third attempt to render this passage was made by Howard Davies for the 1973 York Festival:

> For woe my wit is in a whirr
> That moves me mickle in my mind
> That godhead that I saw so clear
> Some kind should grace, but angelkind disdained he,
> And to himself hath ta'en mankind,
> Whereat have I great envy.[14]

Here we have a different approach from Purvis', part translation and part paraphrase. The eleven lines of the original are condensed to six, Davies' version being an edited text of the cycle for acting purposes. The modernization is partial – less than Purvis' first text, greater than his second. Davies sees nothing wrong with rhyming 'whirr' with 'clear,' as in the original, keeps 'mickle' and 'kind' but does away with 'degree' and gets around the syntactical difficulties of the last six lines by reducing them to a two-line paraphrase, written in archaic style ('hath ta'en,' 'envy' as an iamb to rhyme with 'he'). In explanation of his practice, Davies observed that 'such language as is inscrutable has been turned only into other words already current by the mid-16th century, the period at which these plays were last performed. Later language would be as obtrusive as new colors in an old canvas.'[15]

These three versions taken together illustrate some of the dilemmas facing translators of the cycles. Enough of the original Middle English is intelligible so that each translator finds it desireable to retain as much of it as possible. Purvis' guiding principle in his *Complete Version* was 'to alter nothing that could possibly be retained, either in the words, the arrangement of words, the verse-forms, or the rhymes and the alliteration.'[16] But while this aim may be laudable from a literary view, it is difficult to extract from the resulting text anything that sounds like living drama, either medieval or modern. Though he intended his work for performance, Purvis approached his task more like a museum curator than like a playwright, his main purpose being to 'preserve a national monument of medieval thought.' One recent critic has accurately called the resulting script an example of 'Modern Archaic, a language that no one ever spoke,' a judgment verified by the experience of actors at York.[17]

Of the two Purvis versions, the first, more modernized one is by far the more actable, but the vague religiosity of its tone introduces its own share of distortions of the original meaning. The enraged tyrant here becomes only 'troubled,' and that because he has lost not a deserved promotion but 'favour in his sight,' as though Satan were conscious of a Dantesque loss of beatitude. The Davies version is the most easily intelligible of the three and avoids Purvis' linguistic mistakes, but only at the cost of sacrificing much of the content of the speech (deliberately, of course, since it is an abridgment) and changing its emotional nuance into flat statement: Satan tells us that he has 'great envy,' but he does not sound as though he does. Most importantly, all three translations, even in trying to remain 'faithful' to the original language, succeed only in making it sound quaint, and hence induce, perhaps unintentionally, a condescending attitude toward the plays. In Purvis, this condescension is expressed explicitly in his Preface: the most that he can find to say about the dramatic quality of the York Cycle is that its 'crudeness is not so great as we might have expected ... considering the early date of the Cycle and ... the embryonic state of Engish literature at that period.'[18] It is little wonder, therefore, that he is content to print passages in his 'modern' version that are little more than nonsense with an agreeably archaic sound. Davies clearly understands the original text better and reproduces its meaning more clearly, but as he is preparing his version for the same type of production as Purvis, in which the spectacular beauty of the Abbey ruins and the miracles of modern stage lighting will bathe the plays in medieval nostalgia, he is equally obliged to keep his language decorously quaint and archaic.

While it is easy to criticize the failings of these translations, it is not easy to find examples of better ones or to formulate the principles by which the problems they demonstrate might be overcome. Sheila Lindenbaum has recently proposed, as an antidote to 'Modern Archaic,' the kind of free adaptation devised by Gordon Honeycombe in his composite version of the cycle plays called *The Redemption*, published in 1964. Honeycombe assumes a different kind of setting for the plays than that used at York, a situation more like that of the medieval pageant wagon in a noisy city street playing to a restless, non-paying audience. In such an atmosphere he strives not for a 'reverential' approach but for a 'sense of spontaneity.' The goals of his translation are to make 'immediate sense to the audience' and to avoid 'tongue-twisters for the actor.'[19] Honeycombe's language is totally modern, and he feels free to rearrange and paraphrase the text whenever it suits him. His shepherds, for example, exchange dialogue like the following:

'Did ever you see such a sight?'

'I? No never no man, by this light.'
'Say, boys, what? Have you found a feast?
Save a bit for me.'
'O holy Moses! Behold in the East!
The strangest thing to see.'[20]

Honeycombe's text does not include Satan, but a similar speech by Herod, denouncing the Three Kings for failing to bring him news of Jesus, indicates how he might have treated Satan's complaint:

Oh, that these villains should mar what I planned!
They shall be hanged when I find them out!
Eh! And that scum of Bethlehem – he shall die –
And thus shall perish his prophecy!

The original lines, from the 'true' Coventry Cycle, reveal the amount of modernization here:

A! thatt these velen trayturs hath mard this my mode!
    The schalbe hangid yf I ma cum them to!
E! and thatt kerne of Bedlem, he schalbe ded!
    And thus schall I his profece for-do.[21]

(Between lines 2 and 3 of this quatrain occurs the famous stage-direction, 'Here Herod rages in the pageant and in the street also.')

An acting version similar to Honeycombe's was compiled by John Bowen in 1968. Designed for indoor staging on a stationary 'stylized pageant wagon,' the version cut most of the dialogue of the divine characters in order to concentrate on 'human' rather than 'religious matters.' Rather than presenting the play straight, Bowen wanted the audience to be aware of 'a group of actors presenting a Mystery Play,' thus skirting the problem of dramatic verisimilitude in much the same way that the National Theatre's York *Passion* was to do a few years later. The cast wore plain rehearsal clothes, some of which they changed in sight of the audience when preparing to double parts. Bowen's language, though less pungent than Honeycombe's, is equally modern. His Satan announces:

I shall tell thee wherefore and why
I did all this felony.
For I am full of great envy

> Of wrath and wicked hate,
> That man should live above the sky
> Where at one time dwelled I,
> Who now am cast into hell's sty
> Straight out at Heaven's gate.[22]

There is obviously much to be said for this type of acting version of the mysteries. If nothing else, it is bound to appeal to a wider audience than a conservative text of the Purvis type, and to be more immediately intelligible to them. It is even possible to agree with Lindenbaum that this kind of free modernization is closer to the spirit, if not to the letter, of the original texts than Purvis' version:

Honeycombe, I would say, implies a relationship between the play and the modern audience that more effectively translates the terms of the medieval text. Rather than distancing the play through archaic language ... Honeycombe finds an equivalent for the original language and a style of production that makes the medieval plays newly contemporary.[23]

'Newly contemporary' is an apt phrase for the style that most recent translators of the cycles have aimed at. As a reaction against the nostalgic tone of earlier productions, this movement was to be expected, and should perhaps be encouraged. Tony Harrison's Yorkshire dialect version of *The Mysteries* for the National Theatre is the latest attempt to contemporize the language of the plays, in the manner of Honeycombe and Bowen.

At the same time, however, we may wonder if the mysteries can ever be made to sound to our time as they sounded to theirs. T.S. Eliot was probably right in holding that only new plays, written and conceived in modern terms, can do this. It is noteworthy that the most successful portions of the 'newly contemporary' scripts are just those parts of the plays that most appeal to modern audiences no matter how they are translated – the comic scenes and the scenes of physical violence. It is scarcely accidental that both Honeycombe and Bowen emphasize the comic and the violent at the expense of the devotional and the celebratory. Honeycombe leaves the Resurrection 'optional' for producers and puts it in an appendix. Bowen omits it altogether in order to end the play as he had ended his first act, with 'an execution and a mourning parent' (in the first act it had been Herod mourning for his dead son).[24] Modern colloquial English is well suited for such themes. We have, however, no contemporary equivalents for the devotional, didactic, and ceremonial styles of other passages in the plays. What, for example, could a modern equivalent be for Mary Magdalen's expression of joy at seeing the risen Christ, and what would be the point of searching for one?

> Alle for joye me likes to synge,
> Myne herte is gladder thanne the glee,
> And all for joye of thy rising
> That suffered dede upponne a tree.[25]

For such passages as these there is little alternative but to fall back on the sounds and rhythms of the original, to allow the plays what Tom Driver has called 'the privilege of their own idiom,'[26] and to accept whatever price in aesthetic and historical distance that practice may entail.

Such an admission may be seen as leading to the conclusion that there is no satisfactory substitute for performing the plays in their original language. Experiments at Oxford, Toronto, and elsewhere have indeed shown that actors can learn their parts in Middle English, and that audiences can understand more than they think they are going to, particularly if the action is suited to the word.[27] The most extensive attempt to give medieval plays in their original language has been made not in England but in Canada, by the *Poculi Ludique Societas*. This group, affiliated with the Centre for Medieval Studies at the University of Toronto, has since 1967 mounted more than forty productions of plays from the twelfth to the sixteenth centuries, with representatives from all the major genres of medieval drama. These have been staged in various locations, indoors and outdoors, in Toronto and on tour in other Canadian, American, and European cities. Excerpts from the mystery cycles were among the earliest of these productions, and in the late 1960s gave academic audiences their first chance to hear the plays acted in Middle English.

In October, 1977, the PLS achieved the remarkable feat of mounting all forty-eight plays of the York Cycle on pageant wagons for outdoor performance over the course of two days. Each play was given by a different group, drawn principally from universities and churches in the Toronto area but also coming from as far away as British Columbia to take part. The enterprise suffered from some predictable logistical difficulties – lack of adequate rehearsal time on the eight available wagons, lack of co-ordination and differences of skill among the participating groups – as well as some unpredictable ones, such as the rainstorm which drove more than half of the plays indoors. The excitement of the event itself and the high standard of many of the performances, though, offset these defects and made it possible to experience some of the festive atmosphere that must have prevailed in medieval cities when the wagons rolled into place and unfolded their story of the history of the world. Most noteworthy in the present context, however, is the fact that the PLS abandoned, on this occasion, its usual policy of performing in Middle English. Instead, the Purvis translation was adopted for convenience, since the task of teaching some four hundred different actors from different parts of the continent to speak in Middle English seemed scarcely practical. It was also apparent that a wider audience would be attracted to the performance if the language were modernized, as well as to the videotapes of the plays that were later distributed for educational use.

This decision points up the fact that, in the foreseeable future at least, performance in Middle English, however desireable, is likely to occur only in relatively limited productions aimed at limited, mostly academic audiences. University productions will go on, in order to make the kind of experiments that have been undertaken at Perranporth, Leeds, and Toronto. The equally desireable goal of reaching a wider audience and keeping the mysteries alive in the modern theatre, however, can almost certainly only be accomplished by giving the plays in translation. If so, we can expect our acting versions of the mysteries to continue to make them into the plays we think or wish them to be.

It is significant that in our survey of the present state of mystery-play production we have had to speak only of how, and not whether the mystery play should be performed. Few other works of art have won such a major victory against such widespread prejudice and misunderstanding as have the mystery plays in our century. There is no longer any organized opposition to the mysteries on religious grounds, as there was only forty years ago. Among the theatre-going public they are no longer condescendingly dismissed as 'old plays,' nor do academics any longer relegate them to the status of mere 'influences' on later, more interesting works. It is now impossible to teach the history of English drama as beginning with the Elizabethans, as was the custom only a short while ago. The merits of the plays have been so amply demonstrated by modern productions that they need no special pleading to gain them a place in either the curriculum or the repertoire.

As a result of this change in their fortunes, we are now in a position to look at the mystery plays freshly and objectively, without the obscuring veils of preconception and misinformation which distorted their image for so long. Indeed, it would be tempting to conclude this study with the claim that modern productions of the mysteries have brought us to the point where the true nature of the plays has become clear at last, and that theirs is a case that therefore can be marked closed. But such a claim would be only partly true. Productions such as that of the Cornish Cycle have come as close to historical accuracy as is possible in our present state of knowledge. Such productions, however, have been exceedingly rare. Few productions have historical accuracy as their main goal, for all of the reasons, both practical and philosophical, that we have noted in the preceding pages. Even for those few which do, 'accuracy' tends to be a will-o'-the-wisp. As one recent commentator has noted, 'it is inescapable that the drama must function in a contemporary context.'[28]

We must close, therefore, by asking what it is that we as modern audiences have seen in the mystery plays that touches our contemporary needs. Since the dramatic variety of the plays is almost as great as in Shakespeare, there is bound to be more than one answer to this question. All of them, however, are implicit in what we have seen in the course of this study.

First, the religious content of the plays was uppermost in the minds of those who first revived the mysteries, and remains a main source of their appeal. All the early producers of the mysteries were devout Christians, who took advantage of the English Church's decision to revive religious drama in order to win new converts. For such people the plays were not mere historical curiosities or aesthetic experiments, but statements of belief. They revived them not because of the plays' style, which they often misunderstood, but because of their content. The question raised by the success of this revival is why our own playwrights have not been able to create dramas that fill the same religious need for us that the mysteries did for their time. T.S. Eliot called for the creation of such a drama in 1937, but it cannot be said that he or any other modern dramatist has succeeded in composing works of universal appeal comparable to that of the mysteries. Until they do, the mysteries will continue to serve as our chief dramatic statement of the Christian myth.

Second, there has clearly been an element of nostalgia in the revival. Wistful memories of England's past glories have been a marked feature of English popular culture since 1945, accounting as much for the popularity of *Elizabeth R*, *The Forsyte Saga*, and *Upstairs, Downstairs* as for that of the mystery plays. If the nostalgia aroused by the mysteries has sometimes been of the condescending type, allowing today's Englishman to feel enlightened and sophisticated in comparison to his naive, childlike ancestors, it has also been genuinely envious of an age more spiritually unified than ours, one that could give expression in its drama to hope rather than despair.

Third, there has been the aesthetic appeal of a drama whose style is so different from that of conventional West End plays, though that difference is fast disappearing. The development by Brecht of a concept of 'epic theatre' at the very time when the mysteries were making their first appearances on English stages was not a coincidence, as Brecht's own acknowledgment of his debt to medieval theatre indicates. Both German and English audiences of the 1930s were ready for a drama that would do more than entertain. In so far as expressionism has come to be the rule rather than the exception in today's theatre, the mysteries may be said to have ridden the wave of the future and in their own way to have helped propel it.

Fourth, there has been the appeal to both scholars and producers of working with material of obvious historic importance and dramatic interest which had lain untouched, like buried treasure, for centuries. The novelty of such a drama was considerable: it was not commercial, not designed for a theatre, not realistic – in short, not any of the things which most other English plays are. This sense of rediscovery still permeates many productions today. And it is possible, as the experience of the Bristol, Leeds, and Toronto productions show, that the process of rediscovery has only just begun.

Last, there has been a strong element of local pride in the mystery play revival. We must not forget that these plays are closely tied to place. Since the time of Shakespeare, English drama has meant London drama. But each of the mystery cycles belongs to its own city, and most modern productions in England have taken place in or near the original location. The fact that London has no remaining cycle of its own to perform is a sweet irony to provincial residents who can point to the mysteries as their contribution to English drama at a time when the London theatre was undreamed of. In the present atmosphere of regionalism and 'devolution' in Great Britain, the mysteries, however timeless and universal their subject matter, have helped maintain the identities of cities such as York and Chester, which once ranked among the chief cities in the country. The pride which we are increasingly attaching to home-grown artisanry has few enough stimulants in an age of standardization. The history of the Festival of Britain shows how important this consideration was in the first revivals of the mysteries, and also helps to explain why the export of the plays to North America, despite scholarly interest there, has so far failed to find much popular appeal. For those fortunate enough to be the direct heirs of the tradition of the mystery plays, and for those others who have been able to share it vicariously, the inheritance has been a precious one.

Chronology of Principal Productions

The following list of principal productions of the medieval mystery plays in England from 1901–80 has been kept as brief as possible, as most of the entries are discussed in the text. It will enable the reader to see at a glance, however, the development of mystery-play production during these years, as well as to identify some references in the text more quickly than by using the index. Each entry contains the following information: year of production; cycle or cycles from which the plays were taken; names or number of individual plays performed; performing company; director; name and location of the playing-place.

1901 Chester Cycle, Abraham and Isaac, Elizabethan Stage Society, William Poel, Charterhouse, London

1904 York and *Ludus Coventriae* cycles, Nativity Plays, Amateur Dramatic Society, St Philip's Church, Newcastle-on-Tyne

1906 Chester Cycle, Nativity Plays, English Drama Society, Nugent Monck, Bloomsbury Hall, London, and Old Music Hall, Chester

1909 Chester Cycle, Nativity Plays, Benson Company, F.R. Benson, Guildhall, Stratford-upon-Avon

1909 *Ludus Coventriae*, Passion Play, English Drama Society, Nugent Monck, Fortune Playhouse, London (rehearsals only)

1910 Norwich Paradise Play, Norwich Players, Nugent Monck, Nugent Monck's Drawing Room, Norwich

1910 Wakefield Cycle, Annunciation and Flight into Egypt, Norwich Players, Nugent Monck, Nugent Monck's Drawing Room, Norwich

1912 Wakefield Cycle, Nativity Plays, Nugent Monck, Abbey Theatre, Dublin

1914 Chester Cycle, Nativity Plays, Norwich Players, Nugent Monck, Old Music House, Norwich

1914   Chester Cycle, Nativity Plays, Birmingham Repertory Theatre, Birmingham

1915   Wakefield Cycle and others, Nativity Play, Old Vic Company, Old Vic, London

1919   Wakefield Cycle, Nativity Plays, Norwich Players, Nugent Monck, Old Music House, Norwich

1921   Wakefield Cycle, same as 1919 above

1923   Chester Cycle, Shepherds Play, Old Vic Company, Robert Atkins, Old Vic, London (revived in 1924)

1925   York Cycle, The Nativity, York Everyman Theatre, Edith Craig, Guildhall, York

1926   Chester Cycle, Noah's Flood, Old Vic Company, Old Vic Theatre, London

1931   *Ludus Coventriae*, The Play of the Maid Mary, Chichester Diocesan Players, E. Martin Browne, Bishop's Palace, Chichester

1932   *Ludus Coventriae*, The Play of Mary the Mother, same as 1931

1937   York Cycle, Assumption of the Blessed Virgin, E. Martin Browne, Tewkesbury Abbey, Tewkesbury

1938   *Ludus Coventriae*, Passion Play (called the Norwich Passion Play), Norwich Players, Nugent Monck, Maddermarket Theatre, Norwich

1951   York Cycle, selection, York Festival Society in association with the Arts Council of Great Britain and the Corporation of the City of York for the Festival of Britain, E. Martin Browne, Yorkshire Philosophical Society Museum Gardens, York

1951   Coventry Cycle, Shearmen and Tailors' Play and Weavers' Play, Religious Drama Society and Coventry Cappers' Company, Carina Robbins, Coventry Cathedral, Coventry

1951   Chester Cycle, selection, County Drama Committee of the Cheshire Rural Community Council, Christopher Ede, Chester Cathedral Refectory, Chester

1951   Wakefield Cycle, Nativity Plays, Surrey Community Players, Reigate

1952   Wakefield Cycle, same as 1951; site: wagon stops in the City, London

1952   *Ludus Coventriae*, same as 1938

1952   Chester Cycle, same as 1951

1954   York Cycle, same as 1951

1954   Wakefield Cycle, Nativity Plays, Bretton Hall College, Martial Rose, Woolley Hall, Wakefield

1956   *Ludus Coventriae*, Passion Play, Glynne Wickham, Tewkesbury Abbey, Tewkesbury

1957   York Cycle, same as 1954
1957   Chester Cycle, same as 1952
1958   Wakefield Cycle, twenty plays, Bretton Hall College, Martial Rose, Bretton Hall, Wakefield
1960   *The Redemption*, by Gordon Honeycombe (composite cycle), John Duncan, University College, Oxford
1960   York Cycle, same as 1957, director David Giles
1961   Wakefield Cycle, eighteen plays, Mermaid Theatre Company, Colin Ellis and Sally Miles, Mermaid Theatre, London
1962   Chester Cycle, same as 1957; site: Chester Cathedral Green
1962   Wakefield Cycle, fourteen plays, Lambeth Drama Club for the City of London Festival, Jean Claudius, Westminster Abbey, London; also Edinburgh Festival
1962   *Ludus Coventriae*, selection (called 'The Lincoln Cycle'), E. Martin Browne, Coventry Cathedral, Coventry
1963   *The Redemption* (see 1960), members of the Royal Shakespeare Company, Gareth Morgan, St George's Church, Notting Hill Gate, and Southwark Cathedral, London
1963   York Cycle, same as 1960, director William Gaskill
1964   *Ludus Coventriae*, same as 1962
1965   Wakefield Cycle, fifteen plays, same as 1961
1965   *Ludus Coventriae*, same as 1962; site: Winchester Cathedral, Winchester
1966   York Cycle, same as 1963, director E. Martin Browne
1966   *Ludus Coventriae*, selection, Council of the Parts of Kesteven, Margaret Birkett, St Wulfram's Church courtyard, Grantham, Lincolnshire
1967   *Ludus Coventriae*, same as 1962; Director Robert Prior
1967   Chester Cycle, same as 1962; director Peter Dornford-May
1967   Wakefield Cycle, complete, Bretton Hall College, John Hodgson, Bretton Hall, Wakefield
1968   Wakefield Cycle, fifteen plays, Derby Playhouse and Derby Cathedral, John Williams, Derby Playhouse, Derby
1969   York Cycle, same as 1966, Corporation of the City of York, director Edward Taylor
1969   *Ludus Coventriae*, selection (called 'The Lincoln Cycle') Lincoln Theatre Royal, Clare Venables and Rhys McConnochie, Lincoln Cathedral, Lincoln
1969   Wakefield Cycle, Creation through Nativity, St Peter-upon-Cornhill Players, John Everett, St Peter-upon-Cornhill Church, London

1969   Cornish Cycle, complete, Bristol University Drama Department,
        Neville Denny, Piran Round, Perranporth, Cornwall
1969   Wakefield Cycle, Nativity Plays, City of London Festival,
        Young Vic Company, London
1970   Wakefield Cycle, Passion Play, St Peter-upon-Cornhill Players,
        St Peter-upon-Cornhil Church, London
1971   *Ludus Coventriae*, Marian plays, Joculatores Oxonienses,
        Meg Twycross and Christopher McAll, University Church, Oxford
1971   *I Am* (composite cycle), East Riding County Youth Theatre, Paul
        Vaughan-Phillips, Hampstead Theatre Club, London
1972   Cornish Cycle, Passion Play (day 2), Northcott Theatre,
        Kevin Robinson, Exeter
1973   Wakefield Cycle, selection, Ely Festival, John Boylan,
        Ely Cathedral, Ely
1973   Chester Cycle, selection, Chester Festival, James Roose-Evans,
        Chester Cathedral Green, Chester
1973   York Cycle, same as 1969
1975   York Cycle, thirty-six plays, Leeds University, Jane Oakshott,
        Leeds
1976   York Cycle, same as 1973, director Jane Howells
1977   York Cycle, Passion Play, National Theatre Company, Bill Bryden
        and Sebastian Graham-Jones, National Theatre, London
1978   York Cycle, Passion Play, same as 1977
1979   York Cycle, Passion Play, same as 1978
1980   York Cycle, same as 1976, director Patrick Garland
1980   Wakefield Cycle, complete Wakefield Festival, Jane Oakshott,
        Wakefield

Cast Lists

1954

God the Father	John Jacob
Archangel Michael	John Westbrook
Archangel Gabriel	Michael Vonberg
Satan	John van Eyssen
Adam	Kenneth Parsons
Eve	Jane Southern
Mary	Jean Buckle
Joseph	Leonard Pickering
Jesus	Joseph O'Conor
Judas	John Heu
Caiaphas	John Kay
Annas	Reginald Dench
Pilate	Alec de Little
Mary Magdalen	Henzie Raeburn
Angel of the Resurrection	Judith Dench
Producer	E. Martin Browne
Associate Producer	Henzie Raeburn
Director of Movement	Geraldine Stephenson
Designer	Norah Lambourne
Musical Director	Denis Stevens
Text	J.S. Purvis

1957

God the Father	Frank Shelley
Archangel Michael	John Westbrook
Archangel Gabriel	Eric Goodall
Satan	Robert Rietty
Adam	John White
Eve	Sheila Barker
Mary	Judi Dench
Joseph	Norman Tyrrell
Jesus	Brian Spink
Judas	Claude Ogelthorpe
Caiaphas	Alec de Little
Annas	Laurence Ward
Pilate	John Gatrell

Mary Magdalen	Jean Buckle
Producer	E. Martin Browne
Designer	Norah Lambourne
Director of Movement	Geraldine Stephenson
Lighting Designer	Percy Corry
Music edited by	Denis Stevens
Text	J.S. Purvis

1960

God the Father	Robert Eddison
Archangel Michael	Andrew Kane
Archangel Gabriel	John White
Satan	Harold Lang
Adam	Peter Brett
Eve	Bernice Stewart
Mary	Louise Liversidge
Joseph	Reginald Dench
Jesus	Tom Criddle
Judas	Eric Goodall
Caiaphas	Cyril Livingstone
Annas	Robin Wilson
Pilate	Stanley Ratcliffe
Mary Magdalen	Susan Lee
Producer	David Giles
Designer	Kenneth Mellor
Music	Frederick Marshall
Lighting	Peter Woodham
Text	J.S. Purvis

1963

God the Father	Alan Dobie
Archangel Michael	Keith Wallinger
Archangel Gabriel	Martyn Jackson
Satan	Ian McShane
Adam	Jon Cross
Eve	Rita Nixon

Mary the Virgin	Morag Butler
Joseph	Alfred Bristow
Jesus	Alan Dobie
Judas	Val Gallagher
Caiaphas	Peter Bowles
Annas	Henry Woolf
Pilate	Shay Gorman
Mary Magdalen	Louise Liversidge
Mary the Mother	Edna Shann
Producer	William Gaskill
Set and Lighting	John Bury
Costumes	Annena Stubbs
Assistant Director	Peter Gill
Music	Marc Wilkinson
Text	J.S. Purvis

1966

God	John Westbrook
Archangel Michael	Graham Corry
Archangel Gabriel	Leader Hawkins
Satan	David Henshaw
Adam	Christopher Kitching
Eve	Karin MacCarthy
Mary the Virgin	Loretta Ward
Joseph	Derrick Parr
Herod	John de Frates
Jesus	John Westbrook
Judas	John Heu
Caiaphas	Derrick Parr
Annas	Norman Tyrrell
Pilate	Nigel Forbes Adam
Percula	Teresa Forbes Adam
Mary the Mother	Henzie Raeburn
Mary Magdalen	Jean Buckle
Producer	E. Martin Browne
Set Designer	Michael Cain
Costumes	Alix Stone
Music	Denis Stevens

Movement	David Henshaw
Text	J.S. Purvis

1969

God the Father	Peter Blanshard ⎫
Jesus	Gerald Lomas ⎬ in rotation
Judas	John White ⎭
Archangel Michael	Eric Hewes
Archangel Gabriel	Nigel Forbes Adam
Satan	Christopher Butchers
Adam	Paul Lally
Eve	Anne-Marie Hewitt
Mary	Teresa Forbes Adam
Joseph	Douglas Waft
Herod	Michael Wilson
Caiaphas	John Shaw
Annas	Frank Higgins
Pilate	Cyril Livingstone
Mary Magdalen	Elizabeth Baxter
Producer	Edward Taylor
Assistant Director	Reiner Sauer
Set Designer	Patrick Olsen
Lighting	Percy Corry
Text	J.S. Purvis

1973

God the Father	David Johnson
Gabriel	Charles Martin
Michael	Peter Brammall
Satan	Joseph Copley
Adam	Andrew Spence
Eve	Ann Willis
Mary	Andree Pugsley
Joseph	Peter Aughton
Herod	Douglas Waft
Jesus	John Stuart Anderson

Jesus	John Stuart Anderson
Mary Magdalen	Mary Lloyd-Owen
Pilate	Richard Grayson
Caiaphas	John Ramsden
Annas	Louise Tate
Producer	Edward Taylor
Set Designer	Alison Chitty
Musical Director	Edward Jones
Movement Director	Louise Brown
Lighting	Jonathan Allen
Text	Howard Davies

1976

God the Father	David Johnson
Gabriel	Mary Eyeington
Michael	Dave Hill
Satan	Raymond Platt
Adam	Patrick Wildgust
Eve	Melanie Longster
Mary	Jo Woollons
Mary the Mother	Betty Doig
Joseph	Harry Bridge
Herod	Richard Grayson
Jesus	David Bradley
Mary Magdalen	Ruth Ford
Pilate	Dave Hill
Caiaphas	John Shaw
Annas	Raymond Platt
Producer	Jane Howell
Associate Director	Kevin Robinson
Designer	Hayden Griffin
Music composed by	Edward Gregson
Musical Director	Alan Gout
Lighting	Rory Dempster
Text	J.S. Purvis

1980

God	James Park
Adam	Roger Yorke
Eve	Vary Goodwill
Mary	Penn Charles
Joseph	Harry Bridge
Herod	Peter Aughton
Jesus	Christopher Timothy
Mary Magdalen	Julia Martinez
Pilate	John White
Caiaphas	Duncan Savage
Annas	Peter Jackson
Producer	Patrick Garland
Assistant Director	David Clarke
Designer	Saul Radomsky
Music	Edward Gregson
Musical Director	John Hylton West
Lighting	Les Broughton
Text	J.S. Purvis

B   THE CORNISH CYCLE, 1969

God	Boris Nicholson
Jesus	John Sinclair
Satan	Nick Day
Gabriel	Jean Brantingham
Michael	Jo Sutcliffe
Adam, Moses, Peter	Christopher Stanley
Eve, Mary	Janet Rhodes
Serpent	Jane Bedale
Noah, Judas, Tiberius	Peter Leiberman
Seth, Annas	Alan Corduner
Pharaoh, Caiaphas	Barry Whitefield
Solomon, Pilate	Alastair Moir
Mary Magdalen	Susie Pike
Mary Jacobi	Rachel Stabb
Mary Salome	Jane Hughes
Veronica	Anita Finch

Producer	Neville Denny
Assistant Directors	Sara Yeomans, Kevin Robinson, Sidney Higgins
Theatre Advisor	Richard Southern
Costume Advisor	Iris Brooke
Designers and Technicians	Jenny Bolt, Glynis Davies, Tim Hatcher, John Daniell, Claire Lyth, David Machlin
Text	Markham Harris and Neville Denny

Produced by the Bristol University Drama Department

Sponsored by the Cornwall County Council and Perranzabuloe Parish Council

Acknowledgments

It is a pleasure to express my thanks to a number of people and institutions whose assistance and generosity have been indispensable in the preparation of this book.

To the many people in England who welcomed me and shared their knowledge and experiences with me I owe the substance of this book. I think especially of the late E. Martin Browne and his wife, Henzie Raeburn, who gave me access to their files, patiently answered my questions, and kindly read my early drafts. Mr and Mrs John Hall of Norfolk provided the single most exciting adventure of my quest, the discovery in the attic of their farm house of the papers of Nugent Monck, for which I had searched in vain over two frustrating years. Stewart Lack, Edward Taylor, and Mr and Mrs Nigel Forbes Adam gave me much valuable information about the York Festival. The late Jack Wood, chairman of the York Festival Committee and afterward Lord Mayor of York, kindly allowed me access to the Festival Committee minutes, while also giving me an example both of personal courage and of dedication to the arts which I shall long remember. The late Neville Denny and his wife Shirley let me share in the excitement of the planning and execution of the Cornish Cycle at Perranporth. I owe advice and encouragement of various sorts to: Richard and Marie Axton, Professor A.C. Cawley, Howard Davies, Anne Fitzpatrick, Jane Oakshott, Martial Rose, Meg Twycross, and Professor Glynne Wickham.

On the American side there are also many pleasant debts to record. To the members of the Medieval Drama Seminar of the Modern Language Association of America I owe the first stirrings of my interest in the mystery plays. For continued stimulation and encouragement over the years I wish to thank especially Arnold Williams, O.B. Hardison Jr, Stanley Kahrl, Martin Stevens, Alexandra Johnston, Sheila Lindenbaum, and Robert Potter.

Others who have been of assistance are Alan Nelson, Kevin Roddy, V.A. Kolve, Clyde Smith, Paul Bosch, and the members of the Seventh Heaven Players in Syracuse, New York, who cheerfully acted as guinea-pigs on whom I could test various theories about producing mystery plays for modern audiences.

To the National Humanities Foundation, the American Council of Learned Societies, the University of California and Syracuse University I am grateful for providing financial assistance and time off from teaching duties, without both of which my frequent trips to England in search of the mysteries would have been impossible. Lastly, I wish to thank the staffs of the following libraries and archives who often went out of their way to make my researches profitable: the British Drama League Library, the Religious Drama Society Library, the Enthoven Theatre Collection, the York Public Library, the Chester Public Library, the Bodleian Library, the British Library, the Harvard Theatre Collection, the New York Public Library, the Folger Shakespeare Library, the Huntington Library, and the National Theatre Press Office.

Notes

The following abbreviations are used in the Notes:

EETS Early English Text Society (ES: Extra Series)
HMSO His (Her) Majesty's Stationery Office
LC Records of the Lord Chamberlain's Office
OED Oxford English Dictionary
PRO Public Record Office, London
RORD *Research Opportunities in Renaissance Drama* (Kansas)
SPCK Society for the Propagation of Christian Knowledge
YL York Public Library

The Times is the London *Times* unless otherwise indicated.

PREFACE

1 Anonymous review of a Nativity Play drawn from the York and *Ludus Conventriae* cycles, performed by the Amateur Dramatic Society, St Philip's Church, Newcastle-on-Tyne, in 1904. *Church Times*, 12 Feb 1904, p 195.

2 Dorothy L. Sayers, 'Types of Christian Drama,' *New Outlook* (London), no 3 (1952), 104–12; reprinted in *Seven: An Anglo-American Literary Review*, 2 (1981), 84–99.

In this book I follow the customary terminology used by Sayers, reserving the term 'mystery' for Biblical dramas, 'miracle' for plays about saints' lives, and 'morality' for allegorical dramas like *Everyman*. Not every medieval religious play, of course, can be made to fit into these arbitrary moulds, which are of modern rather than medieval origin, but which remain useful nevertheless.

3 Harold C. Gardiner, SJ, *Mysteries' End: An Investigation of the Last Days of the Medieval Religious Stage* (New Haven 1946), p 72.

4 From the accounts of Trinity House, a guild of master mariners and pilots in Hull, Yorkshire, detailing expenses for a 'Play of Noah' in 1483; cited in E.K. Chambers, *The Medieval Stage* (London 1903), II, 370.

CHAPTER ONE

1 V.A. Kolve, *The Play Called Corpus Christi* (Stanford 1966), p 36; Stanley J. Kahrl, *Traditions of Medieval English Drama* (London 1974), pp 13–52.

2 For the full text of this letter, which is now lost, see *Records of Early English Drama: York*, ed Alexandra F. Johnston and Margaret Rogerson (Toronto 1979), II, 649–50.

3 Frank Fowell and Frank Palmer, *Censorship in England* (London 1913), p 9.

4 Gardiner, *Mysteries' End*, p 72.

5 Virginia C. Gildersleeve, *Government Regulation of the Elizabethan Drama* (New York 1908), pp 10–11.

6 Fowell and Palmer, *Censorship*, pp 14–15.

7 Ibid, pp 26–7.

8 Gardiner, *Mysteries' End*, pp 43–78.

9 Fowell and Palmer, *Censorship*, p 19.

10 *The Dramatic Records of Sir Henry Herbert, Master of the Revels, 1623–1673*, ed J.Q. Adams (New York 1917).

11 William Prynne, *Histriomastix* (London 1633), p 113.

12 John Rainolds, *The Overthrow of Stage Plays* (London 1599).

13 Prynne, *Histriomastix*, p 113.

14 Jonas A. Barish, 'Exhibitionism and the Antitheatrical Prejudice,' *English Literary History*, 36 (1969), 1–29.

15 Proclamation to the *Ludus Coventriae* cycle, line 309, ed K.S. Block, EETS (London 1922).

16 Kolve, *The Play Called Corpus Christi*, p 32.

17 Patent issued to William Davenant and Thomas Killigrew by Charles II in 1662. Text printed in *1832 Report* (see note 34).

18 Proclamation by Henry Herbert dated 25 July 1663 (Adams, *Dramatic Records of Sir Henry Herbert*, p 125).

19 Shakespeare, *The Winter's Tale*, IV.iii.102.

20 Gordon Crosse, *The Arts of the Church: Religious Drama* (London 1913), p 140.

21 William Hone, *Ancient Mysteries Described* (London 1823), pp 230–1.

22 Crosse, *Arts of the Church*, pp 144–6.

23 Hone, *Ancient Mysteries*, pp 242–5; Christina Hole, *A Dictionary of British Folk Customs* (London 1978), p 123.

24 J.W. Robinson, 'Regency Radicalism and Antiquarianism,' *Leeds Studies in English*, ns 10 (1978), 121–44.

25 *The Critical Works of Thomas Rymer*, ed C.A. Zimansky (New Haven 1956), pp 145, 170.

26 J. Dodsley, *Old Plays*, 2nd edition (London 1780), I, xxxvi.

27 Jeremy Collier, *A Short View of the Profaneness and Immorality of the English Stage* (London 1698), p 62.

28 Public Record Office, London: Records of the Lord Chamberlain's Office, LC. 5/152. Abbreviated hereafter as 'PRO, LC' followed by the classification and volume numbers.

29 Alfred Jackson, 'London Playhouses, 1700–1705,' *Review of English Studies*, 8 (1932), 294: 'We are credibyly informed that yesterday a Trial was brought on in the Court of Common Pleas against one of the Players, for Prophanely using the Name of God upon the Stage, contrary to an Act of Parliament made in King James the First's time; and that the verdict was given against the player, according to the Tenor of the said Act.' (Notice in the Flying *Post*, 13 June 1700).

30 For a detailed account of the workings of the censorship system from 1660 to 1737 see Arthur F. White, 'The Office of the Revels and Dramatic Censorship During the Restoration Period,' *Western Reserve University Bulletin*, ns 34 (1931), 5–45.

31 P.J. Crean, 'The Stage Licensing Act of 1737,' *Modern Philology*, 35 (1938) 239–55.

32 See Dougald McMillan, *Catalogue of the Larpent Plays in the Huntington Library* (San Marino, Calif 1939). The scripts were sold as personal property by John Larpent in 1825 upon his retirement after forty-six years as Examiner of Plays.

33 For a general study of the censorship of the Larpent plays, see L.W. Connolly, *The Censorship of English Drama 1737–1824* (San Marino 1976).

34 *Report from the Select Committee of the House of Commons on Dramatic Literature, with the Minutes of Evidence* (London, HMSO 1832), appendix.

35 *1832 Report*, pp 59–60.

36 Ibid.

37 R.K. Greville, *The Drama Brought to the Test of Scripture and Found Wanting* (Edinburgh 1830), pp 51–2.

38 *1832 Report*, p 36.

39 These verses are from a satiric poem called 'Sense and Censorship' by Mostyn T. Pigott, printed in *Stage Year Book 1908* (London 1909), pp 12–3. The words are allegedly spoken by G.A. Redford, the current Examiner of Plays, to an author who has submitted a play on the subject of David and Goliath. So far as I have been able to determine, the author was no relation of E.F.S. Pigott, who preceded Redford as Examiner of Plays.

40 *An Act for Regulating Theatres*, 6 & 7 Victoria, c 68; printed in J. Isaacs, *Law Relating to Theatres, Music Halls, & Other Public Entertainments* (London 1927).

41 *Report from the Select Committee on Theatrical Licenses and Regulations; together with the Proceedings of the Committee, Minutes of Evidence, and Appendix* (London, HMSO, 1866), p 306.

42 PRO, LC 1/582.

43 PRO, LC 1/731. For the full text of this and similar latters, see John R. Elliott, Jr, '"Feeling Hot": Victorian Drama and the Censors,' *Victorian Newsletter*, 49 (1976), 5–9.

44 PRO, LC 1/58. The case occurred in 1858.

45 PRO, LC 1/277.

46 Stewart D. Headlam, *The Function of the Stage* (London 1889), p 10.

47 *Theatre*, 1 Dec 1879, pp 245–8.

48 Headlam, *Function of the Stage*, p 18.

49 For other attempts to perform the Oberammergau play in England, see chapter 2.

50 PRO, LC 1/639, dated 8 Nov 1895.

51 PRO, LC 1/639.

52 PRO, LC 1/657. The author of this letter was one William Griggs. It is dated 24 Jan 1896.

53 PRO, 1/675. *The Conversion of England* was eventually performed privately in a church setting in 1898: see chapter 3.

54 PRO, LC 1/417.

55 *Report from the Joint Select Committee of the House of Lords and the House of Commons on Stage Plays (Censorship); together with the Proceedings of the Committee, Minutes of Evidence, and Appendices* (London, HMSO 1909), p 111, paragraph 1971.

56 PRO, LC 1/564.

57 *1909 Report*, appendix A, p 351.

58 *1909 Report*, pp 14, 23–4; paras 194, 428.

59 *1909 Report*, pp 15–6, 28–9, 31–2; paras 526–34, 254, 550, 590, 592–3, 623.
   In 1911 Reford resigned from the Lord Chamberlain's office to become Britain's first film censor. Not surprisingly, his first act in his new job was to lay down a rule that 'all Biblical scenes are to be watched very carefully – particularly anything from the New Testament,' a rule he then invoked to prohibit the showing of the American films *King of Kings* and *The Sign of the Cross* (Fowell and Palmer, *Censorship*, p 317).

60 *1909 Report*, p 300; para 5422.

61 *1909 Report*, pp ix–x.

62 E. Martin Browne, *The Production of Religious Plays* (London 1932), pp 25, 27.

CHAPTER TWO

1 Alexander Craig Sellar, *The Passion Play in the Highlands of Bavaria* (London and Ediburgh 1871), p 20.

2 Matthew Arnold, *Cornhill Magazine*, Dec 1871; reprinted in *Essays in Criticism*, 1st Series, 1895, pp 223–4.

3 *Church Times*, 25 Oct 1901, p 481. By 1900, in fact, Englishmen had come to feel so much at home in Oberammergau that they first started complaining about the rude manners of the Americans there; L.C. Morant, 'The Vulgarising of Oberammergau,' *Nineteenth Century*, 48 (1900), 820–24.

4 F.W. Farrar, *The Passion Play at Oberammergau 1890* (London 1890), p 6.

5 Ibid, p 17.

6 Anna Mary Howitt, *An Art Student in Munich* (London 1854), I, ch 4.

7 Archibald Henderson, 'The Most Impressive Spectacle Ever Set upon a Stage,' *Theatre Magazine*, 12 (1910), 146–50. For a more sceptical view, and a detailed summary of the history of the play, see A.W. Ward, 'The Oberammergau Passion Play,' *Cornhill Magazine*, 102 (1910), 200–14.

8 The 1662 text has been printed in *Das Oberammergauer Passionspeil in seiner altesten Gestalt*, ed August Hartmann (Leipsig 1880). This text was a revision of the original script of 1634, which has been lost. An English summary may be found in Hermine Diemer, *Oberammergau and Its Passion Play*, tr Walter S. Manning (Munich 1900), pp 90–105.

9 Rosner's text of 1750 has been printed in *Bibliotek des Literarischen Vereins in Stuttgart*, no. 282, ed Otto Mausser (Leipsig 1934).

10 A.P. Stanley, *Essays* (London 1870), pp 506–8.

11 Quoted in Elisabethe H.C. Corathiel, *Oberammergau: Its Story and Its Passion Play* (London 1934), p 70.

12 Howitt, *An Art Student in Munich*, p 17.

13 Karl Hase, *Miracle Plays and Sacred Dramas: An Historical Sketch*, tr A.W. Jackson (London 1880), p 84. The materials for the costumes were actually imported from Palestine, and their designs based on drawings made in Palestine museums.

14 Henry Scott Holland, *Impressions of the Ammergau Passion-Play* (London 1880), p 11.

15 John P. Jackson, *The Ober-Ammergau Passion Play* (London 1880).

16 The charges of anti-Semitism against the Oberammergau play have perhaps been exaggerated in recent years, fuelled by the horrors of the Nazi period. But there is no doubt that it was an important ingredient in the play in the nineteenth century. A Scotsman wrote of the feelings excited in the audience by the 1860 performance as follows: 'With strange emotions you gazed upon the executioners as upon wild

beasts when they tore Christ's mantle into shreds, and cast lots for his vesture; and the Jewish race appeared hateful in your eyes, as you watched them gathering round the cross, looking on the man they had crucified, and railing at him, and taunting him with his powerlessness and his pain. Then for the first time you seemed to understand the significance of those ungovernable explosions that in the history of the middle ages one reads of, when sudden outbursts of hatred against the Hebrew race have taken place, and have been followed by cruelties and barbarities unexampled in history. Just such a feeling seemed excited in this Ammergau audience by this representation.' (Sellar, *Passion Play*, pp 45–6). There is no evidence connecting the medieval English plays with such 'explosions,' though they cannot be said to be totally free of anti-Semitic feelings. A movement to 'reform' the Oberammergau text in 1970 failed, but a similar movement was successful in 1980.

17 Holland, *Impressions*, p 22.

18 Hermione von Patruban, *Erinnerung an Oberammergau* (Vienna 1871), quoted in Jackson, *The Ober-Ammergau Passion Play*, p 67.

19 Stanley, *Essays*, pp 528–9.

20 Farrar, *Passion Play*, p 23.

21 Ibid, p 60.

22 Henry Blackburn, *Art in the Mountains: The Story of the Passion Play* (London 1870), p 148.

23 L. Clarus, *Das Passionspiel zu Oberammergau* (Munich 1860), quoted in Jackson, *The Ober-Ammergau Passion Play*, p 54.

24 Eduard Devrient, *Ueber das Passionspiel im Dorfe Ober-Ammergau* (Leipsig 1880), quoted in Jackson, *The Ober-Ammergau Passion Play*, p 68.

25 Archibald Henderson, *Theatre* 12 (1910), 146–50.

26 Holland, *Impressions*, p 11.

27 Stanley, *Essays*, p 527.

28 Sellar, *Passion Play*, p 55. For the continuation of this conception of Pilate in twentieth-century religious plays, see below, chapter 3.

29 Holland, *Impressions*, p 17.

30 Stanley, *Essays*, p 530.

31 Farrar, *Passion Play*, p 88.

32 Quoted by James Agate, *Sunday Times* (London), 10 April 1932.

33 The so-called 'Daybooks' of the Lord Chamberlain's office, now housed in the British Library (Mss Add 53702–8), record the receipt of ten letters of protest against the Oberammergau play, including a petition from the Masters of Winchester College urging 'the extreme profanity and impropriety of its transference from its natural home to a place of Entertainment in London' (vol 342, letter 222). (Quoted in Marylin C. Mattson, 'Censorship and the Victorian Drama,' Ph D. Diss, University of Southern California 1969, p 88.)

34 *Theatre*, 1 May 1879, pp 215–16.

35 *Theatre*, 1 June 1879, p 322.

36 PRO, LC 1/435.

37 PRO, LC 1/638.

38 PRO, LC 1/638. The Queen's letter is dated 30 Jan 1895.

39 *1909 Report*, p 300.

40 George Bernard Shaw, *Saturday Review*, 13 Feb 1897.

41 W. Dubbers, *Das Oberammergauer Passionspiel nach seiner geschichtlichen, kunsterlischen und culturhistorischen Bedeutung* (Frankfurt 1872), quoted in Jackson, p 85.

42 Virtually alone among his contemporaries, the Nonconformist journalist William T. Stead drew a more sobering historical lesson from the play: 'If the illegitimate son of a Bengalee peasant, hanged by order of our Lieutenant-Governor in the North-West provinces because of the mischief he was making among the Moslems of Lahore, were to establish his faith in the ruins of Westminster Abbey and install the successor of his leading disciple on the throne of the British Empire, we should not wonder at his Apotheosis.' (William T. Stead, *The Story That Transformed the World* [London 1890], p 156)

CHAPTER THREE

1 *The Times*, 23 March 1902.

2 Lines 715–27, 735–49, and 761, in Poel's promptbook, in the Enthoven Theatre Collection, Victoria and Albert Museum, London.

3 C.E. Montague, *Dramatic Values* (London 1911), p 236; *Sketch*, 2 April 1902. For a fuller description of the performance, see Robert A. Potter, *The English Morality Play* (London 1975), pp 1–5.

4 *1909 Report*, p 30, para 556.

5 Nugent Monck, 'William Poel', *Plays and Players*, I (1954), no 6, p 8.

6 *Church Times*, 7 Dec 1906, p 760.

7 Monck recounted his experience in an article for the *Eastern Evening News* (Norwich), 26 May 1939.

In 1909 Blasphemy was a Common Law offence, punishable by fine and imprisonment without hard labour. It consisted of '(1) scoffingly or irreverently ridiculing or impugning the doctrines of the Christian faith; (2) uttering or publishing contumelious reproaches of Jesus Christ; or (3) profane scoffing at the Holy Scriptures or exposing any part thereof to contempt or ridicule' (Halsbury's *Laws of England* [London 1909], IX, 530–1).

8 *The Times*, 8 April 1909; Lord Chamberlain's files, St James's Palace.

9 Unidentified press clipping, 1909, in the files of the Maddermarket Theatre, Norwich.

10 A copy of the poster for the 1909 Passion Play, together with other materials related to the production, has been preserved in the papers left by Nugent Monck at his death, now in the possession of Mr and Mrs John Hall, Pulham Market, Norfolk.

11 Monck Papers. The manuscript is dated 'Norwich April 1910.'

12 *The Times*, 6 Dec 1906.

13 Boston *Transcript*, 9 Jan 1907; unidentified press clipping, dated 6 Dec 1906, in the Harvard Theater Collection. The plays produced were numbers 6, 7, and 8 from the Chester Cycle: the Annunciation and Nativity, the Shepherds, and the Three Kings. They were performed first in the Old Music Hall, Chester, and then in Bloomsbury Hall, London.

14 Monck Papers, unidentified press clipping dated 8 April 1909.

15 Letter to the author from the Lord Chamberlain's office, 19 Aug 1971.

16 M.J. Rudwin, 'Modern Passion Plays,' *Open Court*, 30 (1916), 278–300.

17 *Playgoer and Society Illustrated*, 5 (1911); *Pall Mall Magazine*, Jan 1912; *Literary Digest*, 49 (1912), p 336. A drawing of the set of *The Miracle* may be found in Phyllis Hartnoll, *History of the Theatre* (1970), pp 246–7. The play was revived at the Shrine Auditorium, Los Angeles in 1927, and again in London at the Lyceum Theatre in 1932.

18 George Bernard Shaw, *On The Rocks* (London 1933).

19 Titles and descriptions of many other modern Passion plays may be found in *A List of Selected Plays for Passiontide and Easter*, compiled and published by the Religious Drama Society of Great Britain (London 1955 and 1969). A valuable collection of scripts is housed in the Religious Drama Society Library, George Bell House, 8 Ayres St, London SE1.

20 Hettie Gray Baker, 'The Religious Spirit in Some Recent Plays,' *Theatre Magazine*, 12 (1910), 50.

21 E. Martin Browne, *The Production of Religious Plays* (London 1932), p 25.

22 Denis Bablet, *Edward Gordon Craig* (London 1966), pp 51–4. The use of lighting as a substitute for divine characters is extensively discussed by A.H. Debenham, *Religious Drama: A Practical Guide to the Production of Religious Plays* (London 1935).

23 *The Way of the Cross* was translated from French into English in 1938 by Frank de Jonge (Dacre Press, Westminster).

24 M.C. O'Byrne, 'A Modern Mystery Play,' *Open Court*, 1 (1887), 290–2. Bethlehem tableaux had already been staged as early as 1871 by the Rev N.O. Nihill at St Michael's School, Shoreditch, who was also inspired by the Oberammergau play (see June Ottaway, 'The Development of Religious Drama in England in the

Twentieth Century,' MA thesis, University of London 1952, p 39). The Oberammergau tableaux may, in turn, have derived from a performance at Strasbourg in 1816, in which events in the life of Christ were represented after paintings of the Masters while hymns were played on a harmonica (Alfred Bates, *Drama and Opera* [New York 1909], IV, 35).

25 Browne, *Production of Religious Plays*, p 16.

26 John K.C. Chesshire, *Bethlehem Tableaux from Behind the Scenes, with Practical Hints and Illustrations* (London 1913), pp 1–2, 11.

27 A typescript of this play is to be found in the British Drama League Library, Fitzroy Square, London. I can find no evidence that the play was ever produced.

28 George Bernard Shaw, 'Church and Stage,' *Saturday Review*, 22 Jan 1898, pp 106–8.

29 *Church Times*, 29 Sept 1905, p 363.

30 *The Times*, 28 Jan 1924, p 8.

31 Fred Eastman, *Christ in the Drama* (New York 1947), p 143.

32 Dorothy L. Sayers, *The Man Born to Be King* (London 1943), with a foreward by J.W. Welch, Director of Religious Broadcasting for the BBC. According to Welch, one angry letter to the BBC attributed the fall of Singapore directly to these broadcasts.

33 *Acting the Gospel: The Meaning of Religious Drama*, by the Lord Bishop of Bristol. Religious Drama Society Pamphlets no 10 (London 1947).

34 Robert Speaight, 'The New Director,' *Drama*, ns no 8 (1948), 8.

35 'The Church and Religious Drama,' by the Bishop of Chichester, *Drama* (1930).

38. Browne's own account of his career may be read in *Two in One* (Cambridge 1981).

36 *The Play of the Maid Mary*, ed E. Martin Browne, Religious Plays Series, no 3 (London 1932). A review of the Chichester production appeared in *The Times*, 13 Aug 1931, p 8. The production was first performed in the parish church of Alfriston, near Brighton, before being moved to Chichester.

37 Religious Plays Series, no 4 (London 1932).

38 Browne, *Production of Religious Plays*, pp 9–10, 23, 24.

39 Ibid, p 29.

40 Browne, Preface to *The Play of the Maid Mary*.

41 E. Martin Browne, 'Lighting,' Religious Drama Society Pamphlets no 8 (London 1947).

42 Browne, *Production of Religious Plays*, p 53.

43 Charles Mills Gayley, *The Star of Bethlehem: A Miracle Play of the Nativity, Reconstructed from the Towneley and Other Old English Cycles and Supplemented and Adapted to Modern Conditions* (New York 1904).

44 Gayley, *The Wakefield Second Nativity Play* (Weybridge 1917).

45 *A Shepherds' Play*, paraphrased by R. Nash, Religious Plays Series no 9 (London 1932).

46 Robert Withington, *English Pageantry, An Historical Outline* (Cambridge, Mass 1920), II, 218–19.

47 Unidentified press clipping, Enthoven Theatre Collection, Victoria and Albert Museum, London. Another unidentified clipping in the Harvard Theatre Collection, dated 23 Dec 1923, refers to the 'Shepherds Play' as 'poignant and moving by contrast with this present century of cinema and advertisement and jazz.'

48 A program for this production may be found among the J.S. Purvis Papers in the archives of the York Public Library. Photographs appeared in the *Delineator*, December 1925, p 5.

49 Browne, *Production of Religious Plays*, pp 25, 27.

50 *Bucks Free Press*, Wycombe, 1 Aug 1930. The play was performed in West Wycombe Park on 26 July and repeated on the vicarage lawn on 22 August.

51 Ernest J.B. Kirtlan, *A Little Drama of the Crucifixion: Being a Modernization of the 'Crucifixion' in the Towneley Mystery Plays Circa 1400 A.D.* (London 1920), p 8.

52 *The Word of God: A Miracle Play Adapted from the York Cycle*, ed Paul H. Wright (York 1926), p iv.

53 Reviewed in the *Church Times*, 19 Jan 1912, p 85.

54 Norman Marshall, *The Other Theatre* (London 1947), p 25.

55 Ibid.

56 M.S. and F.W.W., *The Norwich Players: A History, An Appreciation, and a Criticism* (Norwich 1920), pp 28–9.

57 Reginald F. Rynd, 'Nugent Monck and "Mystery" Plays,' *Eastern Daily Press* (Norwich), Dec 1910.

58 Bristol *Times*, 19 Aug 1929.

59 *Daily Chronicle*, 20 Aug 1929.

60 Charles Rigby, *Maddermarket Mondays: Press Articles Dealing with the Famous Norwich Players* (Norwich 1933), p 19.

61 Nugent Monck, *The Norwich Mystery Play of 'Paradise': A Sixteenth Century Mystery prepared for Modern Representation* (Norwich 1910), p 4.

62 *Eastern Daily Press*, 24 July 1939.

63 *Eastern Daily Press*, 18 March 1952.

64 *Sphere*, 5 April 1952.

65 *Eastern Daily Press*, 17 March 1952, and 10 March 1952. An example of the hostile correspondence shows how little the opinions of some Englishmen had changed over the years: 'It is a most blasphemous play, whatever the outward sanctity of the appearance of the players ... To reduce the Passion of Calvary to the level of a sensuous play for the gratification of onlookers is but an aggravation of man's guilt in the sight of God ... Have I seen the play? I would rather lose my sight than do so. To make the agonising sufferings of the Saviour of sinners material for a Passion

Play is too revolting for words. It is a disgrace to the clerical profession which supports it.'

66 'J.M.,' *Theatre*, 6:144, 29 March 1952, pp 21–2.

67 *Eastern Daily Press*, March 1952 – clipping in the Maddermarket Theatre files.

68 A letter to Monck from the Lord Chamberlain's Office dated 10 Sept 1951 informed him that 'there will be no objection to *The Norwich Passion Play* being publicly performed in your Theatre, on the understanding that the text is fundamentally unchanged from the original version.' (I am grateful to Mr Hilary Gardner, Monck's legal executor, for furnishing me with a copy of this letter.)

CHAPTER FOUR

1 B. Seebohm Rowntree, *Poverty and Progress: A Second Social Survey of York* (London 1941), pp 476–7. Other volumes are: *Poverty: A Study of Town Life* (London 1901); and (with G.R. Lavers) *Poverty and the Welfare State: A Third Social Survey of York* (London 1952). For a critique of Rowntree's work see Russell Kirk, 'York and Social Boredom,' *Sewanee Review*, 61 (1953), 664–81.

2 *The Times*, 6 April 1951, p 3.

3 Program note for the first performance of Christopher Fry's *Sleep of Prisoners*, Pilgrim Players, St Thomas's Church, London, 1951.

4 Tyrone Guthrie, Introduction to Sir David Lindsay's *Satire of the Three Estates*, ed Robert Kemp (Heinemann Drama Library 1951) p x. See also Guthrie's description of the production in his *A Life in the Theatre* (London 1961), pp 274–80.

5 Winifred Bannister, *James Bridie and his Theatre* (London 1955), pp 237–8.

6 Letter to the author from Keith Thomson, 30 Aug 1971: 'I have to say that I think the York Festival Committee accepted the Mystery Plays as part of the Festival more because of their uniqueness and their "draw" than because of any deep-seated religious feeling.'

7 Letter to the author from R.J. Hill, Secretary of the Lord Chamberlain's Office, 16 April 1971: 'By 1950 the rule [barring stage representations of the Deity] had been relaxed to the extent of considering immune from censorship a Medieval Mystery Play involving the Deity which had been modernized only to the extent of word for word substitution of modern for archaic English. In this regard Mr. E. Martin Browne told the Lord Chamberlain on the 18th October, 1950, that the York Festival would consist of the Cycle of Mystery Plays in their traditional form abridged for presentation in a single performance. This was accepted as sufficient justification for the avoidance of the need to submit.'

8 E. Martin Browne, 'Religious Drama: Past, Present and Future,' *Religious Drama Society Pamphlets*, no 1 (London, SPCK 1947), 6.

9 Minutes of the York Festival Committee, City Clerk's Office, Guildhall, York, 5 April 1950 and 9 May 1951. Canon Purvis' remarks were printed in the Yorkshire *Post*, 8 Feb 1951.

10 Unidentified press clipping, York Festival Collection, York Public Library.

11 Festival Committee Minutes, vol I, p 114; *Church Times*, 29 Dec 1950; *News Chronicle*, 23 Nov 1950.

12 *Manchester Guardian Weekly*, 14 June 1951.

13 York *Evening Press*, 25 June 1951. The text used in the 1951 production was published as *The York Cycle of Mystery Plays: A Shorter Version*, ed J.S. Purvis (London, SPCK 1951). This is now out of print and should not be confused with the currently available *Complete Version* by Purvis (SPCK 1957), which is an entirely different translation. See below, chapter 6.

14 See Eli Konigson, *La Représentation d'un mystère de la Passion à Valenciennes en 1547*, Éditions du Centre National de la Recherche Scientifique (Paris 1969). Konigson reproduces all twenty-five manuscript miniatures as well as the frontispiece painting, and gives a detailed description of the staging of the play.

15 The wheeling in of the Hell-Mouth wagon cannot be verified by pictorial evidence, but was reported by J.C. Trewin, 'York Revives Her Mysteries,' *Everybody's Weekly*, 9 June 1951, p 17.

I say 'presumed' original staging because it has recently been questioned whether pageant wagons were actually used to perform the York plays in the middle ages. (See Alan H. Nelson, 'Principles of Processional Staging: York Cycle,' *Modern Philology*, 67 [1970], 303–30.) New evidence discovered since 1970 tends, however, to support the traditional pageant-wagon theory. (See Alexandra F. Johnston and Margaret Dorrell, 'The Doomsday Pageant of the York Mercers,' *Leeds Studies in English*, 5 [1971], 29–34; and Margaret Dorrell, 'Two Studies of the York Corpus Christi Play,' ibid, 6 [1972], 63–111.)

16 See the contemporary descriptions quoted in Konigson, *La Représentation*.

17 Flying machines, for example, are indicated in both the Ascension and Appearance to Thomas plays:

> *Jesus.*   Sende doune a clowde, fadir! for-thy
>   I come to the, my fadir deere.
> *Mary.*   A! myghtful god, ay moste of myght,
>   A selcouth sight is this to see,
>   Mi sone thus to be ravisshed right
>   In a cloude wendande uppe fro me.   (Ascension, lines 175–82)

> *Mary.*   Go saie them sothely, thou saw me assendinge.   (Appearance to Thomas, line 162)

(*York Plays*, ed Lucy Toulmin Smith [London 1885], pp 461, 485)

18 York *Evening Press*, 25 June 1951.

19 E. Martin Browne, 'Religious Drama,' Community House Pamphlets, Iona Youth Trust (Glasgow 1948), p 4.

20 Roy Walker, 'The Mystery Plays,' *Theatre Newsletter*, 6:126, 7 July 1951, p 6.

21 Herbert Read, 'The York Mystery Plays,' *New Statesman and Nation*, 9 June 1951.

22 Harold Matthews, *Theatre World*, July 1951, pp 31–2, 35–6.

23 Leeds *Guardian*, 15 June 1951.

24 The actor who played God the Father was Noel Shepherd, a painter and decorator from Wakefield, whose name survives on an autographed copy of the 1951 program now in the possession of Mrs Audrey Browne.

25 Conversation with the author, 6 April 1971.

26 Herbert Read, *New Statesman and Nation*, 9 June 1951.

Martin Browne later defended himself against Read's criticism by explaining that 'even in York itself when I wanted to leave some passages in broad dialect I could not find people to speak them' ('Producing the Mystery Plays for Modern Audiences,' *Drama Survey*, 3 [1963], 5–15).

27 *The Times*, 5 June 1951.

28 Browne, Yorkshire *Post*, 18 Oct 1950.

29 *Punch*, 27 June 1951.

30 *Sphere*, 23 June 1951.

31 *Church Times*, 8 June 1951, p 387.

32 Eric Keown, 'Festival Time,' in *Theatre Programme*, ed J.C. Trewin (London 1954), p 195.

33 Read, *New Statesman and Nation*, 9 June 1951.

34 York *Evening Press*, 25 June 1951.

35 Archives of the York Public Library, Purvis Papers, no 468.

36 York Public Library, Festival Collection.

37 Ibid.

38 The adjectives are from the Yorkshire *Post*, 14 June 1954.

39 Festival Committee Report, 26 Sept 1952, in the Purvis Papers, YL/592.

40 *The Times*, 14 June 1954, p 5.

41 John Buckingham, 'Returning One Day from the Middle Ages,' *British Weekly*, 22 July 1954.

42 Hans Hess, 'Report by the Artistic Director on the Festival of 1954,' York Festival Collection, York Public Library.

43 *The Times*, 24 June 1957, p 14.

44 Robert Speaight, *New Statesman and Nation*, 29 June 1957, p 838.

45 Festival Committee Minutes, 13 Nov 1957, vol III, p 9.

46 *The Times*, 24 June 1957, p 14.

47 Speaight, *New Statesman and Nation*, 29 June 1957, p 838.

48 Festival Committee Minutes, 27 Sept 1957.

49 Report to the Festival Committee, March 1958.

50 Festival Committee Minutes, 14 Jan 1959, vol III, p 40. A proposal by an American company to stage the York Cycle in New York in 1960 with Charlton Heston as Christ fell through when Hess demanded a $5000 fee for the use of Canon Purvis' translation.

51 York *Evening Press*, 2 March 1960; also quoted in Festival Supplement, 1960.

52 York *Evening Press*, 12 July 1960.

53 Purvis Papers, YL/625.

54 *New Statesman*, 18 June 1960, p 890; *Guardian*, 15 June 1960.

55 York *Evening Press*, 15 July 1960.

56 Bamber Gascoigne, *Spectator*, 21 June 1963, p 810.

57 *Stage and Television Today*, June 27 1963, p 15.

58 York *Evening Press*, 15 June 1963.

59 York *Evening Press*, 5 July 1963.

60 Festival Committee Minutes, Jan 1964, vol IV, p 95.

61 Festival Committee Minutes, Oct 1964 – June 1966.

62 Browne, York *Evening Press*, Festival Supplement, 1966.

63 Ibid.

64 Festival Subcommittee Minutes, City Clerk's Office, York.

65 Press release from the Festival Manager's office, *Daily Telegraph*, 28 Jan 1969; *Times*, 6 Feb 1969.

66 York *Evening Press*, 23 June 1969.

67 Ibid.

68 Program, *The York Cycle of Mystery Plays*, 1973, p 1.

69 Ibid, p 5.

70 Ibid, p 3.

71 John Barber, *Daily Telegraph*, 14 June 1976, p 8.

72 Desmond Pratt, *Yorkshire Post*, 12 June 1976.

73 Ibid.

74 Barber, *Daily Telegraph*, 14 June 1976, p 8.

75 Reprinted with permission of the York Department of Tourism.

76 For a selection of reviews of the 1980 York production see 'Census of Medieval Drama Productions,' *RORD*, 23 (1980), 81–4.

77 Robin Thornber, *Guardian*, 14 June 1976.

CHAPTER FIVE

1 Quoted in Kevin P. Roddy, '"Who is This King of Glory?" The Epic Element

in English Cycle Drama,' PH D diss, University of California (Davis) 1972, p 206.

2 *Guardian*, 20 June 1951, p 48.

3 Roy Walker, 'The Mystery Plays,' *Theatre Newsletter*, 6:127 (July 1951), 4–6.

4 E. Martin Browne, 'The English Mystery Plays,' *Drama*, 43 (1956), 34–6. For a further description of the visual effects of the Chester production, see J.C. Trewin, 'The Drama of Daybreak,' *Drama*, 22 (1951), 28.

5 *The Chester Plays*, ed Hermann Deimling and Dr Matthews, EETS, ES 62 (1892), lines 5–20; Roddy, '"Who Is This King of Glory,"' p 208.

6 Chester *Courant*, 17 July 1957. John Lawlor's views on translation were presented in a program note to the 1962 performance, and in a lecture at Bristol University, January 1969, attended by the author.

7 T.S. Eliot, 'Religious Drama: Medieval and Modern,' *Edinburgh University Journal* (Autumn 1937), 8–17.

8 Natalie J. McCracken, 'Medieval Mysteries for Modern Production,' PH D diss, University of Wisconsin 1969, p 231.

9 For a further description of the 1973 Chester production, see John R. Elliott, Jr, 'Playing the Godspell,' *RORD*, 15–16 (1972–3), 125–30.

Other performances of the Chester plays took place in Montgomery Hall, Sheffield, November 1955; and at the Bryanston School, July 1955. See Eleanor Prosser, *Drama and Religion in the English Mystery Plays* (Stanford 1961), p 43.

10 Peter Lloyd, *Memorandum to the Joint Committee on the Censorship of the Theatre* (London 1966), p 3.

11 For the wording of this rule, see above, chapter 4 note 7.

12 *Plays and Players*, June 1968, p 58. The script was John Bowen's *The Fall and Redemption of Man*, a composite version of the four English cycles (London 1968, p 28). The original phrase reads 'Com kis myne ars!' (*The Wakefield Pageants in the Towneley Cycle*, ed A.C. Cawley [Manchester 1958], p 2).

13 Browne, *Drama*, 43 (1956), 34–6.

14 *Minutes of Evidence Taken Before the Joint Committee on Censorship of the Theatre* (HMSO, London 1967), p 132.

For a general review of theatrical censorship in the twentieth century, see Richard Findlater, *Banned* (London, 1967).

15 Interview with J.W. Lambert, *Sunday Times*, 11 April 1965.

16 File of clippings and programs, Religious Drama Society Library, London. No names are given for any of the personnel connected with this production.

17 Martial Rose, *The Wakefield Cycle of Mystery Plays* (London 1961), p 5; and Rose, 'Bretton Hall College of Education Foundation Lecture' (Wakefield, 1967).

18 See the records of payments to actors listed in E.K. Chambers, *The Medieval Stage* (Oxford 1903), II, 139. Chambers is probably wrong, however in concluding that 'all the actors received fees, on a scale proportionate to the dignity of their parts.' For a recent discussion of this question see William Tydeman, *The Theatre*

in the Middle Ages (Cambridge 1978), pp 196–7.

19 *Guardian*, 4 April 1961.

20 Ibid.

21 *Daily Mail*, 4 April 1961.

22 *The Times*, 4 April 1961; *Theatre World Annual*, 12 (1960–1).

23 Martial Rose, *The Times*, 4 April 1961, p 5.

24 Alan Simpson, *Plays and Players* (June 1965), 44.

25 Philip Hope-Wallace, *Guardian*, 9 April 1965. Pasolini's film appeared in 1964.

26 The Derby production was directed by John Williams; text by Martial Rose, adapted by Peter Jackson. The Lincoln production was directed by Claire Venables and Rhys McConnochie; text (unpublished) by Martial Rose.

27 Hull *Daily Mail*, 30 July 1971. *I Am* was written and directed by Paul Vaughan-Phillips and produced by the East Riding County Youth Theatre. It was performed in Hull, York, and London in July and August 1971.

28 See, for example, the instances of 'real-life' audience reactions recorded by Thomas Heywood in *An Apology for Actors* (1612). These include spontaneous confessions of murder by a woman who had poisoned her husband and by another who had driven a nail through her husband's head, in response to seeing similar acts depicted on the stage. A summary appears in E.K. Chambers, *The Elizabethan Stage* (Oxford 1923), IV, 253.

29 Tony Harrison, *The Passion: A Selection from the York Mystery Plays* (London 1977), pp 54, 56. The passages read in Purvis' version: 'This bargain will not be, / For surely I want wind' and 'At first was it made over wide, / That makes it wave, thou mayest well wit' (pp 287–8). ('Gormless get' = 'witless brat' in northern dialect.) The critical comment appeared in the *New Statesman*, 6 May 1977.

30 Iriving Wardle, *The Times*, 22 April 1977.

31 Linette Martin, *Crusade*, Sept 1978.

32 Benedict Nightingale, *Harpers and Queen*, Sept 1977; John Walker, *International Herald Tribune*, 23 Aug 1978, p 5.

The Passion was directed by Bill Bryden and Sebastian Graham-Jones. It opened 21 April 1977 and, in an expanded version called *The Mysteries*, continued to be performed at regular intervals through 1985.

33 For the principles on which these and other medieval dramatic texts have been edited, see Stanley J. Kahrl, 'Editing Texts for Dramatic Performances,' *Leeds Medieval Studies*, 1 (1975), 39–52.

34 Hardin Craig, *English Religious Drama* (Oxford 1955), p 9.

35 Markham Harris, *The Cornish Ordinalia* (Washington 1969).

36 Quoted in *The Parochial History of Cornwall*, ed Davies Gilbert (London 1838), IV, 204–5.

37 Richard Carew, *Survey of Cornwall* (London 1602), p 71.

38 Quoted in Charles Thomas, 'Piran Round and the Medieval Cornish Drama,' *Souvenir Programme July 1969*, Cornwall County Council, p 8.

39 *Gwreans an Bys: The Creation of the World*, ed Whitley Stokes (Transactions of the Philological Society, London 1864), p 34.

40 Neville Denny, 'Arena Staging and Dramatic Quality in the Cornish Passion Play,' *Medieval Drama*, Stratford-upon-Avon Studies 16 (London 1973), p 133.

41 Neville Denny, 'The Staging of the Cornish Cycle,' unpublished lecture, 1970, communicated to me by Mr Denny.

42 Denny, 'Arena Staging,' pp 146, 148.

43 I quote from the acting version, by Neville Denny, which remains unpublished owing to the author's untimely death.

44 This point was noted by Kevin Roddy in his review of the Bristol production: 'Clearly it is Judas and Pilate, the ecclesiastic (as all the apostles were bishops) and the magistrate, who deserve the most frightful vengeance for Christ's death; medieval society, more interested in its own cohesion than in the nature of Roman Palestine, concentrated on those elements in the gospel narrative which defined Christ's rule, the superiority of which must be recognized by every bishop and sheriff.' ('Revival of the Cornish Mystery Plays,' *New Theatre Magazine*, 9 [1969], 16–19).

45 See the *Sunday Times*, 19 March 1972; and Glynne Wickham, *The Medieval Theatre* (London 1974), p 225.

46 A 16 mm colour film of excerpts from the Cornish production, entitled *The Cornish Ordinalia*, is available for rental or purchase from the Extension Media Centre, University of California, Berkeley, California, 94720.

CHAPTER SIX

1 Letter to the author, 12 Nov 1980.

2 Tom F. Driver, 'Misdirected Medievalism,' *Christian Century*, 77 (1960), 927.

3 Alexander Franklin, *Seven Miracle Plays* (Oxford 1963), p 18. I am grateful for this reference to Professor Sheila Lindenbaum, whose unpublished paper, 'Translating Medieval Drama,' is frequently drawn upon, with permission, in this chapter.

4 Gordon Honeycombe, *The Redemption* (London 1964), pp 101–2.

It should not be assumed that the older views on the matter have totally disappeared, however. Joseph O'Conor, the original Jesus at York in 1951 and still active on the London stage, wrote to me in 1976 that 'One fact I think is undeniable. The plays work only if the director and (at least) leading actors are believing Christians. They depend on and flow from faith. This I think is sufficiently proved by some of the later Marxist attempts to make political capital out of plays that exist only in a religious context.'

5 University of Toronto Press, under the general editorship of Alexandra F. Johnston.

6 Twycross' method was derived from visual material published by Bertram Joseph in *Elizabethan Acting* (London 1964), and from earlier stage experiments by Christopher McAll at Oxford. For a discussion of her performances, see *RORD*, 20 (1977), 89–90. J.W. Robinson also argues, on the basis of a study of medieval stage-directions, that 'both the gestures and elocution of the early actor were formal, rather than naturalistic' ('Medieval English Acting,' *Theatre Notebook* 13 [1959], 83–8). William Tydeman reaches a similar conclusion (*Theatre in the Middle Ages*, p 215).

7 Bertram Joseph, *The Tragic Actor* (London 1959), ch 1; Thomas Heywood, 'An Apology for Actors' (1612), quoted in Chambers, *The Elizabethan Stage*, IV, 251.

8 *The York Cycle*, ed Lucy Toulmin Smith (Oxford 1885) p 22.

9 J.S. Purvis, *The York Cycle of Mystery Plays: A Shorter Version of the Ancient Cycle* (London, SPCK 1951), p 24.

10 J.S. Purvis, *York Evening Press*, Festival Supplement, 1957, p iv.

11 A study of Purvis' two translations leads one to conclude that many of the difficulties encountered in them are due to the fact that his knowledge of Middle English was simply not very extensive. In the present passage, for example, he incorrectly translates 'there-at' (literally 'at that' or 'because of that') as 'yet,' and more seriously, translates 'dedeyned me' as a transitive verb rather than a reflexive, gives it the wrong subject, and assigns it the wrong lexical meaning.

12 J.S. Purvis, *The York Cycle of Mystery Plays: A Complete Version* (London, SPCK 1957), p 31. I have corrected what I take to be a printing error in this edition, the division of line 6 into two separate verses.

13 See OED 'disdain' v 3; 'deny' v 10.

14 The Davies version has not been published. I am grateful to Edward Taylor for furnishing me a copy, and to Mr Davies for permission to quote from it.

15 Davies, York Festival Program, 1973, p 4.

16 Purvis, *Complete Version*, p 10.

17 Lindenbaum, 'Translating Medieval Drama' (see note 3).

Purvis himself admitted that 'the cast found the new lines hard to get used to' (*York Evening Press*, Festival Supplement, 1957, p iv).

18 Purvis, *Shorter Version*, pp 8–9.

19 Honeycombe, *The Redemption*, p 13. The script was performed in 1960 at University College, Oxford, and in 1963 at churches in London.

20 Honeycombe, *The Redemption*, p 37.

The original text, in the York Cycle, reads as follows: 'And tell me than / Yf you sawe evere swilke a sight!' / 'I? nay, certis, nor nevere no man.' / 'Say, felowes, what! fynde yhe any feest, / Me falles for to have parte, parde!' / 'Whe! hudde!

be-halde into the heste! / A selcouthe sight than sall thou see / uppon the skye' (Toulmin Smith edition, p 119).

21 Honeycombe, *The Redemption*, p 46; *Two Coventry Corpus Christi Plays*, ed Hardin Craig, EETS, ES 87 (London 1957), p 27.

22 John Bowen, *The Fall and Redemption of Man* (London 1968), p 24. Bowen's script was prepared for the use of students at the London Academy of Dramatic Arts, and was subsequently performed by various amateur and regional repertory companies.

23 Lindenbaum, 'Translating Medieval Drama' (see note 3).

24 Bowen, *Fall and Redemption*, p 13.

25 *York Plays*, no 39, Toulmin Smith edition, p 425.

26 Driver, *Christian Century*, 77 (1960), 927.

27 Hamlet's advice on this matter, derived from Cicero's *De Oratore*, also had its medieval adherents. The author of the twelfth-century *Jeu d'Adam* ordered all of his actors to 'speak coherently and make gestures agreeing with the thing they are speaking of' (*ut composite loquantur et gestum faciant convenientum rei de que loquantur*).

28 Peter Happé, 'Mystery Plays and the Modern Audience,' *Medieval English Theatre*, 2 (1980), 98–101.

Index

Note: the index does not include pp 145–58.